# How Can I
# Keep From Singing?

# Loretta Cobb

**Livingston Press**

**The University of West Alabama**

Copyright © 2016 Loretta Cobb
All rights reserved, including electronic text
ISBN 13: 978-1-60489-166-9 trade paper
ISBN 13: 978-1-60489-165-2 cloth
ISBN:1-60489-166-1 trade paper
ISBN:1-60489-165-3 cloth
Library of Congress Control Number 2016931474
Printed on acid-free paper.
Printed in the United States of America,
Publishers Graphics
Hardcover binding by: Heckman Bindery

Typesetting and page layout: Joe Taylor
Proofreading: Norman McMillan, Maggie Slimp, Hannah Evans, Tricia Taylor,
Jesse Gonzalez, Chloe Pritchett, Anne Hamilton, Joe Taylor,
Jessie Hagler, Cierra Destiny
Cover design and layout: Amanda Nolin
Cover photo: Loretta Cobb
Special thanks to

Joe Taylor, Tricia Taylor, William Cobb, Annette Culver,

Sid Vance, Mary Horton,

Cassandra King, who read the manuscript,

Pat Conroy, who saw the beauty in Pearl and Priscilla's story,

and

All the members of the King John Version Writing Group

This is a work of fiction.
Surely you know the rest: any resemblance
to persons living or dead is coincidental.

Livingston Press is part of The University of West Alabama,
and thereby has non-profit status.
Donations are tax-deductible:
brothers and sisters, we need 'em.

first edition
6 5 4 3 3 2 1

# How Can I
# Keep From Singing?

*To*

*Harley and the moms*

# Chapter One:
## An Echo in My Soul

### 1944

BEFORE I AM born I know. In utero, already the narrator/observer making notes, I warm to the fragile beating of my half-formed heart as I web my way toward life inside a woman whose own heart races to the beat of my father's whims. He wants me aborted. As soon as she figures out what he's up to, however, she grabs her clothes and runs out of the doctor's office—down the back alley of the strange quarter of town.

### *1949*

AT FIVE, I COULD SEE THE CRACK begin in the kingdom of my child-hood. I didn't trust the comfort, but watched for signals from the deer heads mounted on the wall—their trapped horror, their haunting eyes. Too many shadows covered my life, causing me to turn inward in my quest for truth.

I lived with my eight-year-old sister Lucinda and my parents in a white house with green shutters on Heather Hill, the showpiece for a development of "sensible" houses my father had built. We had a snug, comfortable home: door knobs new and shiny, hardwood floors with no scratches, and walls with fresh paint. I knew the clean simplicity wouldn't last even before I had the words to shape the thought.

Priscilla was the mother of our half-brothers. Doc Carson, her father, directed a private sanatorium at the top of the hill where people went crazy or where crazy people went. I couldn't keep that part straight.

The boys lived with their mother in a secluded brick house at the foot of the hill in the woods on the other side of the hospital. Even then I was struck by Doc and the crazy folks being at the top of the hill with my daddy's two families lower—in opposite valleys. The boys wanted us to feel lower than them in every way, but we were all lower than the lunatics, as Mama called the patients at the asylum.

Lucinda and I walked up toward the sanatorium at night sometimes, though we were not supposed to. Our half-brothers made us go. Doc was supposed to be somebody great, but he wasn't our grandfather and was quick to let us and the world know he wasn't my mother's father. The Gothic building perched on the hill like a castle, soft light from its barred windows holding secrets and mystery.

Robby's eyes looked as scared as mine; his mouth fought to maintain a smirk. "Let's walk to the asylum; I dare you, Bonita." He tried to act so big and bad.

"Mama told us never to go up there," Lucinda said, blonde hair looking silver in the moonlight, bare shoulders shivering, "especially not at night. Mama says I'm too pretty, I'll get kidnapped."

Junior's voice was gruff, threatening, "Huh! We'll walk behind you. Come on. I'm the oldest. Do what I say. We'll tell her we made you do it because our mother said you could."

They tried to make us do a lot of things—every chance they had. They were bigger and stronger than us. I tried to escape from fear by focusing on the beauty around me. The night was soft and dark, lightning bugs everywhere making golden magic—the scent of honeysuckle an opiate. I smelled Doc's pipe smoke, saw the round orange circle glow in the bowl, and crept toward the shrub. The boys, unafraid, waved at a woman in the shadows on the porch of Doc's residence, a stone cottage across from the sanatorium. Her skin was the color of hot chocolate under the dim porch light except for her legs in white stockings. Doc always acted as if Lucinda and I were invisible. Priscilla, Daddy's first wife, was Doc's only daughter. Mama said Doc had spoiled Priscilla, claimed the old man was jealous of his own son-in-law.

When we rounded the curve above the valley, the lights of eastern Birmingham were breathtaking. "Like jewels . . ." I murmured.

Lu looked like Shirley Temple, smiling at me.

"You better quit talking to yourself. There are crazy people in there," Junior said, his blue eyes cold, angry. "They'll come out here and get you!"

I rubbed my goose bumps, felt my shoulder tense. The sanatorium smelled like rubbing alcohol, even outside the iron gate. Disfigured faces at the barred windows frightened me.

On the damp grass, we sat on the other side of the hill to watch the lights glitter. We had just settled ourselves when we heard a scream from the main building, followed by groaning. We huddled closer, looking back up the hill. Then we heard yelling. We froze. We couldn't make out the words. A gigantic shadow banged on the French door that opened on the terrace off Doc's office. Just as the alarm went off, someone clicked lights on throughout the building.

"Somebody's trying to break out. Run!" Junior commanded. We ran. Knots in my tummy, I was terrified. A cigarette glowed in the shadows at the edge of Doc's shrubbery, then flicked toward the road. The nurse's white stockings and heavy shoes ran toward the door of the cavernous old building.

"That's Doc's mistress this month," Junior snickered as he tore out down the hill ahead of us.

"What's a mistress?" I asked with the little breath I had left, running as fast as I could back down the hill. They howled with laughter ahead of me. I flushed. The boys were faster, their legs longer. They may have been more afraid.

Once inside my warm, uncluttered house, I brushed my hair, smiled into the mirror and then into Mama's soft eyes. "You have my eyes, but your daddy's golden hair," she said, a smile of pride relaxing her face as I brushed while I counted—a hundred strokes. "I'm so proud of your counting." Mama tucked me in under a frilly spread and soft, warm blankets. The window frame smelled like fresh paint as the moon spilled through organdy curtains.

A few weeks later, the boys set up cots in their attic, "Like a ward at the sanatorium," Robby told us. The youngest, I had to be the lunatic.

Junior locked my sister and his little brother in one attic room and tied me up in another. "It's called a straight-jacket," he explained, a wild look overtaking his eyes as he wound the dirty jump rope around my arms. He was almost ten years older, had a man's body already when I looked up from my three-foot height. "He's filling out, becoming a man," I had heard my daddy say proudly. Junior unzipped his pants. I cringed when I saw the stiff protrusion from his legs, bigger than his fingers.

"Touch it," he commanded, his voice husky. "Kiss it."

"No! I don't want to," I said.

He yanked me on the cot then and tied the rope to the bed post. Panicked, I screamed, then tried to think of splendid jewels, Cinderella's shoes, anything. I gagged, as he shoved his "mess" down my throat. I saw stars. I struggled, kicking.

"If you ever tell, I'll kill you," he pressed hard—his voice low, sinister. I knew the salty taste of hatred for the first time. I bit Junior hard and he jerked away from me.

Lucinda and Robby banged on the door just like the crazy people did. I screamed louder, kicking and scratching as much as I could with my arms tied. Lucinda plugged in an old iron and had the courage to start a fire by burning some newspaper clippings. I smelled the smoke before Junior did since he was having what appeared to be a fit, jerking and breathing hard. He unlocked their door, but he didn't untie me. Lucinda did, her eyes terrorized. By that time Priscilla, returning from the grocery store, called up the stairs, "What are y'all up to? I smell smoke! Can you smell it?" I can still hear her shrill voice and feel the anguished relief.

Junior stomped the fire out, then bounded down the stairs and told his mother, "We were using an old iron up there to press some of Doc's war letters and newspaper clippings. Yes ma'am, I'm making a scrap book," he lied, blue eyes sweet as apple pie.

None of us told what happened, locked into the sweetness of denial that Southern children learn early. There was nothing sweet about anything for me that day, but I knew already that too much truth turned sour. Before I even asked about things, much less told on anyone who was bigger and meaner than me, I knew truth could punish as quickly as lies. And yet, I knew better. I pushed back vomit from my gut. I couldn't look at Priscilla because we had not told her the truth. She hummed as she stacked groceries in the pantry, but peeped out to smile at me, her pale eyes clear and trusting. Somehow, I convinced myself that it was all my fault.

When I got home, I was exhausted. Lying down for a nap, I felt flat inside. Though I had kicked and screamed and tried to defend myself, I had been defeated. I didn't know words like polluted yet, but I sensed the slime of it. I couldn't understand why the inevitable shame of the violated covered me like a second skin, but I knew something worse than lying had happened to me.

Junior came over to play a game of cards after nap time as if nothing had ever happened. I must have decided to turn myself in like a criminal in the movies. I took the cover off the furnace vent and tumbled downward toward the hot coals where the boogey-man lived. Lucinda, looking up from her cards, screamed in horror.

Junior, thinking fast, tied that same jump rope around his ankle and crawled into the narrow vent, reaching for me. Robby and Lucinda tugged at the other end of the frayed rope. Numb with fear, I realized he didn't want to kill me after all. That same brother who had done me harm risked his life to save me.

That night, tears streaming, I clung to my mother's neck which smelled like wild roses and told her, "Junior did bad things to me in the attic."

Her voice was calm, soothing, but her heart beat fast against my chest as she assured me, "You aren't the one who did wrong, baby. You've told the truth to the right person." I could hear her teeth grind when she promised me, "It won't happen again!" I fell asleep soon afterwards.

Next morning I awoke to commotion: loud, angry voices, sobbing, slammed doors. Doc came to our house to speak to Daddy, "In private," Doc insisted, glaring at us. It seemed silly since we could hear their gruff voices growing louder with each exchange.

Then Mama was called in for interrogation by Phil. "Junior is my first-born son; how could you accuse him of such—"

"The girls are our daughters, Phil, for God's sake!" It went on that way for some time. I caught the drift, no matter how noisy my mom was in the kitchen later, nor how many spoons she let me lick as she cooked. Then Doc, all gentleman again, announced formally when they came out of Daddy's home office, "My son-in-law will accompany me to Priscilla's. Perhaps my daughter can make some sense of all this."

Suddenly that afternoon, Mama threw our belongings into boxes. We filled a truck with them and moved to a boarding house on

Southside that Daddy owned. "Why, Mama, why?" my sister and I pleaded.

"Just because, baby. I'm gonna run that boarding house near the medical center Daddy's been talking about. It's close to Highland Avenue where all those beautiful old houses are. Remember? We don't want to live here anymore. We want away from this crazy place."

I struggled with the shame that hung over me like a cloud, assuming, no matter what Mama said, it was all my fault. Lucinda didn't help either, "If you hadn't told, blabber-mouth, we wouldn't be leaving our new home. I loved my room, waking up looking toward Ruffner Mountain."

Nobody had time to explain what was happening, but I figured it out. I compared our lives to the boil that sprouted on my arm: the poison in our lives, which I sensed though I couldn't understand yet, had brewed and festered to a feverish head that had to be relieved.

It amazes me the way families survive sadness through silliness. On the way to our new home, Lucinda pouted but Mama chattered nervously while Daddy drove. Mama wanted to distract me or entertain me. "I swear to get anywhere in Birmingham you have to pass Sloss Furnace, which looks and smells like hell."

"Ah, woo. Mama, you're cussin' like a sailor."

"No, I'm not."

"Yes, you are."

"Another way to find your way home if you ever get lost is to remember that all the hillbillies live on the Eastern side of Birmingham because that's where folks first started coming down from the hills into the city. Now look at the sun. Where will it set?"

"Right there."

"So that's West End."

"What's on your left, Lucinda?"

"The South," Lucinda answered flatly.

Then Daddy interrupted, "—and on the right, North and damn Yankees like me."

"Oh, no! Here we go again! Cussin' parents." I guessed you could make anything fun if you tried really hard.

We turned left, headed to South side. Our Spanish-style boarding house had smooth, round arches and tile floors and hidden passageways. The mahogany staircase squeaked under my feet a little, under my daddy's feet a lot—when he was there. We were special, somebody, because we owned the boarding house even if it did need repair. The massive oak table seated twenty boarders who raved about the good cooking. Mama and Ida, her cook, basked in the compliments from men about the steaming vegetables, fried pork chops, and cat-head biscuits.

Rhett, a handsome boarder, took Mama down to Merita's day-old bakery several times a week. He was the tallest, most muscular man I had ever seen, way over six feet tall with coal black hair that glistened in the sun. Like my daddy, he was handsome but in a different way. Rhett always had time to talk to me, and he brought me chewing gum. He was thoughtful like that toward Mama, too. That's why he insisted on giving her a ride to the bakery, "There's no reason for you to walk four blocks with all that bread," he told her. "Besides, I need to wind down a little when I come in."

I enjoyed the scent of fresh bread from Merita's as I splashed in a washtub on the back porch, making fragile, rainbow-swirled bubbles in the suds. You could smell the bread baking every morning. Besides, Mama had just brought in a load of bread and stacked it in the pantry.

We weren't poor yet. We had indoor plumbing, unlike my country cousins at Phil's sister, my Aunt Shannon's, who still had to bathe in wash tubs. I just liked to play in mine. The water was cool; I liked a refreshing contrast to the humid, sticky air. I pretended my tub was a sink, that I was helping Mama cook. I could see and hear everything she did in the kitchen from my imaginary world on the back porch. Methodically, I ripped the eyes off my potatoes and threw the waste over the crumbling rock bannister, which needed repair as much as the cracked porch. Ida, making bread pudding, talked about her husband's union meetings. "I done told him he's gonna get in trouble going to those meetings if that boss at the ore mine finds out, but he won't pay me any mind. Then he comes home drinking that rot-gut whiskey, shaking his head. I worry about my children."

"I know what you mean," Mama sighed. "You can't tell a man a thing when he gets his mind set. I hear talk, too. There's gonna be trouble. My sister works at the mill out in the country, and they've been talking about unionizing, too. Seems like the little man can't seem to break even."

"Um hm," Ida agreed. "What they need is to be reading The Good Book and listening to the preacher."

While Mama began washing and Ida drying the dishes, I pantomimed cleaning dishes in my washtub's suds. Mama smoked a cigarette, held it in her mouth at the sink, the yellow smoke curling up toward her nose.

There was a crack in the sagging, unstable porch that had grown wider each week like a snake getting fatter and fatter. I thought of the crack in my childhood kingdom on Heather Hill. Sometimes the crack made me think of a snake. Junior's stiff "thing" had swollen as big as a snake. It still frightened me to remember, and as usual I thought of something else quickly. I blew iridescent bubbles through a holder Rhett had given me one morning.

One minute I was content with the aimless bubbles, pleased that Mama had given in to my begging to play in the washtub. The next minute I crashed through the cracked porch, which opened like an earthquake to swallow me. The noise was like a shotgun blast; the porch floor opened instantly, and my tub and I dropped through. The concrete shell, too thin, finally collapsed. I shrieked in terror. I gripped the tub, trembling.

Mama flew down the fire escape so fast we got to the bottom patio simultaneously. "Damn his soul to hell," Mama yelled, "Phil ought to be ashamed to call himself a builder and dump us in an old dilapidated house he never gets around to fixin'. I've told him a thousand times about that crack . . ."

The metallic clang of the tub terrified me. I kept screaming hoarsely. Mama picked me up and pulled me to her breast, rocking me. Her heart pounded under her softness. I craved the reassurance of her soothing, no longer angry, voice.

Ida was right behind her, grumbling too. "Folks better pay attention to what needs fixing. I'm telling you the truth! Folks don't take care of things, lots of innocent children gonna get hurt. Yes, Lord, I see it coming. Just like a war, right here in this city with innocent babies like yours playing one minute, their lives shattered the next. All this talk about bombs and dynamite." Ida's eyes streamed with tears. Then she started humming, which soothed us all while she picked up the potted plants that had fallen and re-potted them, patting the soil gently. Mama rocked me on an old metal glider stirring up a bit of a breeze. I survived without a visible scratch, and Daddy's repairman showed up before the sun went down. I didn't see a doctor, but 50 years later a psychologist told me the impact from that fall may have caused my attention deficit disorder, finally providing an explanation for my tendency to wander off into the world of imagination.

OUR CHRISTMAS TREE fit the bay window like an embrace, its tip reaching the ceiling that year. Mama's eyes reflected the blue lights she circled around the tree. The brightly colored bubbling lights enticed me because they were dangerous. I watched the hot blue liquid bubbling, wondering if it were as hot as the molten pig iron we saw every time we crossed the viaduct downtown. I wondered if Sloss Furnace had real pigs in it.

Daddy moved his office to our boarding house where he built an additional apartment complex. He liked having his office close to Mama again because she kept his books and filed for him though they were separated. He had moved back to Priscilla's, but he still spent a lot of time with us during the day. He was moody: Sometimes he was affectionate and playful, fluffing my soft blonde curls, but other times he didn't notice me or Lucinda for weeks at a time. I liked it when he wasn't there at night because I could sleep with Mama, snuggling against her warmth.

On Christmas Eve, Daddy came in through a secret doorway from his office through the dining room to the tree-filled room. My mother's face lit up when she saw him. He took her in his arms and held her for a long time. Tears streamed down her face. "I'm so happy you're here," she sighed. I felt a burst of relief. I knew he would cheer her up. I tugged at his shirt until he patted my head, and Lucinda gave him a grudging hug. We liked having Mama to ourselves.

Daddy followed Mama into the kitchen, saying, "Let's have a cup of tea." The scent of his warm tea made me feel cozy, snug.

Mama protested, "No, thanks. I like my tea iced and my coffee hot. Period." He also tried to get her to drink iced coffee sometimes, but she'd frown, her lips parting enough for her to bite the lower one, her eyes all scrunched up. He didn't even notice she reached in the refrigerator, bringing out cold giblet gravy, dressing and turkey. He unloaded the packages he'd brought: a basket of fruit and nuts, several long loaves of bread, spaghetti and canned pumpkin.

"Oh, Phil," Mama sighed. "It's too late to cook again."

"I make my own schedule, my own rules," he declared, eyes cold under thinning hair.

"Oh, all right," she said, "I guess you've already had turkey and dressing today. You'll have to tuck the girls in, though." Then she announced, "Girls, fifteen minutes till bedtime!"

I rushed to my playhouse under the stairs until he called us. Lucinda sang off-key from the bathtub upstairs, showing off that she knew the words to all the carols. I set my table with tiny, metal teacups, then pretended to pour hot tea with the small flowered pitcher because I knew Daddy loved hot tea. He stuck his head in the half-sized door, calling in his Chicago voice that made the i's sound like *ai yai yai yai* in cowboy movies, "Punkin Pie, where are you? Time for beddy bye," When I offered him a cup of tea, he patted me on the head, then gently picked me up, "You're Daddy's girl, aren't you?" I savored the cinnamon smell of him.

He wasn't as gentle as Mama about tooth brushing. Impatient, he looked at his watch a lot. My sister was sullen, thought she was too old to be supervised while brushing her teeth. A whole head taller than me, she enjoyed the spitting part, the white foamy bubbles lingering in the sink as her silky hair fell toward them. Her pout confused me, made my neck hurt.

Daddy was in a good mood. He told us a bedtime story that didn't make sense to me. His never did—always about snow and being frozen blue or something crazy. Then it was lights out and goodnight. I lay awake a long time savoring the aroma of onions and garlic simmering in olive oil. I chanted to myself: *The children were nestled all snug in their beds while visions of garlic bread danced in their heads*. Content, I counted spaghetti noodles instead of sheep until sleep finally came.

In the middle of the night, startled awake by a thunderous noise above us, Lucinda and I sat up. "What is that?" Lucinda whispered.

"I'm scared," I answered, and she put her hand on mine. She squeezed my hand when we heard heavy footsteps, someone running in the hall. My mouth was dry with fear, my heart racing.

"Wake up, wake up," my father yelled. "Santa's on the rooftop, come see!"

We squealed, delighted by the sudden change. My heart thumped when Daddy took Lucinda's hand and carried me out on the landing, pointing toward the sky. "See him," he said. I strained to see, but I couldn't. Then I saw sparks flying upward, and I let out a blood-curdling scream. "What?" Daddy was gruff.

"Santa's on fire!" I yelled. I sobbed, reaching toward the sky, arms shivering.

Then he laughed and laughed, holding me up in the air. "Santa's fine. You're such a little angel." He rubbed my goose bumps.

I hoped I'd be able to fly like an angel because I didn't like it up this high—still afraid of the orange sparks that flew across the sky. "Look, there's the fire again," I shrieked. My body tensed, eyes widened, fists clenched.

"Oh, baby, the janitor is stoking the furnace. It's all right now," he said, stroking my blonde curls, the same shade as his. "It's all right, Punkin. Let's go downstairs and see what Santa left."

Mama's family always celebrated Christmas dinner on Christmas Eve so that my aunts could visit their in-laws on Christmas day. Most of our boarders were gone home somewhere, too, so Mama made a platter of turkey sandwiches and told everybody to help themselves. She kept the tree lit all day and sat in a rocker beside it, leafing through the Sears catalog and the newspaper, checking out sales. She wore the dark chenille robe Daddy had given her, looking leisurely but tired. When I asked how she felt, she said, "Oh, a little blue . . ."

I played with my new stove, concocting imaginary treats for her, but none seemed to cheer her. Late in the afternoon, as the winter darkness took over the sky, Grandmother Byrnes, Daddy's mother, arrived. Her stern face was permanently creased into a frown under her saffron-streaked hair. She lived in Chicago, but she planned to stay with us awhile. Under a veiled hat, she peered at me with menacing, blue eyes. The eyebrows seemed to reach to the top of her long forehead.

We had turkey sandwiches and fruitcake and coffee since Grandmother and Daddy had eaten lunch with Priscilla, but Mama had set a pretty table and it was very nice. Grandmother gave us all knitted sweaters and caps, which we wore on a walk to see neighborhood decorations after Daddy left. Mama winked at us after the fortieth time Grandmother carried on about how much more it seemed like Christmas in Chicago because it was colder and snowy. I thought it was nice that we could walk at night without freezing.

It was chilly, however, and by the next morning, I developed a terrible sore throat. Grandmother was skeptical when Mama put her hand on my forehead, checking for a fever.

"You worry too much, Pearl. She has the sniffles, not the croup," Grandmother said, her condescension clear even to a five-year-old. When Grandmother rose to her full height of almost six feet, peering down her nose, Mother let the older woman bully her into not checking my temperature. I didn't need a thermometer; I knew I was sick.

Always, a cigarette dangled from Grandmother's mouth. Mama didn't smoke like that until she met Grandmother, who looked silly poking slowly across the room with a cigarette in her mouth. Lucinda snickered, pointing at Grandmother's heavy legs, "She's slower than Christmas . . . one foot in the grave already." We called her Granny Creeps because the boys did.

When Mother did check my temperature, an hour later, she called the doctor immediately. He was there in five minutes.

I thought Dr. Paterson had a crush on my mother. He was nice. His salt-and-pepper hair matched his beard. He was the only man we knew who had a beard. Through a feverish haze, I saw the mouth in the middle of the beard moving, and I could hear the voice but they didn't seem connected. "You'll need to make a croup tent; use Vick's salve in steaming water to help her breathe," he instructed.

My grandmother lurked in the corner, still leery, suspicious of my mother and the doctor. I hated Grandmother and felt knots in my tummy. Grandmother didn't like anybody who was nice to us. I imagined I was a princess in a fancy bed with curtains and Dr. Paterson was a knight.

Mama made a tent with sheets. Then she set up a new gadget that melted the salve, sending into the air dramatic puffs and hisses of menthol. Ah! I pretended there was a dragon in my tent, but a charming prince was on his way. I enjoyed the attention I attracted in my castle/tent. Lucinda was jealous.

Sometimes, I'd wake up in a fog to see Grandmother in a rocker with a book. She'd glance at me every now and then, but I didn't let her catch my eye. I wished she'd go back to Chicago. Being ill cramped me and intensified my dislike of Grandmother. When I didn't sweat, I froze. I feared she'd put a spell on me.

As soon as my voice quit sounding like a duck's and the coughing died down, I pleaded to go outside. Mama made me wear a coat, along with the toboggan and scarf Grandmother had knitted, and rain boots—though it wasn't raining. I didn't care. The captive was free. I basked in the fresh air, filled my lungs. The sun shone so brightly I felt as if an angel had sent it straight to me. My chest swelled with joy, a sense of power. I knew I wasn't supposed to run hard and make myself breathe fast, but I did it anyway. I liked the flush of disobeying. I felt warmer, my heart beat faster, and my face was red enough to make my nose tingle. I ran faster, my corduroy-covered legs moving fast like the blades of a fan. I wanted to prove to myself and anyone in the neighborhood who might see that I was not a puny weakling but a normal healthy girl. I slowed until my breath came easy.

Mama made me lie down to rest and brought me cold, pulpy orange juice. "I just squeezed this," she said. "Thought you'd like it."

"I do." I gulped the thick, sweet juice. It soothed my throat, which was still raw and scratchy.

"Try to take a nap." Mama pulled the sheet over my shoulders. Tears filled my eyes at her tenderness. Later in the afternoon, she brought chicken noodle soup to the bed and read me a story, something she didn't often find time to do. Then we played Go Fish with her cards for a long time. Ordinarily, she only used them to play Solitaire, smiling ruefully while she dealt the cards. I watched her shuffle and spread them out, enjoyed watching her face in concentration, the way her eyebrows moved.

Grandmother glared from her rocker. I shivered, but Mama smiled toward her, informing me, "Grandmother can tell fortunes by reading the cards."

That news stiffened my neck with fear. She looked like a witch already with those long fingernails, but now I knew. I watched with morbid fascination as Grandmother took our cards and turned them over slowly, saying, "I see the card of death." I saw a dark face card, one of the kings, then she turned over the Queen of Diamonds, "Here's the lady in love. Hmmm." Grandmother shot my mother a knowing look. Eyes hooded, I tried to tune her out, but I was drawn to the mystery of fortune telling. The warning of death lingered. Even before D.W. showed up.

Grandmother reached for another deck of cards, "The Tarot cards keep bringing up the four horsemen. There's going to be an uprising . . ."

Mama looked pale. She interrupted Grandmother, "That's enough. Just the playing cards, please. The girls have seen enough for now. Thank you." We moved into another room.

I was mesmerized by D.W. Lucinda was even more so. From the start, I was curious about Grandmother's mysterious relative, who had once owned one of the steel mills. Lucinda knew he had a story, didn't know what, just knew. Since he was Daddy's uncle, we gave him our nicest apartment until he "could get settled." Lucinda and I sat on his balcony and listened to stories for hours. Mostly, they were scary stories about street fights and shootings by "the Mob." Or love stories where the guy loses.

Mama told us one day we couldn't go down there anymore, which increased my curiosity even more. I listened as Mama and Grandmother washed dishes, both cigarettes moving as they talked. "D.W. looks like Bing Crosby," Grandmother said.

"Saddest eyes I've ever seen," Mama answered. When they saw me in the pantry, they talked about the weather. I didn't know what was up, but I had overheard enough.

Lucinda had too. She gloated, "It always amazes me that grownups don't know that kids catch on. D.W.'s in love with Grandmother, even though Granddaddy was his brother." In a way, our eavesdropping prepared us for the shot we heard one afternoon. It boomed worse than thunder.

Suddenly, all the adults in my life were running toward D.W.'s apartment, but we were ordered to stay out. My grandmother was the first to come back out—blood splattered on her apron. Eyes wide, she looked angry like Mama does when she's really sad. "What happened?" I asked my mother.

"Nothing, baby," she muttered, her hand on my head as if I were her puppy. I imagined a pat on the head and stifled a bark. It seemed clear to me that something plenty happened. Exhilarated, my heart raced.

Lucinda's eyes were filled with tears. "Is he gonna die?"

*How Can I Keep From Singing*

"I think so," Mama answered wearily.

"Would he have done it if we'd spent more time with him?" I asked.

The question seemed to jerk Mama up. She said, "No matter," defensively, her eyes still struggling with questions not answers. Then she took us back to our apartment where we watched from the window when she left. We heard the blaring siren, a familiar sound since we lived a block from the hospital, but I'd never heard it scream so mournfully. We saw the ambulance arrive. When they took the body out, there was a sheet over D.W.'s face. I thought of Grandmother's death card.

"That means he's dead, when they cover up the face," my mother announced, her thin voice solemn. "I think he shot himself."

That's the extent of the explanation I got. Even when I asked Mama later, all she said was, "D.W. was real depressed."

Maybe my grandmother could depress anybody. Right after D.W.'s suicide, she was gone, for good I hoped. She said she had to take care of legal matters. Once she left, the house smelled only half as smoky, but the fear lingered. Then, Mama told us Daddy Phil had inherited some money, but it was tied up in the steel mills, and we would never see a penny of it.

# Chapter Two:
# *A Roof Over Our Heads*

FIRST, MAMA SCARED US TALKING SO loud on the phone to Priscilla, our daddy's first wife. They were both furious, but not at each other. My older sister got scared and went to ask our neighbors, a married couple, if they would come over, play like they were just dropping by. Boy, did they get an earful!

"I'm gonna kill her, Fred, I mean it," Mama screamed to our neighbor who'd come over with his wife. Mama's hair was falling softly around her face. Usually her bangs looked fixed. The red highlights shone like copper in the lamplight above the green flowered dress she had thrown on. Her high heels clacked when she stamped across the room, her nostrils flared like an angry horse's. I expected to hear a whinny any minute. She slapped her purse and laughed, a crazy shrill sound I'd never heard before. "Before the sun comes up, Phil's new tart is one problem I can solve."

Fred was married to Mama's friend Helen, but he was older. They laughed about him when he wasn't there. He looked defeated, but he kept trying: "Pearl, listen to me. It ain't worth it, I'm telling you. What will become of these children if you're sitting your butt in some prison cell?"

Mama looked like he'd slapped her for a second. She looked nervously at us, huddled in the corner, my tears streaming. Lucinda held my hand, squeezing it tight. Tears ran from Mama's eyes under the penciled brows.

When Fred touched Mama's shoulder, she sobbed—loud, moaning sobs. "How could he bring another woman into this, Fred? He spends half the time with his first wife. Didn't he have two families already? More freedom than any man I know!"

Fred rubbed her shoulder, then patted her back gently, as if she were a baby. "Some folks are just greedy, I guess. Don't realize what they have until they lose it, you know?" He tried to take her purse but she held on to it fiercely, clasped it under her arm like a bird hiding treasure under its wing.

Mama's face struggled with the cloud that came over it. She glanced toward Helen for support from her best friend. Then Mama said, more to herself than anybody, "All these years, I've told myself that Phil couldn't help the way things are, that his meanness just grew out of being trapped in a hopeless situation. Now I know he's just a sorry son of a—"

Fred cut her off. "You may be on to something; his mama's pretty mean." His hollow, forced chuckle fell flat. Mama didn't see the humor, just kept pacing the floor—high heels going clack, clack, clack; ducks in the room going quack, quack, quack.

Helen pulled on my arm, "Come on, girls, let's go read a story. What do you say?"

Lucinda jerked my other arm, yelling, "I'm not going anywhere, and if you make me leave, I'll tell my daddy. He says you're a slut, anyway!"

Helen's hand flew to her mouth, then to her neck, tucking in the stray hairs at the nape of her long, slender neck. Face flushed, lips trembling, Helen yelled at Lucinda, "Don't you talk to me like that, girl. If I light into you, you ain't gonna know what hit you! You don't sass me!"

"I sass anybody I want to," Lucinda made the s sound like a hiss.

"Now listen here, young lady," Mama started, but Fred pleaded with her,

"Let it go, Pearl. No point gettin' into all that right now. Helen loves the girls. She can handle them."

"That's right," Mama whispered. "I've got business to take care of. Give me that telephone book."

She called the Greyhound station. "Yes," she said, overly formal, "when does your next bus leave for Selma?" She waited, then answered, "Um hmm. Well, thank you very much."

Mama looked across the room toward Fred, glanced at her watch and announced, "I've got to hurry."

She ran outside, high heels clacking loud and fast, ducks flying into the night. Fred ran out, but when Mama took her shoes off he was too slow. "You stay here and keep the babies," Helen called to Fred. We were on the porch where we'd all run after them. Then Helen took off, her long legs overtaking Mama before she got half a block down the street toward the city bus stop.

I could see Helen shake Mama, could hear Mama yell at her, yanking her purse back. It made me nervous to see them jerk that purse around with a gun in it. I wailed then, making old Fred's forehead wrinkle into a look of helplessness. He was a short, squatty man with a red face, but Helen seemed to adore him. I couldn't understand why. I studied the ugly mole under his eye to keep from watching my life fall apart up the street.

In the dark, we could see the two women silhouetted against the sky, like they were playing tug of war, until all of a sudden Mama won. She shoved Helen down on the sidewalk. Lucinda and Fred both had their mouths open, like baby birds.

Mama threw her high heels at Helen, who struggled to get up as Mama ran down the sidewalk. Helen said, when she returned—out of breath from running as fast as she could—that she had reached the top of the hill in time to see Mama—barefoot and wild-eyed—board the city bus.

Fred looked a lot wearier. Shoulders stooped, he rubbed his weather-beaten neck. Pulling hard on a Lucky Strike, he grabbed a flannel jacket that made him look like a hobo. "I believe I can catch her at the Greyhound station. We can't let her get to that woman in Selma," he said to Helen, ignoring us.

He cranked several times before the old Packard started. Then we heard it chug chug down the street. Helen took us inside, to her apartment. "How about we finish mixing these cookies and find some cold milk, girls."

Her blonde hair was thick and shiny. Mama said Helen had a model's figure, but she didn't look that pretty to me. Right now I strained to find something besides the conflict to focus on—staring at Helen's legs, my eyes level with what must have been the top of her thigh. I wondered what my daddy meant when he said Helen had legs all the way to Heaven.

After the warm cookies, Helen brushed my hair. "Let me brush yours," I offered, the scent of cookies still a comfort.

"Okay," her eyes—green with flecks of blue and brown— registered surprise. She unpinned her hair, let it fall down on her shoulders. I told her softly, "I like that story in the Bible where the girl washes Jesus' feet with her hair. I bet hers was just like yours."

She smiled sadly, mopping the corner of her eye, "Let me tell some bear stories, okay? Did I ever tell you about the bear who got in your mama's trash can up in the Smokies?"

We were almost settled down when we heard Mama and Fred come in. Mama slumped in defeat. "Let's go home, girls," she said hoarsely. She went to the window and looked out, waiting for us. Her back to us all, she whispered, "I'm sorry."

"Hey, what are friends for?" Helen assured her.

"I've got no education. We have to have a roof over our heads, you know?"

Helen put her hand on Mama's shoulder. "I know, sweetie. Remember how it broke my heart to leave my son with his daddy. I still can't stand to think about Little Ed calling somebody else Mother. You better continue to think about that roof and keeping all three of you together."

Fred muttered, "There are roofs, and then there are roofs."

When we got home, we went through the motions of an orderly life, brushing our teeth and saying our prayers, but there was no bedtime story. "Y'all can sleep with me tonight," Mama said, bolting the bedroom door.

I wondered who she was afraid of since she was the one with the gun. After she thought we'd gone to sleep, I heard her cry softly into the pillow. I went over and over the words to a song we heard on the radio, "Frankie and Johnny," picturing Nellie Bly and the man who did Frankie wrong.

The next day, everything happened so fast it's hard to tell about. At first, Mama got up, looking normal except for the puffy eyes, like two emeralds swollen by bee stings. She made cinnamon rolls and squeezed fresh orange juice. Then she started a big pot of vegetable soup, replacing the aroma of cinnamon with cloves and tomatoes.

One hour later, when Phil charged through the door, he rushed with a frightening urgency to his office where Mama was typing statements. Lucinda and I could tell by the way he slammed the door, there was gonna be trouble. "You had no right to call her!" Phil yelled.

Without ever saying a word, Lucinda went up to their bedroom, found Mama's purse with the gun, and hid it under our bed. Then we sat on the steps to listen some more. "But I love you more than any woman on Earth," Phil said, though his tone didn't sound loving to me.

"That's what any woman expects when she's the mother of your children; it's a given." Then Momma added spitefully, "Ask Priscilla."

"Don't bring her into this," he yelled, then we heard a loud slap. I was off to the world of make-believe by the time my mother slammed the other door, which led to the dining room. Her face had a red hand print.

Phil stayed in the office, talking on the phone all morning. He was overly busy, but he made time for lunch with us, casting a cold silence over the steaming soup.

After lunch, Mama suggested, "Why don't we all take a nap today. What do you say?" Lucinda groaned, but I wanted a nap. My eyes were scratchy from lack of sleep. Phil allowed a flicker of warmth in the blue eyes that peered at Mama like he was asking her a question. His thin hair was the color of honey. I hoped they would hurry and make up.

Maybe an hour of peace passed before we heard the commotion. Lucinda checked under the bed to be sure the gun was still there. This time he didn't just slap her. When we heard her scream, followed by a loud crash, we ran to their room and opened the door. Phil picked her up the way Prince Charming carried Snow White. Only he wasn't charming right now, and she kicked and scratched like a panther. His eyes were insane, popping out of the red angry puff of his face as if they might burst. "I'll teach you," he screamed. "I'll throw you through this goddamn window."

"Phil, please," Mama pleaded. "I lied to make you jealous."

In the brief second that he paused, I rushed toward him screaming, "Please, Daddy, please."

I'm not sure which of us convinced him, but suddenly he turned from the window and threw Mother on the bed like a basket of laundry. He stalked out of the room and down the stairs.

When Mama called Dr. Paterson, she struggled for each asthmatic breath, wheezing. And when he arrived, he glared at my dad, telling him, "You'll need to leave the room, please, so that we can calm her."

Dr. Paterson's jaw was set, the muscle twitching above his neatly trimmed beard. He glanced at us huddled like puppies in the corner. I thought for a minute he was going to cry. "You know we should report this," he said when Daddy left. "He is a dangerous man."

"No," my mother said, a tear rolling down her cheek. I wondered if she meant No, I won't tell on him or No, he's not dangerous. I focused on her tear which seemed to get bigger, changing from a tear shape to a big ball and then, all of a sudden, it was flat like an old blister—just water on her cheek.

Dr. Paterson wiped her cheek. "You'll need to stay in bed a few days with this broken rib. Call me if you need me." He nodded toward us.

It seemed like a month that Mama lay in bed—flat, lifeless. Her eyes stared blankly out the window, the dark purple circles under them the same color as the bruises all over her body. I was relieved she stayed home. I didn't want anyone to see her like this. I crawled in her bed to comfort her. She scratched my back, but the absent stare still controlled her face.

When Ida brought Mama's stew to the bed, she scolded us, "Leave your mama alone, let her get some rest." They closed the door and whispered together in the afternoons, the way they did when they talked about labor unions. Their whispering changed over the next week, as if they were plotting a revolution.

Once, I heard Mama tell Ida she didn't think preachers should talk about politics in church, and Ida didn't like that one bit. She didn't whisper about that either. "Where else colored folks gonna talk about it? In y'all's newspapers? On y'all's television stations?"

I could hear that dust mop banging behind the closed door, but I didn't hear a peep out of Mama. Mostly, they seemed to go over the want-ads and talk about different neighborhoods.

Some days they talked about Ida's husband Sam or Daddy Phil. Sam drank a little when he got discouraged, but he was a dependable husband and father. If Daddy came to his office, Ida kept Mama posted at least every hour. I also stayed in my room right next to hers as if I could do anything besides run for help. All their whispering really kept my curiosity up.

# Chapter Three:
# *Moving on*

*1949*

Eventually, Mama's bruises turned to brown, then to yellow. Her eyes began to come alive. The first morning I smelled fresh biscuits again, I sensed the sadness passing even before I saw her smile. "We're going shopping," she announced.

Lucinda and I hated the matching suits of red wool with pleated skirts and jackets fastened by tabs. I loved the leopard skin coats, though.

Lucinda rolled her eyes. She had been withdrawn ever since the fight. "Why are you mad?" I asked her.

"Never mind," she answered, her face the same mask as Mama's when she was depressed. Lucinda knew how to stare vacantly into space already. I was confused by the mood swings around me. I wanted to be normal.

When Lucinda came home from school, she always said she had homework to do. She used to wait until dark to do that.

My dolls were well fed. I spent lots of time in the playhouse. Mama poked her head in every now and then and asked, "How's my girl?"

Mama showed Ida all kinds of things in the kitchen: where she stored the pressure cooker and the canning jars, how to operate the fuse box, where she kept the mouse traps. My mother's voice had energy; she walked lighter. Daddy Phil didn't come home or use the office like he used to. Mama hadn't been in the office since the day he broke her rib.

One morning Mama woke me up with a silver breakfast tray. "Breakfast in bed. Special treat." She waved French toast under my nose. Cinnamon invaded my nostrils. Conquered, I was immediately in a good mood, loving the attention. "Baby, I haven't told you because I didn't want your daddy to pump you with questions about our business, but we are moving today!"

"What about Lucinda?" I say, my throat tightening in fear. Surely we wouldn't leave her behind because she was at school.

Mama smiled uncertainly. "She's not too happy about it, I know," she answered, "but she'll come around. We're leaving as soon as she comes home from school. That gives us just about the right amount of time to load the trucks."

"What trucks?" I asked.

"Your uncles are coming to move us," she said brightly. "You'll have a lot of packing to do this morning, won't you? I've packed most of your clothes in boxes I moved downstairs last night, but I want you to fold the things in your room and put them in this suitcase, ok?"

"OK," I tried to sound as cheery as she was. "Where are we going? Chicago?" That's the only place I knew where people moved to or from.

"Heavens no!" Mama laughed, too enthusiastically. "We're moving across town to Lakeview. It's really still Southside, but it's about 10 blocks down Highland Avenue where you like to walk by all the beautiful older houses. You're gonna love it."

I dressed, put my other clothes in the suitcase and then remembered my tea set. I hurried to my playhouse to pack all those things. I wrapped my pink-bordered dishes in newspaper the way Mama had wrapped her plates and glasses. I was far into the task before I accepted fully that you can't move a playhouse from under the staircase. You have to pack what you can and abandon the house as grownups do. I nestled the tea set, damming tears.

Strumming his guitar, Uncle Clyde waved to me from the front porch swing, "*Hola*, Bonita!"

I hated it when he teased me, speaking Spanish because of my name. It tickled him for some reason. He sang about a young cowboy dressed in white linen. I hoped nobody heard that country, nasal tone. Crawling into his lap, I seared into my memory the red tile roof and the crumbling stucco, imagining the young cowboy on a white horse taking me away from the cool tile floors and the airy archways I had come to love.

My daddy said Uncle Clyde caressed his Gibson when he played. I asked him to sing "Red River Valley." As soon as he started singing about going away from the valley and taking the sunshine, I finally cried about moving again, sobs hoarse and deep.

He leaned over and bit my head, another thing he did to annoy me, but at least it made me laugh instead of cry. "Don't cry, baby; everything's gonna be fine. Y'all gonna be a lot happier now; your mama's doing the right thing."

This gentle, balding uncle was the only good man in my life. His posture was funny: he slumped over like a question mark, probably from strumming that guitar. I couldn't believe the stories about his courage during the war. How could this gentle singer kill other men, I wondered. Mama said he drove a burning tank until all his buddies had escaped at some place in France. "Tell me the story about Normal Beach," I said.

He chuckled. "Nothing normal about it, Bo. Sounds like somebody else has been telling stories. I don't like those stories myself. It's Normandy though, baby."

Uncle Clyde lived with my good grandmother, Granny Connor. He took care of Granny, but she wanted him to get married. He dated a beautiful girl a lot younger than he was, too young to get married yet he said.

I liked the way he talked to me like I had good sense and sang when things were sad. He rarely treated me like a puppy. Today, we sat on the porch until my grumpy uncle arrived. He was married to Mama's pretty sister, but he was ugly and fat. He poked his chest out like he was somebody bigger than he was. I liked Uncle Clyde's posture better.

Uncle Bill had a worse than usual sneer on his face. "I got something for Phil if he shows up," he bragged, flashing a pistol under his vest. Chill bumps sprouted on my arms. I rubbed them.

Uncle Clyde just grinned, "Shoot, you can put that thang up, Bill. We don't need a weapon for a coward that beats women. All he needs is good beatin' himself."

Uncle Bill, crestfallen, poked his chest out more. He never even spoke to me. Arf, arf, I wanted to say. Even Uncle Clyde thinks I'm a deaf puppy.

As they went up the staircase, Uncle Bill continued to talk about my daddy, "If Phil had fought in the war like he should have, instead of being a war profiteer and screwing around, neither one of these innocent children would have to be here, living through this kind of hell." I wasn't sure whether to be glad or sad.

Uncle Bill went on to more practical observations, his voice accusing, "That armoire's heavy. You got a dolly?"

I watched all morning for my daddy. Everybody seemed to expect him to show up and try to stop us from moving. When I heard the brakes of a car screech outside my window, I felt my heart race. When I looked out, though, I saw it was only an old man who parked his car and headed down the street toward the hospital. He looked sadder than I felt. I wondered who he was going to see at the hospital. I imagined the frail, thin man going down halls that smelled like rubbing alcohol to a . . . It was easier to make up stories than to live this one.

Mama, chain-smoking and looking out the window every few minutes, seemed to expect Daddy more than anybody else did. When I told her what Uncle Bill had said, I thought she was gonna slap him. Her mouth flew open wide enough to swallow a bird. It made me think of four and twenty blackbirds and those pies for some reason. I heard her tell Uncle Bill, "Don't talk about Phil around Bo. She's real sensitive."

Uncle Bill wanted Daddy to come, I could tell. But I could tell just as surely that Uncle Clyde didn't. I was on Uncle Clyde's side. We won, too, because when Lucinda came in with her book satchel and her long face, we loaded up in Uncle Clyde's car and followed Uncle Bill's truck to our new life without ever hearing from Daddy Phil. I knew he'd find us though.

# Chapter Four:
# *Adjustment*

LUCINDA AND I FUMED WHEN WE REALIZED Helen and Fred were sharing our apartment. They had already moved into it, the downstairs part of a gray Victorian house, now divided into several apartments. "Of course, they took the best bedroom," I grumbled, "lots bigger than ours."

When we crammed all the furniture in, we could hardly move in the tiny bedrooms. Nonetheless, Mama and Helen were thrilled as if this were a fine place to live forever. They went on about how big the kitchen was. "So much sunlight!" Mama said as the winter sun lit her face.

Helen echoed her praise, "Plenty of cabinet space, too." They didn't mention that the long windows from floor to ceiling were drafty or that the linoleum was peeling.

"The thing I love most in a house is the kitchen," Mama prattled. "If the place where you cook is big enough for everybody to pile up in, then it's even better!" She was trying too hard.

I warmed my feet and hands at the gas heater in the living room. Mama had cautioned me fifty times about standing too close to the flame. I hated seeing Fred across the room in his plaid bathrobe and pajamas. Somehow, it didn't seem right.

One night, I woke up in our new apartment and heard Mama and Helen talking in the kitchen. I smelled coffee and the stale cigarettes that Mama now rolled herself with Bugler tobacco to save money. I felt pressure in my bladder that screamed, Go to the bathroom, but

I dreaded putting my feet on the cold hardwood floor. Mama cut the gas heater down when Lucinda and I went to bed, then off when she came to bed. I slept crowded between Mama and Lucinda, but it kept me warm under the covers.

After I'd waited as long as I could stand, I made my way down the drafty hall in the middle of the night. When I opened the bathroom door, Fred sat on the toilet, his trousers around his feet. Our eyes locked in a strange kind of embarrassment I didn't understand for years. Suddenly aware of a terrible odor, my face reddened as I backed out the door. I felt ashamed; he wasn't even kin to us. I lay awake with my legs crossed until I heard the commode flush and the sound of Fred's feet going back to his room. When his door closed, I flew down the hall, holding my nose.

I began to realize we were poor, not good enough somehow. Mama obsessed over Octagon coupons, clipping the eight-sided soap wrappers as if they were gold. "Just wait and see," she beamed, "when we get enough, we'll go downtown and redeem something pretty with these." We also bought powdered milk and ate peas and cornbread a lot.

In the day time, I played outside. I wanted to get away from the cramped apartment, the gas heaters, the shame of living with other people. Here there were no girls my age, but some boys who welcomed me. We played Japanese against GI's. I had a scarf Rhett gave me, white silk with an orange ball in the center. This "flag," of course, flew over my territory, while the boys basked in the glow of Old Glory. I didn't really care because I was mostly making mud pies anyway. I could do that just as easily in Japan as the U.S.

While Mama worked as cashier at the dry cleaners, Helen watched us. I told Mama I didn't like staying with Helen, but she explained, "I have to make ends meet." At night, I heard Mama tell Helen the owner tried to kiss her all the time. She hated that part. I felt a blush of shame as I listened, in pain about such abuse before I knew why.

Eventually, Daddy Phil came to see us. Everybody was really tense again, like the day we moved. I guess everybody assumed he'd want to beat Mama up every time he saw her. Or that he'd kidnap us, but he didn't. He just came by and acted "down and out" as Mama put it.

I'd never seen him slump before. Mama had always said she loved the way he carried himself so proudly. His eyes had red marks like on road maps.

"I hate it here," I told him. "Fred wears stupid pajamas and a baggy bathrobe."

After shooting a quick look toward Mama, he picked me up and swung me around. "Is that so? How about your mother? What does she wear at night?"

"Those old gowns like Granny wears. It's cold here at night." Then, I was spinning and giggling and lost in a rush of love that transcended my troubles for the moment.

# Chapter Five:
# Maintenance

WITHIN A FEW DAYS OF DADDY'S VISIT, he bought us an apartment house across the street in Mama's name, not his. The white-columned house had two separate apartments, one upstairs and another downstairs. There were also single rooms to rent boarders like we had before at the medical center. Daddy told Mama, "I figure the rental income will support you. I'm closing the old boarding house, and I'll send the boarders to you. I suggest you hire Ida to help since she'll be out of a job now."

Mama hesitated, "No strings attached?"

"No strings," he looked away.

Mama certainly knew how to run a boarding house, so our fortune was up again. What Mama didn't know anything about was maintenance, but she tried to learn. The house had a balcony on the second floor at the end of the hall, between two apartments. Mama insisted that Daddy repair the porch, "I don't want some boarder with a good lawyer falling through the porch like Bonita did. You've got to fix this one."

Lucinda squealed, "This house is romantic, like old plantation houses!" It had been so long since I'd seen her happy. The place filled my head with make-believe. I'd go to sleep at night imagining myself on the balcony with a hoop slip under a dress that fit tight in the waist.

However, reality was not so pretty. The house was in constant need of repair: sagging floors, leaks in the roof, cracked window panes that needed immediate attention. The three of us worked together to remove peeling paint and refinish wood, which was fun at first, but we thought we'd never complete the projects. We bought new wallpaper for the dining room, but it wouldn't stick like it was supposed to. However, Mama seemed happier than I'd ever seen her; she even repaired the plumbing herself. She had a wringer washer that never seemed to work right. She was always fixing that washer because we wore it out, cleaning all the linens for the dining room and even doing some laundry for the boarders.

I watched Mama feed the sheets into the roller so much she decided to let me help her. She started the sheets, feeding them slowly to the roller. Then I pulled them out on the other side. When the phone rang, Mama's mouth puckered in a frown.

After she'd gone down the hall to answer it, I decided I could carry on without her. I fed a pillow case to the tiny slit between the rollers, which turned hungrily like some monster's mouth. All of a sudden, my arm followed the pillow case into the mouth of the monster. The pillow case didn't take nearly as long as the sheets had. When I saw what was happening, it was already too late: my fingers were pressed flat. I screamed as loud as I could.

"Oh, my God!" Mother yelled, her eyes big as frying pans. The eyes that had, a minute ago, smiled so proudly were now filled with terror; her hands shook as she jerked the machine and turned it off. Somehow she managed to retrieve my arm. The machine was all the way to my elbow.

The pain burned like a raging fire. My arm was elongated, flattened while Mama rushed to the phone. "Dr. Paterson, please; it's an emergency." Her face went white as she listened. Ida stroked my hair, holding me tight.

Mama slammed the phone down and ripped into the yellow pages, "I'll call a taxi. He said we'd better come to the hospital since we may need their equipment."

"Let's call Helen," Ida commanded. Just before I lost consciousness, I saw Mama give Helen her purse and reach toward me from the passenger side of the roomy Packard, her face creased with concern.

# Chapter Six: Lakeview

WE WERE AMAZED BY THE WAY my arm healed itself, grew strong again, normal. I stretched it to its full length and drew a circle around myself, rusty dust making me sneeze. Instead of the usual summer dog days, a relentless drought set in, parching our red clay and crab grass yard. I loved dirt, always had. In the loose, dusty soil, I drew pictures with a stick and hummed fragments of songs I didn't remember all the words to.

I drew a circle of stick characters holding hands, all red— no yellow or black or white like Granny Connor sang about. I sneezed again, hard. Hands covered with dust, I stuck a sparrow's feather behind my ear and pretended I was an Indian—a different way of being colored. The boys I played war with, claiming to have Indian blood, cut their skin and mingled blood to become blood-brothers. However, we were scared to even think of being "really" colored. We knew it was dangerous.

Most children wanted to be Indians while we played, but in the movies Indians always lost in the end and they did awful things like scalp white people. Colored people you had to watch out for, but Ida was the smartest and kindest person I knew besides my mother. The biggest confusion for me was that Granny Connor was my greatest source of wisdom, the one I spoke to at night when deeper questions occur to even the youngest who dare to question as the stars take over the night, but she was often in direct conflict with my other fountain of wisdom. For after she had gone to sleep, I didn't even have to ask questions to hear answers offered, free for the taking from The Club Rose, a night club next door where jazz mellowed the night air. This was before air conditioning, when we all left our windows open, and you could hear music easily from one house to another. Also, occasionally, the club would set up parties on the side porches, and the tables in the back would be lit with candles where small groups gathered to laugh and talk.

On nights when colored people had parties there, I was magnetically drawn to the window by music. Men in colorful suits and satin shirts danced with smooth-skinned women—sparkling in sequined dresses. Mesmerized, I watched muscular bodies moving smooth as molasses in perfect rhythm. I fell asleep to songs like "Saint Louis Blues" and "Sophisticated Lady," envisioning evening sunsets and ladies with cigarette holders.

I connected to the wailing blues drifting in my window as I closed my eyes and tried to sleep. I understood sadness and survival before I knew what disenfranchised meant. I sensed a bond stronger than most I'd come to know. I recalled the stick figures I had scratched out in the dirt. Puppies can scratch in the dirt, but they can't hum. I was beginning to see that folks can't keep children as puppies forever.

When Fred left, Helen moved in with us again. Mama just moved a single bed from one of the boarder's rooms into our room. I heard her tell Mama, "Fred wasn't any fun once y'all moved over here. Come to think of it, he never was much fun." She giggled. "Just a rebound thing, a fill-in man who offered me security. He never could hold a candle to Big E; I always knew that."

I had no idea until then that Fred had children or that he'd left his wife, and this was the first I'd heard about Helen's ex-husband. She told me that, in Pittsburgh, her son Little Ed's best friend at school was colored. When I asked Mama about it, she said, "Yeah, and you notice Little Ed didn't come home with her to live down here either. He stayed with his daddy. Helen has some funny ideas about colored folks mixing with whites. Maybe she stayed up North too long!"

Helen smeared her scalp with a mud-like substance called henna, which turned her brown hair a deep, rich red—the color of her cherry furniture—moved from storage into our attic. When she unrolled her hair and brushed it out, she cut bangs across her pageboy bob. She pulled a draw from her cigarette, its tip wet at the end like Mama's, and squinted in the mirror, "Don't I look like Cleopatra now?"

"Where on earth did you get all these?" Mama asked, going

through the trunk full of shoes with bright, thin straps and high heels. Big E had shipped them from Pittsburgh. Helen also had glitzy dresses trimmed in metallic ribbons of gold and silver and dresses you could see through.

"Big E did buy me lots of clothes, I'll say that for him," Helen sighed. "He loved night clubs." Her eyes lit up when she talked about her life in that distant place.

Mama always tried to change the subject when Helen started telling me grownup things. I dragged them out of her though when Mama wasn't around. She was like some "wicked woman" from The Club Rose up close—a woman who admitted to drinking and fooling around with men. And she talked to me like I was grown up.

I should have had my nose whacked with newspaper for acting like a puppy myself, begging for her stories. Mama couldn't always edit her own outbursts or keep us from exposure to a lot, but she tried to shield me from Helen's worldliness.

When she and Mama went dancing at a place called Queenstown Lake, I couldn't sleep until they came home. I lay awake imagining myself a queen or a princess with my own lake and a dance hall inside an old stone tower where the music would echo. I played possum when they came in, Mama squealing, "I can't believe we saw Rhett after all these months!"

"He sure is a good looking man," Helen murmured, "and he danced like he meant it." They giggled, taking off their high heels. Then I heard zippers from the shiny, flimsy dresses and springs in Helen's bed squeaking as she crawled in under the stiff, starched sheet.

I snuggled up to the gentle snoring of Granny Connor, who didn't approve of honky-tonk angels. I was relieved she wasn't just playing possum, so I didn't have to feel guilty about exulting in the adult fervor.

"I love Rhett's eyes," Mama said.

"Um hmm, such a physique!" Helen mumbled, soon snoring softly, an echo of Granny. When Granny's snore rose, Helen's fell, in perfect rhythm. Mama tossed and turned on the sofa, which was centered under the window. Moonglow crept across the room until it enveloped her completely in its radiance.

Rhett began to visit us with Helen's new beau, a handsome man named Karl, who was tall and blond and considerably younger.

I overheard Granny on the phone with one of my aunts, a weariness in her voice, "Where I came from, drinking and frolicking brought nothing but heartache."

Granny's pinched mouth registered fear when she saw Mama at the mirror, "Getting dolled up again?"

I liked seeing Mama so happy, so alive. Helen drew rounded eyebrows on Mama and made her put on more rouge. Then she went to work on herself, slipping into a slinky gold dress. Helen poked falsies, little pointed foam rubber cones, into her bra, but Mama didn't need any. Helen told her, "You were blessed with a great figure, especially the bust line." Helen smiled into the mirror at both their reflections. They were ready!

I always felt my stomach tighten when Granny warned, "Now y'all be careful. Don't get into any trouble, and try to get home earlier."

Granny's voice was usually kind and full of laughter, but it took on an edge when she cautioned them. According to Mama, Granny worried too much, had seen too many hard times. Granny sat in the old wicker rocker and read the Bible every night, her soft, pale face aglow. She was so short she'd almost disappear in the rocker, her tiny feet barely touching the floor where she pushed off with the balls of her feet. I crawled up in her lap and buried myself in her warm softness while she sang "Hush Little Baby" and "Jesus Loves Me."

She always ended with "Jesus Loves the Little Children," her favorite, which confused me because nobody was exactly red or yellow or black or white. "Why don't we all love each other like Jesus did?" I asked.

"I don't know, baby, but I know Jesus meant for us to." I caught a whiff of Granny's talcum powder—Avon's "To a Wild Rose." The scent permeated her plain print dresses, often made from flour sacks. We seemed to rock forever.

That morning a letter came from Daddy Phil's sister that made Mama moody.

> *Dear Pearl,*
> *I'm so sorry about the way things have turned out for*

*you and Phil. Please know that I will always love you as my sister and your girls as mine. Who among us understands the human heart? I love my brother, but I can't defend his ways. You've always known that. Summer's almost over, and the children have been begging for a visit. Sammy Joe would love to see the girls while Sam goes to a cattle auction in Nashville in a couple of weeks. Do you think we could work something out? We will always be your family.*

*From my heart,*
*Shannon*

Toward the end of summer, Sammy Joe came to spend a few days. Lucinda told Mama, "He's cute. I love that dark, wavy hair."

Mama's eyes penetrated like a sly fox observing a vixen. "That boy is wild as a buck, just like his daddy. You got to watch him every minute," she warned.

Sammy Joe's sparkling eyes, his height and his swagger made him larger than life. He enjoyed being the cousin from the big farm come to teach the girls a trick or two. He taught us how to squirt lighter fluid on the ground and throw a match on it, flames spurting up along that line of fluid as if they were magic. He also talked Lucinda into smoking a cigarette though she was only eight years old, going on nine next month. He claimed his daddy taught him how to smoke rabbit tobacco when he was my age.

The night before Sammy Joe had to leave, we all peeped through a long, skinny keyhole—one of those made for a skeleton key—to spy on Mama and Helen with their boyfriends, and we saw plenty. They were having a birthday party for Karl at home instead of going out. Whenever they "partied," the door to the living room was always locked, which aroused our curiosity. It had never occurred to me or my sister to spy on them, but Sammy Joe thought of it right off.

"Look here," he said, his bright eyes dancing. His voice was low, guttural, dripping with something that reminded me of The Club Rose and "Sixty Minute Man," a song which always made Granny cringe.

When Lucinda looked, face flushed and eyes sparkling, she exclaimed, "Golleeee!" She and Sammy Joe decided I wasn't old enough, but I said I'd tell on them, so they let me look through the keyhole for a second. Helen and Karl lay on the bed kissing, his hands rubbing her neck and inside her dress, unbuttoned down the front and hanging around her like a raincoat dragging the floor. Mama and Rhett danced close, his hips—shoved against hers—moving back and forth in one motion as if their bodies were one unit.

This was an overload for my young psyche. Maybe I said, "Yip, yip," or wagged my tail or panted fast, my tongue hanging out. I must have shown it was too much somehow because the older kids made me quit looking just before I started barking.

When Granny came down the hall with a cake for us to decorate, we stopped peeping. Lucinda blushed, looked sheepish. Sammy Joe grinned and winked, but I ignored him. Then he had another idea, "Why don't we put on a show, dress up and pretend we're them!"

Lucinda and Sammy Joe imitated the dancers, pulling each other close, her arms around his neck and his around her waist. Sammy Joe, what Mama called a string bean, had sprouted up about 18 inches since we had last seen him. His skinny frame stooped down to reach Lucinda who was a tall girl herself. He tried to move his hips close to hers like the adults did, but they were both awkward. Their bodies weren't the right height, and his long legs ended up in big clumsy feet that had no rhythm. "You'd be a joke at The Club Rose," I told him.

Eyes flashing, he wiped the leer off his face long enough to frown at me, his lip turned upside down. He rolled his eyes at Lucinda who giggled against his chest. "Traitors," I said, but they ignored me. Already, I could see my fate with a beautiful older sister. I would never be danced with or even noticed.

As Helen, I created an outrageous costume from her closet: a sheer red blouse with a sequined top under it, just right for a dress on my short, knobby-kneed body. I clomped around in red satin high heels and found a pair of her falsies. Even Granny laughed about that. I painted round eyebrows, clipped on scarlet earbobs and smeared lipstick across my mouth. When I stuck my hip out and propped my hand on it, I liked what I saw in the mirror. The hazel eyes looked bigger with painted brows, my mouth pouty like Lucinda's. Even my mousy, dishwater-blonde hair looked pretty when Granny poofed it out like Helen's. Most of all, I liked the lively spirit looking back at me from the mirror, the wide red smile that slid across my face.

Once the grownups stopped the music, we knew we'd soon hear the skeleton key click in the lock. When the click signaled, Sammy Joe jerked open the door and yelled, "Surprise!" Lucinda cut the light off while Granny brought the cake in, candles blazing, and we sang Happy Birthday.

Karl seemed shy for the first time, his eyes reflecting the candle light. I saw a tear try to escape, but it never did. He closed his eyes and puckered his nose and mouth when he made a wish, then poked his lips out far enough to blow hard and whooshed the candles out.

Once Granny had served the cake, she said, "The children have another surprise for y'all." When Granny put the big 78 record on, the scratchy music started. She had picked my favorite, "How Much is that Doggie in the Window?"

Sammy Joe and Lucinda danced around the room, moving awkwardly, trying to imitate the pelvic moves Mama and Rhett had made. At first, all four mouths opened like baby birds waiting to be fed, and all eight eyes widened. Helen put her hand over her mouth to stifle a giggle, but her eyes gave her away before the throaty sound of her laughter. Then the others laughed, sipping their drinks too quickly, and gave the dancers a round of applause.

I had to outdo those two! On cue, I strode into the room, modeling my sheer "evening gown." Mama's mouth dropped open as wide as an alligator's when I reached in my bra and pulled out the falsies, squealing, "Ta dah!"

Helen and Karl howled with laughter, and Mama slapped her thigh, rubbing tears from her eyes. Rhett seemed concerned instead. "This ain't the kind of game kids should play. Let's all walk up to the park before bed time."

"But, Rhett, it's already bed time," Mama said.

"I don't care. Tomorrow's a big day for Bonita, first day of school and all. The park will be a good change of scene for the kids, give them a break from being around us all the time," he snapped. It was the first time I'd seen him snarl, but it wouldn't be the last. He was an interesting contradiction: military tough, but soft-hearted, too.

We made our way up the hill on 29th Street, looking at shop windows as we passed: chandeliers shimmered in the antique store, the bakery window was filled with long, skinny loaves of bread, and the neon lights at the Avon Theater where we went to the picture show cast an eerie chartreuse glow on the posters of leggy blondes like Betty Grable dancing in feathers. "Umm, I love the smell of fresh bread," Mama said, breathing in the sweetness.

"If you're hungry, let's get something good," Rhett said as he signaled to the hot tamale vendor whose cart squeaked up the hill.

Mama looked suspiciously at the ground meat. "What kind of meat is that?" she asked the weary man.

"I just sell them," he said, no energy in his voice. Mama forgot her reservations once she tasted the spicy tamale and gobbled the hot food as quickly as she could unwrap the corn husks.

"I've got to hand it to you, Rhett," she cooed, "these things are good enough to take a chance on."

Mama called my attention to the next window, a photography salon featuring portraits of brides, "Look at that bead work." Lingering, Mama eyed the sleek ivory gown, gazing dreamily at the brides with their long, flowing veils. However, Rhett was the one who didn't want to leave the window at the jewelry shop. Behind the burglar bars, rows of diamonds sparkled like rainbows.

The park, actually the school playground where I'd be going in the morning, was even more enchanting at night. Roses filled the air, blossoms pearlescent in the moonlight. Mama and Rhett pushed our swings as long as Lucinda and Sammy and I wanted. The weathered wood smooth beneath my bottom, I held on tight to the cold metal chains, squealing, "Push me higher and higher!" In the breeze against my face, I felt the first cool of summer's end and the rush of what lay ahead in the morning.

Before bed, Mama pinned my hair in tight curls, which I learned to sleep on in spite of the pain. Next morning, Uncle Sam picked Sammy Joe up before dawn though their school didn't start for another week because so many kids were needed to help with the cotton crops.

While Mama enrolled me in first grade, filling out endless papers, she seemed more nervous than I was. Miss Hood, my teacher, was soft-spoken and pretty, her hair piled on top of her head in braids. She was still young enough to be patient and sensitive to shyness. She knew why I studied my white saddle oxfords so hard.

At first, I felt a gnawing hunger in the mornings when the aroma of cornbread dressing, with its onion and sage, permeated the hallway at Lakeview Elementary. Soon, however, hungry for reading instead, I devoured books about Dick and Jane where everybody was happy. The daddy wore a tie to work and drove an ugly, old-fashioned car from the 1940's. The mother—in the kitchen smiling— mopped the floor in high heels. The streets were clean, the neighbors friendly, and the sun was always shining.

I thought all the other first graders must have lived in Dick and Jane's world, or in Lakeview, playing together all their lives. I felt alone.

I dreaded recess because we walked through the dark, scary tunnel to the playground. As if he'd read my mind, Smoky Arrington, a popular boy who sat beside me in reading circle, took my hand and smiled at me.

It was just the way Rhett held my hand when he came to pick me up every day because Mama was still at work. He worked the night shift at Tennessee Coal and Iron, where he loaded ingots of freshly-poured steel. Before that, he had been a miner: first, out west, digging in the mountains for silver and then on Red Mountain, digging for iron ore. Walking along scented streets past the bakery and the barbecue café, I felt a dark, gaping wound inside me begin to heal. I hadn't realized how much I missed my first daddy until I found a new one who waited while I collected acorns, the sound of leaves crunching beneath our shoes.

Miss Hood said sweetly one afternoon, "Bonita, your father's here to pick you up."

"He's not my father." I laughed, my eyes radiating pride. "He's just the man who lives with us."

Miss Hood faltered, the papers on her desk suddenly very important. Such arrangements were not heard of in 1950. Rhett quickly relieved her, "I'm a boarder in their home."

"Oh, I see," Miss Hood stiffened. She could see there was something more.

When Rhett told Mama, she blushed like Miss Hood had. "Maybe we ought to change all that," Rhett said, tousling my hair with one hand and placing the other hand over my mother's.

"Run on and play, baby," Mama said, her voice hoarse, almost a whisper. Feeling as relevant as a puppy, I wanted to paw the air and say, "Yip! Yip!" Like Miss Hood, I knew something was going on.

Before all the leaves fell, Rhett took us to meet his parents. He said that was the best time of year to see their farm. I don't think there could be a bad season. The old wooden house sat across from the greenest pasture I'd ever seen, with the road curving off to the left to embrace a creek as clear as rain, winding on up a steep hill behind the pasture. Just pulling into the driveway by their old 1930's Chevrolet used to make me feel peaceful. Granny Youngblood told us to go ahead and call her Granny as she scooped us into her arms. She was short and spry and full of life, but Rhett's dad was tall and thin and quiet. Lu and I played outside until dark. She taught me about sycamores and sumac and goldenrods, things she was studying at school. Then we went inside and sat by the coal fire with the grownups.

On Thanksgiving, we met the whole family, including Moon who was "afflicted." About 30 years old, he was really tall, red as sumac with coal black hair and a face as round as a moon. He scared me, always wanting me to sit in his lap.

By Christmas, Mama and Rhett were engaged. Just like Granny Youngblood had predicted. Mama said this grandmother didn't need cards to see a lady in love. Granny Youngblood was in touch with the spirit world because her mama was a full-blooded Cherokee who refused to walk the Trail of Tears. Granny claimed the spirits had protected her mother from the Government all the years she hid.

When Daddy Phil heard the news of Mama's engagement, he gave us all a scare, especially Granny Connor, who said he'd lost his manners. He didn't ask, he told us in a loud voice that I could hear from the phone's receiver, "I'm coming over tonight, expect me."

After waiting all evening, visions of broken ribs and purple bruises dancing in my head, we cut off all the lights and crammed into the front bedroom. Lucinda and I piled on our double bed with Granny, and Mama lay on the single bed, her arm reaching behind her to hold Rhett's hand where he lay on the sofa. I was almost asleep when I heard Rhett whisper, "Does he carry a gun?"

Lucinda squeezed my hand. I stole a peep at Granny, who lay on her back, staring at the ceiling as if she were in a trance. I crossed my legs until I couldn't stand it, then got up and used the slop jar, which Mama had put in the closet. I knew they could hear me, so I pretended to be a waterfall.

It must have been midnight when we heard Daddy's car pull up to the curb. I saw the headlights illuminate the room briefly before he switched them off. We heard the sound of his footsteps on the sidewalk, the concrete steps, and then the porch. He knocked softly on the door, then louder and louder. We heard him sigh, then go around to the back door and knock again, calling out, "Pearl? Pearl?" No answer from us. Not a sound. Then we heard him in the grass beside the window. We could see him because of the street light, but we couldn't tell if he saw us. He paused there a few minutes, then went to his car.

We heard the car door open, then the sound of metal clanging. "What was that?" Rhett said, standing at the window, looking out.

"Rhett, don't go out there. I'm warning you," Mama whispered.

Granny's wide eyes still stared at the ceiling, holding on to that trance. Lucinda's hand squeezed mine blue, her sweaty palm slippery. We heard the clop, clop of Daddy's shoes coming back to the porch and then a boom that sounded like a shot. Lucinda's hand was over my mouth before I could scream. We all sat straight up, even Granny. My whole body was trembling, my breath coming in little gasps.

Then we heard the clop, clop again, then Daddy opened and closed the car door. The motor growled, the car lurched forward, and he was gone. We waited, watching carefully out the window, before we went out to see what had caused the noise. On the porch was a wash tub of canned goods: soup, green beans, peas, tomatoes, and several dozen cans of pumpkin pie filling. In the center was a loaf of Italian bread, a pack of spaghetti and the fixings for sauce.

I had never felt so helpless, caught between Rhett and Daddy. I felt guilty, ashamed, because Daddy had brought pumpkin pie, my favorite dessert, for me.

"Some way to make a point," Rhett growled, stalking to his own bed.

A few weeks later, Daddy showed up at my school wearing a three-piece suit and a hat like the fathers in our readers. After he charmed Miss Hood into letting him check me out of school early, we walked twelve or fifteen blocks together to Tate's, the deli where Mama worked. (She had worked there before, when she first met

Daddy, whose crew was building a B. F. Goodrich store across the street.) Dancing and prancing, Daddy sang "Buttons and Bows" and held my hand so I could twist and turn like Ginger Rogers. I pretended I was in a movie with Gene Kelly, but ours would be called *Dancing in the Sun*. It was the most fun I ever had with my father, just the two of us. He adored me enough in that brief stroll to send me in search of adoration for a lifetime. I guess absence had made his heart grow fonder.

When we arrived at Tate's, glowing, Mama's face twisted into anger at the sight of us. Daddy, undaunted by her anger, leaned across the counter, "I love it when you're mad; your eyes get so beautiful, so green. It could be ten years ago, Pearl. You haven't aged a day."

Mama's mouth sprang open, then twitched until she finally found her voice. "I don't want to hear your silver tongue, do you understand me?" Her voice was shrill at the end. "And, I swear to God, if you ever take my baby away from school again, I'll show you pretty anger. I'll choke you till those frozen blue eyes pop right out of your face." She swiped the counter hard with a rag that smelled like bleach, her eyes flashing fire.

Even Daddy could tell she meant it. He straightened his spine, looked nervously around. I wanted to dig a hole to China and crawl in. There were only a few people in the shop, mostly toward the back. "I'll swear out a warrant," Mama yelled louder when her boss came over.

"What seems to be the trouble? Anything I can do?" He eyed my father.

"Yeah, you can let me have some time off to take my baby home," Mama said, untying her apron and jerking my arm like she was madder at me than Daddy. I couldn't stop the tears that rolled like raindrops down my face, but no sound came out with them.

I learned to put my feelings into something like Mama's meat grinder, then freeze them. The tug of war went on and on like a merry-go-round gone wrong while I missed most of the games children around me played. Smokey soon held hands with other girls most of the time, his freckles and green eyes not seen up close anymore.

*How Can I Keep From Singing*

# Chapter Seven:
# The Bubble Honeymoon

I SMELL SMOKE FIRST, as if someone is burning leaves, but it's not that time of year. Then I wake up and see the cross burning in front of The Club Rose, the flames licking wood as if they're hungry. I scream, but Granny is already awake beside me. "Don't worry," she says. "Those men inside will take care of it. They've seen it."

Then I see a man in a dark suit with a white ring around his neck who is motioning to the others to be quiet. That's when I realize there's no music. Outside, men with white sheets over their heads are leaving, mostly in trucks, many of them laughing. Once they've gone, the man with the white collar and several others bring buckets of water and put out the fire. Then he puts his arms around a slender girl in a bride's dress and holds her while she cries. Some people begin to leave, but others mill around talking in small clusters. Some are soft-spoken, others angry. The man sends the bride away with a young man, then draws the others around him and speaks softly to them, and they leave.

"He's a preacher, over there drinking and dancing," Granny says.

"Who?"

"That smart aleck with the white collar."

"Oh. What happened?"

"I don't know, but that was the Klan burning a cross. I know that. They do that when people do wrong. Did you see any white people dancing with colored people?"

"No ma'am. Were they gonna set us all on fire?"

"No, no. Just a warning, honey."

Next morning, Ida was full of news and mad, too. "Crazy folks done burned a cross because the A.M.E. Zion minister's daughter had champagne at her wedding reception. Tell me what's wrong with that. You don't get a thimble full. No more than you get at Holy Communion."

Mama answered, "Some churches use grape juice, but that's not the point. Now, Ida, I don't want to argue with you, but I just don't believe a preacher ought to drink or go places where people do."

"Hmph! We don't criticize our preachers," Ida said, banging the mop.

"I'M TIRED OF POURING all the rent I make into this money trap," Mama said into the phone that afternoon, the cigarette in her mouth moving up and down when she talked. From the sound of it, she was talking to Daddy Phil. "Dream on if you think this dump will support these kids the rest of their lives."

Rhett took us for a ride in his new Ford truck with the early green of Alabama spring peeping through in February. Wild redbud trees bloomed along the road. The air smelled like fresh-cut grass from the back of the truck where Lucinda and I rode.

Rhett was going into business for himself selling knives he made and jewelry he claimed was hand-made on reservations. He got the idea when the Cisco Kid and Pancho came to town and my aunt took me to get their autographs. Rhett was amused by the debate my aunts had: whether Pancho was really Mexican or Indian.

Mama and Rhett's engagement seemed like a fairy tale to me. I couldn't wait for the wedding, envisioning myself strewing rose petals along the aisle. They would be deep rose, almost purple, their scent would fill the church, and I would be dressed in lace like a princess . . .

Reality was different. Mama and Rhett drove off in the baby blue truck, smiling and waving, to get married in Columbus, Mississippi, because it was quicker. I didn't understand the hurry. I didn't smile, but I waved, though I felt as if my arm had been in the wringer again and didn't belong to me. Granny Connor patted my head with one hand and waved with the other. She didn't look happy either. I asked her, "Granny, why do they call it a honeymoon?"

She smiled, then absently turned the gold band on her finger,

"Well, it's a special time when the bride and groom get to know each other and don't include anybody else. I expect they call each other honey and admire the moon, too."

I admired her ring, its simplicity as opposed to Mama's diamond one. Granny's thin band caught the sun as I stroked her palms, seeing the knuckles, the rest of her skeleton under the sagging, spotted hands. "Granny, when you die, may I have your wedding ring?"

She smiled, eyes lighting up at the attention to her one treasure. "I expect I'll be buried with it, hon, 'cause all your cousins want it, too."

"Hmmpp," I muttered.

That night I dreamed of moonglow: the warm water may have been ocean or simply bath water. I swam toward a full moon, feeling my own fullness, the round curves of my barely shaped body and the celebration of being alive.

A few days later, the honeymooners came back, talking of slot machines and Rhett's brother who lived in Mobile. Mama liked her new brother-in-law. Now I was supposed to call him my uncle. Accusingly, I spat out, "I thought honeymoons were only for the bride and groom, so what was Rhett's brother doing there?"

Mama's smile evaporated. Apparently, she hadn't been aware of my resentment. She sat down on the bed, smoothing the chenille spread, and talked to me in a soft voice. "Maybe someday we can take you to see your new uncle, honey," she said. "Your daddy wanted me to meet his brother, so we called him and went out one night."

"How come Daddy told you and Rhett who to call?" I asked, my voice turning into a croak.

"I mean Daddy Rhett," she said, brushing my hair, "not your Daddy Phil. Maybe you need some pampering. It's time to give you a little beauty treatment. Why don't we wash your hair and give it a vinegar rinse?" She said this like it was a treat.

"I hate that stinking stuff," I said, enjoying the drawn look I brought to her face, her mouth turning down at the corners.

"We'll use lemon juice then," she said, "and I'll pin it up so Daddy Rhett can see just how pretty you are when he comes back."

"Where's he?"

"On some business," she answered, going toward the fruit bowl where she kept the lemons. I loved the feel of the cold kitchen sink against my neck together with the warm water she poured on my head. She rubbed my scalp with the sudsy shampoo, then rinsed it twice before she poured the lemon juice, its fragrance prickling my nose.

While she stabbed circular curls with bobby pins, I broke down and asked her to tell me about the honeymoon. She and Granny exchanged a look, their eyes locked briefly in that conspiracy adults have—guarding children from the great mysteries. I hated their patronizing me. I wanted to bark out loud. When Mama saw my anger, she chattered nervously, "We stayed in one of the oldest hotels in Mobile called The Battle House."

"Why would people on a honeymoon want to have a battle?"

"Maybe they figure they might as well get started early," Granny chuckled from the rocking chair.

Mama's voice lilted as her memory kicked in, "It was named for a battle fought during the Civil War when it was built. The rooms had old-timey furniture and heavy brocade drapes. I believe they'd have to hire somebody full time just to polish all the brass and marble in the lobby."

I figured she meant that old war when Granny's mother buried silver in the back yard. And why would anybody want old furniture when they could have some new, pretty things? I didn't ask though because I heard, then saw, Rhett's truck. I ran to hide my pin curls from him.

I heard him say to Mama, "Gotta get an early start in the morning and drive to Neshoba County, where I can get a good price on some beaded moccasins."

"I sure hate to hear you got to get up early in the morning. I had some plans for you tonight," Mama said in a husky voice. Then he kissed her right there in the kitchen. I couldn't claim to be treated like a puppy this time because nobody knew I was hiding on the back porch, which was almost like being in the kitchen. Then he whispered something, and she laughed and made eyes at him, murmuring, "Oh, Rhett, you're a mess."

I felt odd overhearing all their foolishness, so I coughed loud and scraped my feet like I'd just come up on the porch. When they turned to look, I darted toward the stairs, trying to hide the pin curls with my arm somehow, but it's hard to look casual doing that.

Before dinner, Mama combed my hair and fluffed it. She said it was important for this dinner to be special since it was our first as a family. Granny didn't say a word, but she did wear her cameo pin to the table, which she usually only wore on Sundays. Rhett went on and on about the crackling cornbread Mama had made, "This is nearly 'bout good as my mama's."

"Oughtta be. She told me how to make it for you. Said you loved it more than anything," Mama said. Granny ate a few bites, but one was enough for me; it had hard things in it, wasn't soft and sweet like Granny Connor's. I picked at my food, watching the peas roll around on the plate like roly-polies.

"You have to clean your plate to get dessert," Mama said, looking hard at me. I finally finished everything but the cornbread, which she ignored. She brought our dessert in fancy glasses somebody gave her for a wedding present. "Have a highball!" she said brightly, placing the foaming glasses on the table. She had poured Coca Cola over generous blobs of vanilla ice cream, which melted quickly, floating in the carbonated liquid and turning into milky, brown bubbles at the top.

"I thought a highball was a mixed drink," Rhett said.

"It is mixed," I retorted. "You have to use your spoon to stir it if you want it mixed more."

Then they all laughed, even Lucinda. My face felt hot as if I'd stood too long in front of the coals in the fire place, but I tried to look unconcerned. Finally, I gave in, "What's so funny?"

"Nothing, baby," Mama said gently, her eyes telling Rhett to let it pass. She was so busy flirting with him I was surprised she said anything.

Granny piped in, "They're talking about those mixed drinks full of demon rum that folks drink in honky tonks. Of course, me and you don't go to those kind of places, do we?"

Granny hardly ever said much, so everybody got quiet and still. Then Mama whisked the dishes off the table like she was in a hurry. "It's almost bed time," she said cheerily.

I found my best nightie, a pink gown, and brushed my teeth a long time. Then I took my book and crawled up on Mama's bed.

"Oh, no, baby," she said, her mouth turned down in a frown. I saw her make it change, the corners moved vertically, but the smile wasn't real. "This is mine and Rhett's room now," she said, a trace of apology in her thin voice. "You'll be sleeping with Granny from now on."

"But I don't mind sleeping in the middle," I said. "I didn't get a new bed like Lucinda's."

Lucinda, piled up on a roll-away bed with her nose in a book, said sullenly, without looking up, "It's not new. It came from one of the apartments upstairs, and it smells like mildew."

Mama and Daddy Rhett turned our living room into their room. They moved the double bed, which we'd slept in with her for over a year, into the corner. They set up a rickety room divider covered with parachute material Rhett had brought back from the war. The old rust-colored sofa sat catty-cornered, looking as out of place as I felt. I lifted my chin and strode out of the room, trying hard to be as detached as Lucinda, "That old parachute smells like mildew, too."

Granny hummed "The Old Rugged Cross" as she scratched my back under the cool, starched sheets. I pictured the crown I'd wear in Heaven someday. When Granny switched to "Jesus Loves the Little Children," I imagined them: red and yellow and black and white. None of the pictures I called up worked just right. I already knew that skin tones came in a range of shades like paint samples at the hardware store. I thought about the whispers I'd overheard between Mama and Ida about labor unions and meetings and one of Ida's sons. The Club Rose was just getting started, a voice smooth as chocolate sang "That Old Black Magic." I studied the shadows made by the fig tree in the back yard until I fell asleep, imagining different shapes rising out of the shadows.

The more Mama complained about the house being a money trap, the clearer it became that we were headed for another move. I heard her tell Granny that she and Rhett needed more privacy, and they often disappeared after dinner to look at real estate announced in the want ads.

By the time Rhett and Mama told us they were selling our house, we had already figured it out. I hated the FOR SALE sign in our yard and couldn't bear to even think of moving and leaving my teacher Miss Hood and Smoky and my other classmates behind. I tried, instead, to memorize every detail of the house I knew I'd miss: the pale green tile around the fireplace with its columned mantle and beveled mirror, and the elaborate trim on the crown molding. Most of all, I would miss the bay window where the music floated into the room at night from the club next door with its swirl of colors—gaudy by day, enchanting by night.

We had a buyer almost immediately. My aunt said it was because Mama sold too low. Mama glowed with the excitement of being flush. She gave Ida a big cash bonus and a lot of curtains and sheets and furniture we wouldn't need in our smaller house.

When Aunt Mary Alma came to pick up Granny Connor, I overheard her say, "I give those two six months!"

Granny continued packing without a word. Before she left, she held me tighter than she ever had.

# Chapter Eight:
## The First Redbud

IT SEEMED, EVENTUALLY, easier to put Daddy Phil and that part of our life behind us in a new neighborhood we didn't associate with him. We all enjoyed the glow of change and a fresh beginning—extending the honeymoon.

The new house, gleaming white, trimmed with green shutters, seemed fresh and modern after the money trap. Mama and Rhett had picked the house without us one afternoon, but they took us to see it that night. In the cool moonlight, it resembled the house we'd had near the sanatorium enough to make me wonder if the crack of my life could be healed after all. I resented having to peep in the windows like a burglar, but I kept it to myself because Mama was so tickled over it. Her glow rivaled the moon's. Already, I knew not to mention to Daddy Rhett how much the new house reminded me of our old house before everything changed. It was even close by, in East Lake, way beyond the smelly viaduct. We were moving back to the part of town where the sun rose every morning.

Mama installed an awning over the window box at our kitchen sink, made it cozy—an inviting place to wash her new dishes with gold edging around a balladeer lost in a lover's gaze. Mama's gaze was like that, too, in the early days on Division Avenue before I learned, again, about the house divided's inability to stand.

The wide porch had room for a swing and several rockers, but I perched on the floor where I could look through a round hole in the stone bannister. I spied on the new world around me, filled with streetcars and intriguing neighbors.

The sturdy wisteria vine, more like a tree, shaded the porch with its entangled offshoots. The lush purple blooms snuggled up to the roof like a sleeping dragon, not a mean one, I decided, but a girl dragon who would make the fiery dragons settle down. Grabbing a vine and swinging dangerously close to the window, I felt the sweet exhilaration of childhood as I beat my chest to make Tarzan sounds. Lucinda, who always had to be Jane, cut her eyes at me just in time to prevent my crashing into her window, where frilly yellow curtains kept the afternoon sun from her ruffled spread.

I liked to scare my sister, make her think I'd break her window to pay her back for trespassing in my huge closet where I stored my tea sets and other treasures from my old play house. Lucinda arranged my dolls on the wicker bookshelf to hide the amputated arms hanging from the soft, stuffed torsos. She set the dolls so that their blue eyes, covered with lashes unnaturally thick, popped out of the hard faces as if they'd seen a murder. I told Lucinda, "Stop messing with my dolls; they look scared!"

I tilted their heads, which made their eyes open more normally, their expressions less hysterical. I loved having my own room, but I still had to work at sleeping alone. When I tried to go to sleep, I made up a night version of cloud watching. I imagined the silver swirls in my mint green wallpaper as creatures or angels. Sometimes the silver dragons covering the wall would look so real I'd crawl in bed with Lucinda and cuddle up to her warmth. She pretended not to notice, but I suspected she liked the company, too.

When Mama insisted I sleep in my own bed, I wet the bed. I woke up in tears, disgusted by the heavy smell of urine on my gown and sheets. I could almost sleepwalk into a fresh gown and stumble over to Lucinda and her warm softness. Before the bed wetting, Lucinda had welcomed my company. Nowadays, she held her nose and whined in a high nasal voice, "Puuuuuwee! I smell stinking wee wee. Must be a baby around here somewhere."

Mama never criticized me; she simply tucked me in the next night with fresh sheets that smelled like Clorox. When we first moved, she told us stories every night or read to us from *Wind in the Willows*, which I had checked out of the library. I didn't like the book, but I never told a soul because I was sure there was something lacking in me, not the book.

I relished walking to the library, an old stone building with long arched windows. The library's church-like ceiling hovered over the hushed reverence where I learned to worship books. The small tables and chairs fit my body snugly. I always felt like Goldilocks when I sat down, wanting to squeal, "This one is just right!" I was responsible about the books I checked out, never paying a fine for late returns. I felt grown up, important, choosing my own books.

Mama seemed happy, too, always busy. She hosed down the porch, leaving the smell of clean dampness behind. When she washed Venetian blinds in the yard with a cleaner that smelled like pine trees, the water hose made rainbows and a soft cool spray I loved to drink.

Mama must have dusted the figurines on the whatnot shelf in the living room five times a day. I saw her standing once in the sunlight that poured in the front window, holding a porcelain shoe toward the light and smiling as the gold trim glittered. She seemed, for a moment, like a child herself.

Her pleasure in such a simple thing stung my eyes. I wanted to wave a magic wand and take away the pain of her scant childhood. She had only received an orange and a candy cane each Christmas, but my wand would lavish her with toys that sparkled in the sunlight. Instead, I went out and picked her a bouquet. My favorite thing about the new house was the luxury of flowers: dahlias and roses and gardenias that smelled like Mama's perfume.

Mama's favorite thing was the Youngstown kitchen with the swivel cabinet in the corner. "I could store enough food in that cabinet to feed all the starving children in China and then some," she said when she first saw it. At least once a week, she swiveled the shelf until she found her cake ingredients and came up beaming.

After supper, we'd go for long walks to "the end of the loop," where the streetcars turned around and headed back to the city. We lived just on the edge of town, before the suburb of Roebuck. Sometimes the soft summer nights and walks that lasted hours filled me with a peace I thought I'd lost forever when Mama left Daddy Phil.

When school began, Mama hated our separation as much as I did. It's as if we both knew that her opportunity for a normal life with time to enjoy homemaking would be short-lived.

Mrs. Greenhaw, my new teacher, was stern, much older than

Miss Hood at Lakeview. Rumor had it that lots of the stern old woman's pupils wet their pants, which terrified me. One morning, during the second week of class, Mrs. Greenhaw assigned what she called "seat work" and then, as she always did, kept her tight blue-gray curls tilted downward at her desk, reading. Her glasses hung off the edge of her long, skinny nose and always seemed about to fall. I felt panicky when the fullness of my bladder began to press for attention between break and lunch. I raised my hand at least ten times to ask permission to go to the bathroom. When Mrs. Greenhaw failed to notice, I frantically waved my hand. I thought perhaps she'd fallen asleep at her desk, so I began to clear my throat and scrape my feet on the oily wooden floor. My classmates who had noticed my attempts shot me empathetic looks, but we were all afraid to say a word since silence during seat work was sacred to Mrs. Greenhaw.

My face flushed as if I had a fever when the warm oozing spread between my legs, yellowing my white pinafore. When two boys across from me snickered, I was too humiliated to be angry. Still unable to find my voice, I felt as if my heart had stopped. Suddenly, I bolted for the door and ran the whole six blocks to the sweetness and warmth of my mother.

Her perfume enveloped me as I sobbed against her breast. She held me in her lap until I stopped crying, never complaining about her now-wet gabardine skirt. "I'll go up there and give that old biddy a piece of my mind," she scowled. "She don't know who she's messin' with." Mama always talked "countrier" when she was upset.

The look in Mama's eyes convinced me she could scare Mrs. Greenhaw to death, which I exulted in for the rest of the morning while I played. Mama drew me a tub of warm water and called to me in a voice too casual, "Wanna take a bubble bath?"

I made grilled cheese sandwiches when Lucinda came home for lunch. Blowing on her steaming chicken soup, Lucinda told us, her hazel eyes contemptuous, "I nearly died when Mrs. Greenhaw told me. She said to tell my parents she would have done anything she could to make the wee wee monster feel better, but she left too quick."

Mama's voice was soft, "Lucinda, you're embarrassed more than mad at Bonita. Think about your little sister's feelings. That old biddy told you her self-serving version of the story, which you bought without blinking. So maybe you're not as smart as you think you are."

Lucinda blushed, but she recovered quickly. Like a witch reaching inside her evil bag of tricks, she eyed me, sneering, "Mrs. Greenhaw said to tell you not to worry. She's had lots of babies wee wee in her class. It's perfectly normal."

Mama's eyes widened, her mouth turned into a stretched Cheerio screaming, "You mean she called my daughter a baby?"

"No, that was my addition." Lucinda stuffed her mouth with the gooey cheese sandwich.

"I'll march up to that school and teach that ol' fool a thing or two," Mama grumbled, scrubbing the new oilcloth so hard I looked for holes in it. We were all quiet for the rest of the meal. Then Mama told Lucinda, "Run on back to school now," but she told me I could stay home the rest of the day. "We'll make some fudge, ok?" she suggested as Lucinda prissed down the street, golden hair shining in the sun like a crown.

By nightfall I begged Mama to drop it, to just let me go back and act as if nothing happened. "I'm scared enough of Mrs. Greenhaw already, Mama. I don't want to make her mad." (It never occurred to me that it was the old crank's fault, not mine.) Finally, Mama came up with a compromise. She sent a note: *Bonita has my permission to be excused without asking permission if she senses an emergency coming on. Thank you, Pearl Youngblood.*

I walked what seemed the longest six blocks of my life the next morning, marched to my desk and went on with my life. It was not my fault. My waving hand had not been acknowledged. I had a solution. Mrs. Greenhaw looked up from the note delighted, "What a fine idea."

Mrs. Greenhaw's class was different from Miss Hood's; we never planted flowers or used water colors or even crayons. For art, we made a vocabulary book. We spent hours cutting out pictures of words to fill up a page for each letter, the rustling of the worn magazines the only sound allowed.

The only other time my teacher smiled at me that year was the day I glued a picture of Kotex on my K page. "I think you'd better find another picture," she said in the only caring tone I ever heard from her.

I was glad Mama was not so busy, and I got lots of attention at home that fall since my classmates acted like I was from Mars as "the new girl." When I bought Smith Brothers cherry cough drops for a nickel at the store across the street from school, the girls in my top reading group giggled, "Ooooo, look, her tongue is red. She must be diseased."

I envied them when they'd go off to tap dancing or Brownies after school in those cute outfits. I especially wanted a beanie to keep my head warm, but Mama always said we didn't have extra money. She scraped together enough to pay for Lucinda's piano lessons, but she told me no.

Lucinda hated walking the six blocks along the lake to go home for lunch, but I loved seeing the lazy, mossy water any time. Lucinda said it took too long, but the break from school was never long enough for me. Mama always had something good to eat. "Besides," she pointed out, "it's cheaper than those little-bitty school lunches."

I couldn't wait for lunch or the metallic clang of the three o'clock bell. I enjoyed homework, still relished school work, but not school. On the shadowed porch I watched streetcars go by at dusk, when the yellow squares framed passengers like a photograph at each window. I wondered who they were, where they were going.

"Pearl, this girl is a smart cookie," Rhett cried one night when he'd had just enough beer to summon patience. I sat in his lap and spelled every word he could think of. "Get that big ol' Webster's dictionary down." It was almost a foot thick, an edition Mama got for enrolling in a book club she never ordered from. I sat in her lap then while Rhett looked up words to challenge me, giving me a quarter for every one I spelled right. Elated, I counted them before I went to sleep, but early the next morning he crept in my room and whispered, "I'm gonna need to borry these, sugar."

A month or so later, a curly-haired younger boy moved in next door, another runt, somebody newer in the neighborhood. Johnny and his parents were friendly, unlike the neighbors who already knew each other. He and I played house every day. He followed my commands, moving all my playhouse things around the fence that separated our yards. I had finally found a new home under the sheet we tied to the clothesline, making a tent for my teapot and stove. We laughed and sang over tea and mud pies, having our own honeymoon. Then we swept and mopped together before we "broke camp" each afternoon. Bursting with joy and sunshine, I decided this was how it felt to be in love, to be newlyweds.

One day I sneaked Granny's quilt outside to make a pallet for a nap after our Sunday dinner of roast mud and grass sandwiches. The sun dappled our faces, warmed us while the breeze rustled Johnny's curly, golden hair. Overhead, the redbud, our "roof," covered and protected us like a pink parasol. Discretely peeping, we'd watched three eggs in a small, oval nest for weeks. The cardinal, always searching for worms, flew in—his red beauty startling as the sound of his strong wings—and perched above the nest. His mate, a homely color of old blood, fed the scrawny beaks that popped up. I took Johnny's hand as we listened to her song.

Seemingly out of nowhere, Johnny pulled out his penis and said, "Look. Show me yours."

I answered softly, "No, I don't want to," but something in me knew this sweetness felt right, was not threatening.

I knew I'd find the right time to talk to Mama. Later that day, Mama made fudge, letting me lick the spoons as the bubbly goo came to a boil. Mama dropped a blob in the cup of water, but it didn't make a ball. "Not quite thick enough," she said and lit a Pall Mall, still stirring.

"Smells like heaven," I told her, then added casually, "Something must be wrong with Johnny's privacy because it's bruised. You know, the end is purple."

Mama's jaw dropped. She took the cigarette out of her mouth, the inch-long ash falling down her blouse. Leaving her cigarette in the ash tray, she stirred the candy furiously, "How do you know what his 'Christmas' looks like?" she snapped, eyes flashing.

I didn't understand. Since Johnny and I were being the mom and dad, it had seemed natural to look. I didn't want him touching me, but I wasn't shy about looking at something that seemed so harmless. "Why are you mad? He didn't do anything to me like Junior did."

"I'm not mad," she yelled, "and there's no need to bring all that up! Little girls and boys just don't do nasty things, honey. That's all."

After that, I wasn't allowed to play with Johnny. His nice, friendly parents quit speaking to us. This little boy had just been sweet, and I hadn't really done anything but try to understand that stupid honeymoon stuff. I was never trusting anybody again. Except Granny.

The next spring, when the tree bloomed again and spring jumped out of the ground, I tried to understand it as a second grader. I could see the consequences were not as severe as the incident with Junior for sure. Later on, I realized I lost something that day, some sort of hope or innocence. Instead of flowing naturally, I was jerked out of the flow and stunted a few years back when the older boys had been mean and forceful toward me, but this incident with Johnny never made sense. The adults mishandled this lesson; maybe I was deemed the evil older woman as a first-grader. Maybe my mother was terrified by the trauma of what happened before, thus overprotective. Who knows?

Winter in Alabama could be a tease, offering stolen glimpses of spring as early as January, long before the daffodils sprang up beneath the redbud tree. Both so vibrant, they seemed like wild gifts from Mother Nature at the border between Johnny's yard and mine, haunting me with life's possibilities.

Awakened by the poignant birds singing age-old questions, I often pondered questions of my own. Something in their simplicity awakened the memory of Johnny and that innocent moment in my life. I was exposed to life's underbelly by the same people who scolded me away from that first innocent pretense at parenting, at coupling.

I felt the aching irony of it, the same ache I heard in jazz singers from The Club Rose, their heartbroken wailing when they sang "Mood Indigo." I imagined dark blue ink seeping from my heart into my toes when I tried to write about its mystery.

Every spring when I see, in tiny, determined buds, the first sign of a longing to erupt, I think of that soft, vulnerable innocence. Each year, the first blooming redbud reminds me of the redbud of my youth: its purple shadows in contrast to the lavender blooms, dazzling against the gray, barren landscape. Winter's trees like thin, broken pencil lead beneath a pale blue sky predominated, but one burst of orchid couldn't wait to open. That urge toward life, that glimpse of wonder—squelched in the bud.

Maybe children should not be taught to believe in honeymoons. Certainly, they should not be as enmeshed as I was and then have so little explanation as they try to explore and find their own way.

Childhood needs to be a place where little girls around the world could be safe from half-grown brothers who would abuse them, boys in their own grief-stricken journey through the mystery of red buds and honeymoons who would ride them like hobby horses.

# Chapter Nine:
## Peddling to Boxing

I WAS ALSO ENMESHED ALREADY in the trap of monitoring the amount of alcohol Rhett consumed. My imagination soothed the disappointment as I watched the honeymoon wear off and reality set in. He and his brother Moon both had dark eyes and coal black hair like Indians in the movies. If they'd worn braids, they could have been movie stars. I imagined how I'd spend the money when we moved to Hollywood. Sometimes Daddy Rhett was funny and affectionate when he drank beer, but when he drank whiskey he was mean. Mama said it was the Cherokee in him that made him drink "firewater."

One Friday after school, I was on the porch escaping into the drama of the streetcar passengers and their stories I created when I heard Rhett open a beer as soon as he came in the back door. Whenever I heard the sound of that old rusty opener he called a church key making the beer foam, I was relieved. That meant it wasn't whiskey this weekend.

Rhett guzzled a can of Pabst Blue Ribbon, burped and chuckled, "I left ol' Moon selling turquoise rings down in Roebuck. Friday afternoon's a good time to catch folks since it's payday for most of them. Decided to come home and get my family, take y'all out to eat at Bennie's new café when we sell out. How about it?"

Lucinda and I didn't like peddling, but we piled in the truck anyway and went to the tables they had set up on Highway 11. I was ashamed that Rhett was a peddler when other daddies had real jobs at the airport or TCI or Chicago Bridge, places of importance. I hoped my embarrassment wasn't obvious when Reba, a girl in my class, and her mother drove up in a new white Buick polished to a spit shine. Reba's mama had on a bright red dress pleated neatly around her long slim legs, which were planted in a pair of shoes the color of a redbird. Like Lucinda, I buried my face in a book.

As soon as I saw her mother try on a bracelet, her nose stuck up in the air, I told Mama I had to go to the bathroom. As I crept away before Reba saw me, I heard the woman, whine, "Is that the best price you can give me?"

Crimson filled my face as I hurried across the parking lot while Rhett and Moon sold Reba and her mom jewelry. But I felt strangely empowered by the shiny, smooth nickel in my pocket as I found my way through the busy crowd of Friday shoppers at Hill's Grocery Store. Making a purchase would make me feel better about asking to use their restroom. I decided to buy another box of cough drops with my allowance and only eat them on the weekend when I could let the sweetness of cherry flavoring color my tongue if I wanted.

When I returned, Rhett was still griping about that snooty lady trying to get him to bring his prices down. He didn't care about her nose and hadn't budged on his prices. He stuck another feather—bright red like a cardinal—in his headband, grinning. It was a game to him. "Like playing poker, ain't it, Moon," he said, laughing and slapping his leg and swilling beer. "I give her a few earrings in the bottom of the sack that were just silver-plated; serves her right, by God."

I prayed again that Reba didn't see me. My eyes felt the sting, my throat the lump, as I buried myself—again—in my reading. We had sold the jewelry down to two crosses and maybe a dozen bracelets when it happened.

The License Man inched his protruding belly from under the steering wheel and crawled out of the dark, official car. He checked on Rhett all the time, seemed to have more rules than Rhett could keep up with. He lumbered up to the truck, where Moon and Rhett tried to look unconcerned, having stashed their beers as well as their headbands.

"How's it goin'?" the man asked, holding his hands out to the side when he walked as if to balance himself. I figured it was hard work totin' that belly around.

"Some weeks you lose," Rhett whined, hoping for sympathy.

There was no sympathy in the old man's wheezing voice, "I ain't so much concerned about that as I am about your license. Last time I checked you didn't have one, was goin' the next day."

Rhett's eyes registered triumph. "Well, old timer. You're in luck today. I just happen to have that license now." Chest swelled with pride and ivory teeth gleaming, he showed the man the flimsy paper.

"Um hm," the man responded. He walked around the truck, his eyes roaming. He checked everything so closely he needed a magnifying glass. He waddled up close, tipped back as if he might fall over, and pulled out his pad. "I'm still gonna have to write you up, bud. You s'pose to have a permit, too."

Rhett's shoulders sank, his mouth hanging open in shocked disappointment. "How long do I have to pay the fine?" he croaked.

"It's spelled out on your license, bud. You might want to read the fine print next time." The old man sneered as he lumbered toward his car. Rhett cussed under his breath as the fellow stuffed himself back into the car, "That sumbich oughtta be shot."

Mama whispered, "If you know what's good for you, you better quit talking like that." Her eyes studied the fat man to see if he'd heard.

Rhett wheeled around and hollered at her, "You shut your mouth, woman. Stay out of this. Understand me?"

"You kiss my foot," she yelled just as loud, eyes dilated, ready for battle.

"Not right now. I'm mad," Rhett grinned. If the fat man heard them, he didn't show any sign. He left a cloud of red dust as he backed his car around and roared off.

Mama and Rhett didn't care who heard them, but I was glad we were far enough away that most folks couldn't. It had become a ritual by then. Bickering energized them, but it wore me out. They carried on that way for awhile, which made Lucinda grin self-consciously, but I never looked up from my book. Mama tried not to let Rhett's quip stop her, "Don't you take it out on me, Mr. Big Ike," Mama started, but gave in to a grin, "Give me one of those beers."

Why couldn't they be like the parents who were invited to come in and talk at the end of Mrs. Frances' *Ding Dong School*, which I watched religiously on the pale flickering screen in the living room?

As soon as Mama was half way through her beer, the sun began to turn the the sky the color of a Dreamsicle, "Look," I said, "like my favorite popsicle."

She smiled, relaxed, at the beginning sunset and brushed Rhett's arm, "I think we have a hungry girl here."

"I'm ready," he grinned back. He finished his beer in one gulp, packed up, and we drove to the Grill.

Bennie smoked good barbecue, and Martha, who looked more like his daughter than his wife, made thick, greasy French fries. "I could eat just those if they'd let me," I told Bennie, dipping fries in ketchup and savoring the salty taste.

Lucinda looked up at Bennie under long, thick lashes and cooed like she was ordering a kiss, "I want that fried fantail shrimp."

Mama ordered catfish and Rhett had barbecue. I'd eat anything as long as I had fries, but my favorite was chicken, which Martha fried to a perfect crisp after dipping it in buttermilk batter. Martha and Bennie had been married longer than Mama and Rhett, but they still seemed to be honeymooners. He was a jovial, pleasant man with salt-and-pepper hair that always had too much Wildroot Hair Groom in it.

Martha was petite, with a wide smile visible from the front door. No matter how busy, she was always soft-spoken, patient. She let me help her in the kitchen when Rhett got loud out front. We could hear his guffaws as he told the other men about the fat man demanding a permit.

Once the hot grease started popping, Martha let me stir a chocolate pie. I lost myself in the process, the watery mixture turning into a velvety smooth substance that took on a body of its own. It was miraculous, and I was part of the miracle.

When Rhett got loosened up enough to be generous with the nickels after dinner, Lucinda and I played the shuffleboard machine until we hit the big bonus. Lights throughout the machine flickered, bells rang and the boobs on the big, blonde cowgirl painted across the top of the machine lit up.

When Rhett said to us, "Come on, girls. Time to go. Gotta get home for the boxing match," Bennie handed him a bottle of whiskey.

Rhett's dark eyes flickered with hesitation. He knew he couldn't drink whiskey, that it made him crazy. Bennie told him, "This is partly to celebrate the café and partly to commiserate about the permit." Rhett caressed the bottle and looked at his friend a second or two longer than he normally allowed himself to make eye contact with another man.

He cleared his throat, looked to see who was watching, then said in a low voice. "It means a lot, bud. Thanks." The two men joked about whiskey being better company than a woman to clear the air of anything like real emotion. I hoped Rhett would stay jovial, but by the time we got home, nobody laughed.

He turned the bottle up maybe four times, his Adams's apple working hard to make room for the liquid fire. "AAhhhhhh," he sputtered, "stings the eyes, soothes the soul!"

I didn't think so. Whiskey triggered an avalanche of meanness in him, gave him a different personality altogether. He ranted and raved about Mama's cigarettes, our toys in the middle of the floor—anything set him off.

Mama never let him carry on without standing up to him. She yelled as loud as he did, "That firewater makes you look like a wild Indian ready to scalp somebody! Go look in the mirror at that red face, you crazy thing. Why would you drink that poison?"

I couldn't see how that was such an insult since I'd heard her tell Helen he had Cherokee good looks, carrying on about his regal nose and high cheekbones.

Rhett pushed her away from him. "Don't you sass me like that!"

"Don't push me, you heathen," she fired back, shoving him so hard he fell over in the bed, which dissipated the tension. They both struggled to suppress giggles. His mouth fought the curling smile but surrendered, "Well, I be dog, right where I was headed anyway."

"Good," she wheeled around in the navy polka dot dress, high heels underscoring her exit with their clomp, clomp, clomp. She smiled triumphantly, but she didn't giggle with Lucinda and me.

The room was filled with unspoken relief that Rhett passed out early. I knew one of these nights it was gonna go further than pushing, but at least it seemed settled for the moment.

I had already pulled my rocker up to the television as close as I could get to watch boxing. In my soft, pink bathrobe I escaped into the silvery, flickering light. I yelled, "Get him! Kill him! Knock that fool down!"

Mama and Lucinda relished my response, grinning at each other the way adults do as if children are blind as well as deaf. I see now the irony was amusing—me the little peacemaker who was scared of everything and everybody. It was part of that escape into fantasy taking shape, an outlet for my anger. When I went to bed, I heard them laughing at *I Love Lucy*, but I didn't even want to think about Desi Arnaz and carry on with them about how handsome he was. Joe Louis was my hero of the night, and I was asleep in a flash.

# Chapter Ten:
# Beware of Men Who Murder Flowers

THE MORNING WAS UNSEASONABLY WARM. Almost immediately, I heard the usual bickering start, cranking up like the distant rumble of thunder before a storm. No matter how hot it was, I closed the windows when Mama and Daddy Rhett yelled at each other. I didn't want the neighbors to hear. It seemed as if all their fights boiled down to three things: money, his drinking, and her smoking. I didn't understand yet their interrelatedness.

Mama smoked one cigarette after another by then, always had one bobbing in her mouth. "If you'd take that cigarette out of your mouth and hold it between your fingers like you're supposed to, you might not be such a chain smoker," Rhett growled. I had learned to recognize his sailor's voice. Whenever he was really mad at himself he always wanted to straighten somebody else out.

"You ain't really Mr. Clark Gable, you know," she shot back. "How long you gonna primp in front of that mirror?" He didn't answer her but continued to admire his dark eyes in the mirror, the black slickness of his hair. The silence riled Mama.

"Besides, who told you it was your business to tell somebody how to smoke?" Mama said in the shrill voice I'd learned to expect at this point in their arguments. I also knew her next line, "If you didn't drink up every penny we have, we'd be a darn sight better off, I tell you that." Her eyes fiery as the orange coal that bobbed when she talked, she squinted. The smoke trailed by her upper lip into her nostrils and then her eyes. Her tight-lipped smugness indicated she thought she'd had the final word, but the squabbling elevated.

Rhett was irritable, expecting us to tiptoe around until he got "cranked up." After he shaved, I noticed his fingers shook as he smoothed his hair back with Wildroot. He looked in the mirror again, satisfied with the hair, running his fingers across the smooth-shaven cheek, the strong chin.

Mama almost let herself admire his dark good looks, her eyes struggling with the division. She sat on the bed in a creamy ivory slip Rhett gave her for her birthday, her breasts swelling above the lace. She twirled her thick hair at the nape of her neck. The length of his self-adulation at the mirror annoyed her though, so she belted her chenille robe and came into the kitchen and set up the waffle iron.

When Rhett poured his coffee and sat down, Mama returned to the feud, "I told you last night you had no business getting drunk in front of my children. It's irresponsible."

"Well, this is my house. Furthermore, it ain't my responsibility what they see and hear, is it!" Rhett shouted. "Looks like I took on enough responsibility," he added sarcastically. I knew he was talking about us.

Mama shot him an accusing look and said, mostly to herself, "Far as I know, it's my house."

"Who pays the light bill, keeps this place running? Ask Alabama Power," Rhett hissed.

Mama towered over him, while he slumped at the red Formica table picking at the loose chrome trim. "You know good and well you just takin' it out on me because you got outsmarted by that license man, and it ain't my fault!"

"That damn fool," he said, "would have led any man to have a few beers."

"Haaaa," Mama screamed, "a few beers, my foot. You couldn't walk when you came in. No wonder you went straight to bed so early. I had to pour you in it, in fact, in front of these children, and I'm sick of it!" She shrieked so loud her voice sounded hoarse, as if it might give out.

Rhett was on his feet, "Don't tell me what you're sick of with that cigarette in your mouth. That's what I'm sick of. I'll get that cigarette out of your mouth!" He knocked the cigarette out and ground it with his heel into the hard wood floor, grazing her upper lip in the process.

Mama fell to her knees, crying, "My floor, you've ruined my

floor!"

I was surprised she was more worried about her floor than her upper lip bleeding. After Rhett stormed out of the house, I brought her a cold washcloth. Lucinda, on the porch reading a book, never even looked up when Rhett huffed by.

Outside, the lawnmower sounded worse than usual as Rhett shoved it toward the house under the window. On Saturdays, when other daddies puttered in the yard, planting flowers or vegetables, Rhett would be in a foul mood because he either cut grass or was ashamed he hadn't cut it. Either way, Saturdays were not happy times, and this one was worse. Sweat pouring down his face, Rhett pushed the lawnmower so fast I thought the metal blades had disappeared. When he stopped, I saw they were just blurred by his speed. He banged the mower furiously, cussing to himself.

My eyes turned into ice when I saw it, as if I could freeze my vision, refuse to see it. He slammed the mower through the circular flower bed, then the dahlias. I ran outside, sobbing, "Please stop, Rhett, please. I love those flowers."

My pleading spurred him on. "Damn flowers, too much trouble. I ain't got time to fool with this!" The mower was so clogged with thick stems it quit turning. With a pick ax, Rhett chopped the gardenias like a savage. I wondered if he learned to be so brutal in the military, like Mama said. He never even looked at me. I was irrelevant. Maybe I couldn't completely freeze my eyes, but this puppy had begun to freeze a heart to survive.

I froze my hurt so well that Buster and his brother, our buddies down the street, didn't even know how heartbroken I was. The flowers had made me feel like normal people lived in our home, happy people . . . at least some of the time. Buster's mother told me they probably would not come back after that kind of treatment, but she would try to root some. I did salvage a vase or two full of those that weren't shredded beyond recognition. Buster was sweet to me, helping with the flowers, but usually he only had eyes for Lu. I loved his dark, curly hair.

That night, Rhett and Mama went dancing at Queenstown Lake to make up. I thought about their roller coaster love. They looked as dazzling as movie stars when they left . . . and as happy, Mama's rhinestone earbobs pretty as diamonds. They made up faster than I ever could. When I thought of those soft, pink flowers shredded by the mower, tears dampened my pillow. I didn't feel the wet cotton pillowcase against my cheek, as if the tears belonged to somebody else.

Next day at sunrise, I woke up early with damp sheets for another reason. I put on a fresh gown and gave in to an overwhelming urge to snuggle against my mother. I crept into their room where all the shades were drawn against the morning light and crawled into Mama's arms. Her face was relaxed, lovely, when she reached for me. I jumped back when I saw that she was naked, sensing myself out of place somehow. Her eyes registered a fleeting awkwardness, but she whispered groggily, "It's ok, baby," and twisted her sheet into a sort of gown and pulled the comforter over us.

I pretended I was asleep when Rhett woke up; he stretched, yawned and then farted. I had to work hard not to giggle, but I succeeded because just then I caught a glimpse through my slitted eyes of his naked, muscular shoulders slipping into a terrycloth robe. I held on to Mama tight and tried to go back to sleep, though my head was filled with questions and visions of redbuds. Tears streamed from my eyes, slowly at first, then a flood. I couldn't stop them or the sobs. Mama was wrinkled with concern, kept saying, "What's the matter, baby? Tell Mama?"

I couldn't tell her because I didn't understand, myself. "Get dressed and take her outside in the fresh air," Rhett growled, rubbing his temple and turning his back on us.

EVENTUALLY, Mama had to get a job at Greg's Cookies to help with the bills. Rhett gave up on his silver scam business because he couldn't make payments on his truck unless he had a regular income, and the pawn shop supply was just as unpredictable as his luck with selling. He worked nights now, driving a wrecker.

That summer, it rained every day. Katie Mae, Ida's daughter, who took care of us during the day was so scared of thunder and lightning she made us hide under the bed when it stormed. "Mean ol' dog days," she whispered, clutching the bed springs when thunder blasted around us. Otherwise, we loved having somebody not much older than us. We played all day inside and outdoors, too. Lucinda adored her, begged Katie Mae to teach her every sport in school, but

I swear nobody could make me athletic.

Katie Mae did teach me to dance like at The Club Rose though. She would kick off her shoes, and her light colored soles would become magic as her full body swirled me around the floor as if I were light as a feather. We found our music on the radio in the living room, and she sang along with every tune. She taught us steps, but she danced "from her head." Smooth and easy, she became the notes as they flowed from the radio. It was really magic.

When Lucinda told on Katie Mae for making us hide under the bed, Mama thought the girl was scaring us to death. To tell the truth, it was years before I could face a storm calmly or see the beauty in dark clouds gathering.

Once again, Granny Connor rescued us by coming to stay with us a few weeks to keep us during the day. When Granny stayed with us, we always had more money because we didn't have to pay a baby sitter, and Granny gave us popsicle money. When the guy came by, pushing the white cart and ringing the rusty old cow bell, he'd let us touch the dry ice, which would sting if we held on too long, capturing a little skin from our fingers. His crush on Katie Mae didn't help her case. He'd talk too long to her and let my skin peel away. He always chuckled softly, saying weird things like "I be like that witch in Hansel and Gretel, heh heh."

Granny Connor always came to our rescue when she could, but as soon as we settled into a routine that summer, Uncle Clyde's wife had a baby who got all Granny's attention for awhile. I couldn't see what all the fuss was about. She was just a little red thing that squalled all the time, but Granny had to stay with them on the weekend and then for a whole week. I hated that new baby for being the youngest now. I pulled her hair when nobody was watching.

# Chapter Eleven:
# Life on the Farm, a Respite

DURING THE WEEK THAT Lu and I spent with Aunt Shannon, I wondered what was going on at home, why Daddy Phil helped Mama put us on the bus instead of Daddy Rhett, but I didn't say a word. Sammy Joe took us on hikes through the woods, sometimes trooping for miles. We checked on the cows that chewed lazily down by the mossy, green creek. Sometimes we spotted an occasional hawk, but often we saw buzzards. "When you see a buzzard circling around like that, you know there's a dead carcass nearby," Sammy Joe told us casually. It made me shiver.

Every night, we entertained ourselves for hours rehearsing a play to be performed before bed time. Our dramas always unfolded behind the sheet we mounted at the ceiling and lit with the naked light bulb from the lamp. Lucinda wanted to be the boss, explaining that every drama had to have a climax. We managed to end most every one with a murder since we had a long rubber dagger and several cap guns.

Then we, the youngest, piled up pallets of quilts covering the cold linoleum floor. The older cousins always slept together in the squeaky iron beds, leaving the little ones like me lying awake listening to their giggles and whispers.

We were awakened every morning by the hoarse, amused voice of Sammy Joe, "Y'all be careful. Don't let ol' Rawbones ketch you."

In the middle of the night, I heard the rat in the attic. I lay there listening, until I heard gnawing. I could imagine the sharp teeth chewing my bones raw. The heavy bump of the rat's movements convinced me that he was monstrous. His incessant chewing and scratching frightened me. I envisioned the critter far worse than he could possibly have been.

In case we weren't scared enough, when it was time to get up for biscuits and jelly, Sammy Joe came in our room and opened the trap door to the attic. "I'm gonna ketch that rat one of these days," he'd mutter, eyes twinkling the whole time. Every bare foot in the room hit the floor at once. He knew how to wake us up, but I'm not sure I ever even slept that week.

On the day Mama was coming, Aunt Shannon set up wash tubs in the yard and added a pan of hot water to each one. We played as much as we washed, throwing the soap from one tub to the other. The young cousins bathed in panties, but the older ones bathed inside one at a time in the chilly bedroom. I was glad to be younger for once, silly and carefree.

We sang "Michael Rowed the Boat Ashore." Then we sang the one I dreaded, "She'll Be Coming Around the Mountain When She Comes." I missed Mama and fretted about her coming around those hairpin curves on the Greyhound bus to pick us up. I also hated the idea of killing the old red rooster, even though Sammy Joe's rooster was mean and noisy and there was nothing red about him but the rubbery looking stuff that grew out of his head like a horse's mane.

"How much longer before Mama's bus comes?" I asked my aunt, whose rough towel smelled like Tide.

"In about an hour," she answered, humming at my ear.

In less than an hour I grabbed Mama's shoulders and jumped into her arms, my knees jabbing her as I fiercely wrapped my legs around her waist. "I don't know why I missed you worse this time," I cried into her neck.

After lunch, we cut a watermelon that dripped sugary juice all down our freshly-scrubbed chests. "Give me them blouses," Mama said crossly. "Let me wash them quick before the stain sets in." Aunt Shannon didn't say a word, just wiped up the table.

My cousin Merle Ann and I were swinging on the front porch, just the girls, while the boys went to the garden to pick peanuts to parch after supper. Mama and Aunt Shannon sat in the two rockers, shelling peas. Aunt Shannon wiped her thin blonde bangs up toward her forehead just the way Daddy Phil did. They could have been twins with their long arms and fair skin, the same blue eyes.

Suddenly, we heard a high-pitched, agonized scream from Sammy Joe—the worst scream I had ever heard—and he just kept on and on screaming. "That sounded like it came from under the house, didn't it?!" My aunt screeched, her pan of shelled peas going everywhere as she ran toward the screen door, her apron flapping as she ran. Mama was right behind her, barefoot, her arms stretched out toward the older woman as if she could catch her. Merle Ann and I followed right behind as fast as our legs would carry us.

Sammy Joe's little brother yelled, "He's bit! He's bit!"

My aunt dove head-first under the house, but her wide butt got stuck between the concrete blocks supporting the house; however, Mama's slender bottom allowed her to slip between them with ease. My heart stopped until she dragged a screaming Sammy Joe out by his good leg. The other one had started to swell already.

Everything became a blur—both women moaning, screaming, out of control—until Uncle Sam, chest heaving, ran in from the garden with a hoe in his hand and crawled under the house himself. We heard the metallic clang of the hoe as it hit the top of the crawlspace, then a hard thud as it came down. Uncle Sam's feet came into view, followed by his overalls, and then his thinning hair as he slid out from under the house. He pulled his cap back on quickly, "Killed that sucker!" he mumbled, wheezing.

Then he picked Sammy Joe up, slung him in the truck like he was mad at him and drove off, leaving a cloud of red dust and the screeching of tires in our eyes and ears. "What happened? What happened?" I shrieked.

"Nothin', honey," Mama said absently, still trembling herself.

"Was it Rawbones?" I asked, which was met with a chorus of hysterical laughter.

"No, darlin', it waddn' Rawbones. Sammy Joe just had a little accident. Everything's gonna be all right."

Finally, Merle Ann told me it was a snake, which made me not want to go outside again. I stayed right next to my mother, even got to sleep on the sofa with her that night. She told me that Rhett had missed us terribly. "He's even a little jealous of how much y'all love your Daddy Phil and his family," Mama said tentatively.

"No fair," I said, crossing my arms, ready to argue.

"Oh," she chuckled, "of course, it's not fair. Rhett's a grown man. He should know better, but he's just kind of . . . funny. I was surprised, really. I mean we had to find a solution when Granny had to leave so I could go to work Monday."

"Lu said you just packed us off on somebody."

"Did you feel that way?"

"Not really, but I missed you and Rhett."

"We missed you more, sweetie pie. Tell you what, I'll mention this to Lu, too: let's not tell Rhett that Daddy Phil came to the house to pick y'all up, okay?"

"Okay." I had never appreciated more the warm, soft sweetness of her. She even woke me up every time she went to the potty and asked if I wanted to go. Then we'd lie awake and talk until sleep reclaimed us. The last time we woke up, I told Mama, "If I had somebody to wake me up every night like this, I never would wet the bed."

"I know, baby, but the trick is to wake yourself up. You will one day. Anyway, it's been a long time, now. You might never have to worry about it again." Then the soft sound of her breath got slower and slower. I timed mine to hers until I was asleep again. I didn't hear Rawbones a single time that night.

# *Chapter Twelve:*
## *Almost Persuaded*

RHETT POUTED BECAUSE we went to visit our aunt, especially because Mama stayed overnight there. "They're not your family any more," he snapped at Mama after supper. Rhett drank more and more. He started working at the golf course as a caddy. He took up with a doctor named Ledbetter. During the war, Rhett had worked as a sergeant in the medical supply unit, knew a lot of doctors who really liked his wit and his appreciation of their chemical wonders like grain alcohol. Drinking buddies, he learned a lot from them. Mama said he could have been a doctor himself if the firewater hadn't controlled him. Ledbetter introduced him to something quicker: soon Rhett was more interested in pills than booze. That's when Rhett really got mean, his eyes all out of focus and his moods changing from one extreme to the other. He'd be playing around rough and tumble with us, laughing and cutting up one minute and be in the kitchen yelling at Mama the next.

One night, from all the way down in our neighbor Buster's yard, we heard Rhett yell, "Don't you ever go through my pockets again, you stupid nag!" We'd heard our parents grumbling off and on for half an hour after they'd told us to go outside and play. We all pretended not to hear them, never talked about it, but now it sounded dangerous. I locked eyes with Lucinda who had replaced fear with a glaze. Buster and his brother were lost in their own trance, arm wrestling.

When I heard Mama's blood-curdling scream, I felt my stomach tighten. I didn't know which was worse—the embarrassment or the fear. I didn't bother to decide, just wheeled around and ran up the sidewalk, my legs pumping hard as my heart was beating. When I opened the door, I saw bright red blood on the floor. My heart stopped. Then I heard Mama's telephone voice, sounding business like but slightly hysterical, too. I was shocked when I realized she had called the police. "Yes, sir," she screeched, "he's hit me more than once, and I do think he's a threat to the family. I want y'all to get over here and see him while he's like this."

Breathing heavily, Mama lit a cigarette triumphantly without noticing the tip was blood red from her lip, and then stuck the pack back in the pocket of her blouse. The pocket had survived a rip that left the sleeve hanging from her arm. Rhett was at the table, his face in his hands as if he were desperately praying. Smiling wickedly, Mama blew smoke in his face and laughed.

Then Rhett was on his feet again, going for her throat. His eyes bugged out, and the veins in his neck bulged as if they might jump out of the skin as he grabbed her neck and mashed her throat with his huge, dark thumbs. When she kicked him in the crotch, he hit her hard, knocked her to the floor. Without thinking, I jumped on his back, beating him around the head the way I'd seen boxers do. My punches might as well have been from a flea on an elephant, but it shocked him. It might have even stopped the fight except Lucinda decided to follow my lead.

Our help spurred Mama on. We were all energized, emboldened by the knowledge that the police were on their way. Swept up in the heat of the moment, we acted like animals, tapping some dark pool of tacit knowledge—surviving. Lucinda clawed at his skin with her long fingernails, leaving red welts running down his arms. He squirmed and pushed with all the might he could muster in his stupor, but the three of us managed to hold his arms behind his back.

Rhett—eyes popping open now, pupils dilated—registered contradiction: disappointment at the "betrayal" in the deepest darkness of his eyes, but fury and desperation in the dilated pupils. His face was eerie, unreal in its naked emotion, tears streaming from his eyes while his mouth twisted in sinister determination to break loose from our hold. When Mama smacked him across the ear with a Betty Crocker cookbook, his stunned eyes opened wide, then closed in resignation.

"Oh, no," I moaned when I saw Rhett fall in a heap on the cold linoleum, his ear bleeding. I knew if I ever started crying I wouldn't be able to stop, so I tried hard not to. Lucinda didn't look like she even had to try. Sometimes, I didn't think she would ever cry again in her whole life. She just looked out the window with the loneliest look I'd ever seen on her face, her lower lip pushed way forward.

Mama was excited though, revved up. "This will show you, Mister," she yelled. "By God, you can't run over me and my kids without sitting in jail. I wonder what your friend Dr. Ledbetter will think when I tell the police about his dope peddling." She had a butcher knife in her hands now, kneeling down and holding it close to his chest. Its silver blade reflected the naked light bulb overhead.

"Please, Pearl, don't do it. I'm warning you. There'll be trouble if you do." Then he saw me shivering in the corner, my thin arms trying to hold onto each other to stop the jerking of my body. He decided to try me. "Please, baby, tell your mama."

My tears broke loose like a dam overflowing. Maybe I stopped her from cutting him or scaring him to death. We never knew because just then we heard the screech of brakes in the front yard.

When the police rushed into the house, they ignored my crying. They broke up the human pretzel we'd created and made the grownups sit across the room from each other. Then the older one told Mama, "Well, ma'am, we can't really arrest him for disturbing the peace when it looks like he's the one whose ear's bleeding. Maybe y'all oughtta work things out, let this one pass. It wouldn't look too good for you, and it wouldn't set well with these pretty little girls in the morning to have their daddy in jail, now would it?"

So, maybe he hadn't ignored me totally, I thought, hearing my sobs subside. "When you think about all this tomorrow, it'll even seem funny to you maybe," the young officer said, his mouth trying hard not to grin since Rhett hardly looked like a threat. His partner shifted from one foot to the other. They weren't comfortable with situations where the villain wasn't clearly defined.

"If you'll let us get him in bed for you, I swear he won't be able to cause you any more trouble," the older one finally said. "He'll sleep all night."

"At least," the young officer added.

Mama didn't find it funny the next morning, and neither did we.

But something significant did happen that next morning; something had come to a head. You could feel it heavy in the air, almost see Mama stir it in her coffee. Her smooth ivory face was firm, the puffy eyes strengthened, determined when she told him, "I really meant it when I told you, Rhett, that I've had enough. I mean it this time. You need to pack your things and move on. Looks like I've just made another mess, can't seem to get out from under this cloud of doom, but I've got kids to think of, and this is no way for them to live. If you can call it living. Or me either." She rubbed at the heaviness settling into her shoulders.

Rhett touched the scab on his ear, winced, then joined her at the table with a glass of buttermilk.

"At least I won't have to smell that stuff in the morning," she chuckled, the laughter dry, raspy, hollow. Her eyes softened, then hardened again.

Rhett rubbed his eyes, stared out the window at the pouring rain. He spoke softly, "What you gonna do for money? How you gonna get by? These are my kids, too . . . now." He seemed genuinely concerned, his voice tender.

"I don't know," she brushed a tear away defiantly. She stiffened her lip, increased her volume, "I'll find a way. I always have."

He kept the volume low, his voice soft. "I really want to do better, baby, I do. I'm scared of what these pills have done to me. They make the nightmares worse. I see those rotten Jap arms reaching out at me and I stumble over corpses with maggots everywhere, wake up thinking they're crawling on me."

Then they were both quiet. I stood in the corner, still as a statue, pretending not to be there at all. He was quiet because he didn't want anybody to hear that tenderness in his voice, I knew. It was way more important to him than caring if anybody knew he was a dope fiend. "Y'all go out in the yard and play," Rhett said, as if it were the most normal thing in the world to move from such a conversation to a suggestion that the puppies go out and play.

Then Mama joined him. "Yeah, y'all run on outside a little while." Lucinda, primping at the bathroom mirror, rolled her eyes but started moving. I followed, as usual, but I lingered long enough to overhear, "I got an idea, baby. It just might work. You know that place they call Pinecrest? They can get you off these pills . . ."

I wanted to stuff rags in my ears all the way to my toes. I couldn't stand the thought that my new daddy was turning into one of those crazy people at Doc's sanatorium. My old daddy and his snooty family would surely find out. "What do you think Daddy Phil and the boys will say?" I whispered to Lucinda as soon as we were out the door.

Her face turned pale under the streak of sunlight her hair had become, but she sounded nonchalant, "They already think they are so much better than we are. I hate the way they act like somebody pooted when we come into a room. Who cares?"

I knew I'd never be able to stand the jeering from the boys, their taunting questions about Pinecrest and Rhett's treatment. "What will those nurses do to Rhett anyway?" I asked my big sister.

"Put those little electrodes on his brain and make him act retarded for the rest of his life," Lucinda quipped, but when she saw the flood in my eyes, her sneer disappeared. She took my hand in hers and said softly. "Just kidding. They'll make him quit drinking. Let's go for a walk. Walking always helps."

I was full of questions, fear that bubbled in my heart, but I didn't probe any more. I was too afraid of the answers.

After lunch, Mama sent us to the library to check out some books. I came home with a stack of books taller than I was and buried myself deep. I could hear them on the phone with the doctor, so I stuffed cotton in my ears. I could see her folding pajamas and stiffly starched shirts in the old striped suitcase. When they left together in a taxi, I wanted to run after it, howling, but I kept reading about George Washington Carver and how he improved his station in life through hard work and determination. He did great things with something as simple as a peanut.

I never asked about Rhett until he came home from Pinecrest a few days later. I denied it. Now, I realize all they did was dry him out, detox him. They didn't do any rehabilitation or try to help him understand why he drank. The program sounded as compassionate as Doc Carson who ran it. Nervous and irritable, Rhett was even worse to live with in many ways. He quit drinking and popping pills for a while, though, and our family did normal things like play checkers and card games.

One night, Rhett brought in all his change and dumped it in the floor and let me put it in dollar stacks and add it while he lay there smiling at me. He was working for himself again, hauling produce and making two and three day trips into the swamps with truckloads of apples that smelled so, so sweet. Lu and Buster and I sneaked some off the truck on the nights he brought a fresh load home to get a good night's sleep before his early morning departure.

I learned to taste the bitter along with the sweet at an early age. My fantasy of being rescued by a knight in shining armor was challenged. I had thought Rhett would kiss Mama and the memory of my father trying to throw my mother out the window would disappear. I had thought the sweetness of their early love would last forever. Now I knew better. I knew with every sweet bite of apple comes the possibility of biting into a worm.

When autumn came with all its bitter sweetness and contradictions, I walked to school on brisk mornings, collecting leaves— blood red maple and golden sycamore—that fell from the pure silver bark and then wrinkled in the bowl where I kept them for my science project. Walking home, the heavy sweaters Grandmother Byrnes had knitted, which had saved us from the morning chill, were a burden. We shed them as the sun warmed us by mid-morning. "You carry mine," Lucinda commanded. "I have enough to carry with my books and this stupid lunch box."

"I have books, too," I argued.

"Yeah, baby books," she teased, pointing to the small orange biography I carried.

"Well, alright, I'll carry your lunch box, but not your sweater, if we can walk down First Avenue, along the lake." The green mossy lake inside the rock-walled park never changed, but the pool, abandoned for the winter, seemed dead after the summer's frolicking activity. I didn't understand why colored people would want to come over here to swim or why anybody would close the pool if they did. We heard it might never be opened again because all city pools would soon be integrated.

We passed by the house near the drug store where my idol, a famous movie star, once lived. A director/producer had come to town and discovered her, whisking her away to Hollywood. However, her sister who had polio would sometimes be on the porch in her iron lung. My sister and I worked hard to train our eyes to glance sideways without turning our heads, for manners' sake. I cried some-times at night imagining the girl who had to live inside that contrap-tion. What if she were claustrophobic like Mama?

Rhett was doing so well hauling produce into the swamps where there were few roads and fewer stores for folks who lived on the back roads that Phil offered to buy a much larger load and split the profit. "Makes good business sense," he told Mama. "We all win. My money grows, the girls are better off, and Rhett makes more money, which keeps you happy."

Rhett liked the idea of making more money, but he seemed sul-len, moodier than usual. He hired Pete, one of his old sidekicks, to drive a truck twice the size of his, and they headed out one frosty morning before dawn. Rhett was jittery, gave Mama a cold peck on the cheek, but didn't even tell me bye, though I had gotten up early to see him off. He avoided me. We figured out why soon enough. When Pete came back with the big truck and no money, he said there was a woman down there who let the fellas drink and play poker as long as they wanted to at her café. Just put the money in the register on the honor system.

Mama stopped him there. "Honor system?"

"Yeah."

That's all she wanted to hear this time. We never knew what she told Phil about his investment, just that she was furious and that Rhett didn't come back. He had gone almost six months without drinking.

# Chapter Thirteen:
## Give Peace a Chance

THERE'S NO WAY RHETT could have talked Mama into taking him back just by swearing he would never drink again. Not after disgracing us like that and stealing from Phil. This time he played the religion card, and I have to admit it really worked. Once Rhett got religion, we went every Sunday and Wednesday to Cheaha Mountaintop Baptist Church or to its foundation, white concrete blocks that would actually be the basement once the church was built. The structure would sit atop a hill overlooking green valleys surrounded by rolling, Appalachian foothills. There was a large, flat rock called Pulpit Rock that the church would be centered around—to remember the rock that Peter built a church on. The church goers, of Scotch Irish descent for the most part, were good, clean people scratching out a living as best they could on farms or working in mines and factories.

Mama, who didn't want to give up her cigarettes at first, was leery of it all. She quipped, "They're sure fired up, aren't they? They've got that enthusiasm that comes after a split. That zest usually results in building a new church with some persuasive, egomaniac preacher. It will be a while before they begin to tear each other to shreds."

She called the folks malcontents at first, but she came around because their enthusiasm was contagious. Rhett even got his parents involved, and his daddy hadn't darkened the doorway since the last feud resulted in a split twenty years earlier. Granddaddy Youngblood looked just like Rhett except he was taller, thinner, and older with white hair where Rhett's was dark. It turned out that he used to preach, himself, when he wasn't drinking.

Mama got the real family story from Granny Youngblood. She

was the one whose mother was a full-blooded American Indian, and she looked it with her rich dark skin and the thick silver hair braided and piled on top of her head. She was always laughing, which made her dangling turquoise earrings shake. They were a handsome couple, and everyone was elated that Rhett had convinced them to come back to church. The new congregation was on a roll, and soon we were right in the middle of them.

At last, I was included on Mondays when my teacher would ask if we'd been to Sunday school and place a gold star by our names. When she asked why we didn't go to church in East Lake, I told her proudly, "We don't like them highfalutin' city churches where you have to dress fancy."

At Cheaha Mountaintop Baptist, our Sunday school rooms were like a giant storm pit because the congregation built the basement, the foundation, first. The small rooms were cold and musty, which led me to wonder if Hell wouldn't be just as bad if it were cold. Before the sanctuary was built, there had already been a squabble. I heard it whispered that the preacher was messing with somebody's wife, but that seemed a long way from us during this time of Rhett's good behavior.

Since Rhett wasn't drinking, he developed a taste for ice cream. He stopped at the Polar Bear where giant stucco bears held up the building. We licked cones of soft, cold vanilla ice cream, piled up like snow-covered Christmas trees. We sang all the way home, mostly Lucinda and me though Rhett joined in on "Give me that Old Time Religion." Mama didn't sing, but her knee kept time, and her mouth sneaked out to the corners of her face for a smile. We would move on to Christmas songs . . . "Round yon virgin, mother and child, holy Infant so tender and mild, sleep in Heavenly peace, sleeeeeep in Heavenly Peace." Singing, I moved closer to my mother, felt the rhythmic beating of her heart. I felt secure. I believed.

It wasn't regular, but it was passionate. It was a strange brand of religion where we learned the importance of a spiritual life, how it can transform a family into ice-cream eaters and singers. Maybe it was transient, but we saw that life was better that way.

It must have been close to a year before our world fell apart again. Rhett was suddenly toppled from the pedestal, and the ice cream was replaced by whiskey. Just as automatically, Mama's Pall Malls came out of hiding, and our ice-creamed lives melted.

Suddenly one day, Lucinda and I rode in the backseat of Phil's new Studebaker, and he and my mother seemed to be friends again, allies somehow. When he stopped at an architect's office to pick up some blue prints, I felt that old pride in him. He was pleasant, ran a solid company with good workers. One time, when Rhett and Phil were planning to work together, I was happy with the arrangement; I felt a healing of the old wounds not having to choose between two fathers I loved.

However, I began to see that something was amiss. Several times, Mama wiped her eyes with the wadded up Kleenex in her purse. She kept whispering, "I just don't know," when Phil questioned her in hushed tones.

His anger finally resulted in louder remarks: "I told that sorry s.o.b. I was a fool to give him a chance. I met him at the crack of dawn with $1400 and then waited at the office all morning for him to bring the produce by for my inspection. It sounded too good to be true, that slimy, no-good . . ."

"Phil, don't do this to the girls. I mean it." Mama flashed him a warning. It appeared that Phil and Mother were searching for Rhett. Finally, they found out at the airport he had bought a ticket to Texas, taken the money and run, simply disappeared.

By then, Phil had married again, but he seemed eager to be with us, especially Mama. I heard him say, "Pearl, I'd leave her in a minute if I thought there was a chance . . ."

"Don't, Phil," Mother said quickly, "the children . . ."

Why did adults do that! *Woof,* I wanted to bark. We were getting the puppy treatment again. Something was up, but we weren't going to have any explanation. Phil took us up on the observation deck to watch the planes land. They talked while Lucinda and I entertained ourselves, mouths agape, watching as the huge, loud engines revved up and the planes took off. I made up stories to go with people who waited for the arrivals, especially if a couple kissed when one of them arrived.

Lucinda pointed to a beautiful woman, tall and slender, hurrying past us and said, "See how rich people who fly are! Look at that mink coat. I'm gonna be rich someday."

"I'm gonna be a world traveler," I assured her, "maybe a missionary."

"Hmmmph," she growled.

When Phil walked us to our door, he seemed weary and sad. At the doorway, he kept starting new conversations, but he said he didn't have time to drink a cup of tea. Even the droopy wisteria vine seemed blue. I rubbed my eyes and went to bed as soon as we were inside.

Then Mama rented out the big side of the house, with the Youngstown kitchen and the swivel shelf in the corner, and the three of us lived for a while in the two rooms where Irene, our boarder, had lived. The groceries got scantier and scantier.

It was some time around Christmas when we went to ask Priscilla to take us in so that Mama could rent the whole house and make enough to supplement her wages of 75 cents an hour. "It takes a lot of nerve to ask your daddy's first wife for help, girls, but we have to do something. I've tried everything else."

We took the street car downtown, then transferred to a bus over to Southside. "Well, come on in," Priscilla said, her full face glowing. A little plumper, she hadn't changed much, still wore her hair pulled back in a bun and wore no makeup on those trusting blue eyes. She was genuinely glad to see us, but the boys were sullen, downright mean. "I made some brownies," Priscilla opened the door under the stairs to get dish towels for hot pads. She kept her laundry there, piles of smelly clothes. My heart sank when I saw dirty clothes crammed in my playhouse. Nobody would ever have guessed that it had housed a princess who loved to make tea. Priscilla finally found a towel in the basket of clean laundry and plopped it down on the coffee table. She never could keep up with regular hot pads.

Robby glared at me when he saw me peer into the lost playhouse. Junior took one look at us and ran from the room, holding his hand over his mouth. Then we heard him gag upstairs, vomiting. I felt unclean. We never knew whether he was sick or kidding. Lucinda's full lips pouted, her eyes blank. Mama tried too hard to be jovial. It was humiliating.

I played "Rudolph the Red-nosed Reindeer" over and over on their new record player. I identified so much with his loneliness, his sadness, that I cried all the way home.

# Chapter Fourteen:
## The See-Saw

MAMA RENTED OUT THE WHOLE HOUSE in East Lake, furnished completely to make the house payment, and we survived in the back room of Priscilla's eight-room apartment, all of which used to be our home. Mama walked fifteen blocks every day in the dead of winter to a warehouse downtown where she stamped cigarettes for less than a dollar an hour.

Priscilla cooked, and Mama washed dishes, both taking care of their brood of children. What bonded them was warped love for Phil and equal hatred of his new wife. Two strong women, they taught me the power of love that transcends betrayal, that defends our offspring at any cost to ourselves like mother plants in August giving in to seeding.

Not wanting to impose on Priscilla any further, Mama found an after-school solution, which fit neatly into the swirl of circumstances that became our lives. Ms. Harriet Galloway, a lively, white-haired woman, opened her home to young girls for a couple of hours every afternoon after school. Most of us had mothers who worked outside the home. There was no charge, even though refreshments were offered. Ms. Harriett's hair was braided and piled elegantly on top of her head, framing a fine face with keen, intelligent eyes.

The white Victorian house sat atop a steep bank covered with ivy. The shady street was filled with homes that had once been the finest in town. In many ways, the area was in the early stages of white flight. Folks from Birmingham who could afford to had already begun to retreat to the luxury of their cocoon across Red Mountain, away from hoi polloi the iron industry brought to town.

Not long after we took over her house, girls giggling and squealing everywhere, Ms. Harriet moved away and left her home to Birmingham's first Girls Club. Wealthy women from "over the mountain" volunteered to teach us how to be ladies. We could sit in the porch swing and watch sparrows play in the bird bath if we didn't want to participate in classes for flower arranging, cooking, and sewing. We would still get refreshments—my favorite part.

Walking up the steep hill after school to a quaint home and warm cookies, I drank in the beauty around me with a thirst I'd never known. The first bursts of yellow daffodils against the grey winter sky stirred my heart, something like hope was taking shape inside me again.

Passing a stone fortress/apartment building called the Royal Arms, I called up fairy tales of knights and ladies to soothe my broken streak of romanticism. The Gothic lines of the sandstone towers commanded a regal post overlooking the valley that sprawled, in reality, into a cluster of medical buildings. The old Hillman Hospital where I was born was a stark red, the color of iron ore, in contrast to the sleek, modern yellow of the new Veteran's Hospital. From that vantage point, we could see how Birmingham was surrounded by small green foothills on every side, making it a beautiful city geographically. Looking straight, I thought of North Birmingham and Nashville beyond it and all the singers who had made their way from here to there.

In my imagination, at night when I brushed my hair 100 strokes like Lucinda, I'd think of the valley beneath the Royal Arms as lush and green. In the tower, a princess like Rapunzel . . .

After the brief hit of fantasy each afternoon when I passed the Royal Arms, I stored up details for the saga in my head at bedtime. Then, I continued along the ivy-covered crest to Ms. Galloway's house with flowers and the sweet aroma of chocolate.

As soon as I put my book satchel away, I was ready for flower arranging. I picked velvety pansies to thin the blooms around the fountain, its splash sounding approval of my choices. I arranged the flowers in different sizes and shapes of containers, working hard to balance color and proportion. I slipped a bright yellow pansy edged with shades of deep purple into the center of a cluster that reflected its opposite: deep purple blossoms with barely perceptible golden veins. Mrs. Patsy, our teacher, said, "Oh, Bonita, dahlin', that's wuuuuunnnnnnndaful!"

Her skillful hands continued creating a perfect cluster, usually with white in the center. For purity. She pointed out the way the little veins in the white flowers revealed slight shades of all the other colors in her bouquet.

My sister excelled in cooking classes, which I didn't like. My creations never turned out well like the instructor's, who never baked a runny cookie or a pancake that was too flat. The lady who taught cooking had a soft voice, too, like Mrs. Patsy's that could find seventeen syllables in the word *nice*. It seemed the wealthier you were, the more syllables you used. People on our side of the mountain didn't talk that way. Taking that long to pronounce a single word suggested leisure we weren't privy to. I resented our prissy teacher, but I loved Geraldine, the black woman who washed dishes and cleaned up the mess the lady of leisure left behind. I begged to be Geraldine's helper instead of feeling clumsy in cooking class. It felt right to me, comfortable, a reminder of Ida. The cooking teacher never looked Geraldine in the eye, just purred commands to her back. Sometimes, we got tickled, but the teacher never realized we were laughing at her.

I was also reminded of Katie Mae. On the first stormy night after we moved back to Southside, I was scared by the weather's intensity. Rain lashed at the bay window as sizzling bolts of lightning split into forks that lit the sky with an eerie glow. Torrents of water along the curb rushed down the hill into the sewer with the force of a river. I jumped like a jittery rabbit when a clap of thunder followed a particularly dramatic streak of lightning, which struck nearby and caused the lights to go out.

Mama sighed and searched for a candle. When she found one, she lit it and smiled warmly in its glow. "Might as well do the dishes by candle light." She drawled in her exaggerated belle's voice, "It's more romantic." The soap suds bubbled in the sink, making rainbows in the candle glow, and I decided Mama was right. It was romantic. I wondered why Mama didn't talk that way all the time since she knew how, but I didn't ask about it. I knew, without knowing why, it would embarrass her.

I began to feel cozy in the middle of the storm, in the kitchen with two mothers. I felt my body warm to the hypnotic cocoon I created to tune out the storm. As the thunder subsided, I almost hated for the storm to end.

Priscilla invited me to listen to the radio with her when we went upstairs to bed. Mama said I could for a little while. I lay in bed with "Aunt" Priscilla, her freckled, plump arms folded across her chest while she closed her pale eyes and listened to Luigi and Pasquale on the mahogany radio. We visualized faces and bodies to go with passionate voices of Italian men.

I found the nerve to ask her, "Do you think Robby resents us because we took his bedroom?"

"I think Robby is fortunate to be sharing a room downstairs with his older brother. That makes him a big boy." She continued watching the ceiling, but she patted my hand. Then we heard *Fibber Mc-Gee and Molly*, which I didn't find as funny as Priscilla did. When she chuckled, her large sagging breasts moved slightly. Since she rarely opened her eyes while listening to her shows, I could spy on her breasts without detection. She and Phil were ten years older than Mama. I thought they shook like jelly the way Santa Claus was supposed to. We finished the evening with *Amos 'n' Andy*.

One cold Sunday in early February, Priscilla made a batch of cinnamon rolls that filled the house with sweetness and spice. She brought the big, fluffy morning treats to perfection for whoever woke up early enough to enjoy them warm. I was her most faithful customer, never suspecting the aroma might be incentive for church-going. I was also her most faithful companion for church.

She looked at the dripping rain and made a clucking sound in her throat, "Good gracious, what a nasty day to go out," she muttered but didn't consider skipping church. It wasn't an option for her.

"You need some kind of rain gear, girl," she insisted, tying a rain bonnet around my head too tight. When she went to dig up Robby's galoshes, I loosened the headgear and frowned at the mirror. I was all bonnet, no sign of the tight curls Mama had worked so hard to create.

Priscilla stooped, struggled with the yellow rubber boots until they finally slipped over my saddle oxfords, then pushed herself up, breathing heavily. "It's hard for fat ladies to bend and stoop," she told me, her pale eyes twinkling. "No need to worry about Robby needing these for Sunday school anymore. I don't know what's gotten into that boy about church."

It never occurred to me that Robby might have quit going to church because I was taking his place. She took my hand in hers and smiled as we plodded through the mud puddles toward Southside Baptist Church. Its Roman columns and stained glass windows gave it grandeur, accentuated by its dramatic position at the intersection of two of the main streets in the neighborhood. The front entrance to the church, with high marble steps, was set in the tip of a triangle. The slanted street led to an apartment building called Stratford on Avon, which Lucinda said was named for Shakespeare's birthplace. The straight street went back to our house and on down to the hospital.

Priscilla and I always entered through the back of the building where the Christian education rooms reached all the way to the alley. I was too shy to explain to such a practical woman how much more dramatic the front entranceway would be.

At first, I went out of curiosity to see what mysterious clothing people at a "highfalutin'" church wore. I figured out quickly that it didn't really matter what I wore. The dresses weren't that different from those at Cheaha Mountaintop Baptist: mostly plain navy blue or black dresses with a few pastel suits. There were more hats and white gloves, but Priscilla didn't wear those. She wore the same loose dresses she wore at home, almost all in the same style. She did have one navy silk polka dot dress that she wore only to church, but Priscilla wasn't much on fashion.

The serenity of her face in church was a sight worth going to see: the smooth, pale skin with no attempt to hide the freckles like other women—absolutely no make up. I'd heard Lucinda whisper to Mama, "Looks like she would fix herself up," but I liked Priscilla the way she was. While the preacher droned on and on, Priscilla looked entranced, in deep concentration, often amused. She was amused by most of life, a happy woman in spite of her disappointment in Phil.

I couldn't do a thing about Daddy Phil, but I could ease Priscilla's disappointment when Robby quit going to church with her. Besides, I was drawn to it. What they promised seemed worth buying, and they had extensive art supplies: reeds when we studied Moses, ceramics for Rebecca at the well, and water colors in addition to crayons. At junior church, John Jr., the minister's son, led us in rousing versions of songs like "Do Lord." I envisioned my palace as I watched his face glow, eyes full of vision: *I got a home in Glory Land that outshines the Sun, outshines the sun . . .* His zeal was contagious whether he was singing or talking about donations for sending missionaries to Africa.

He planned to run for Congress, and I was proud to inform Mama that I knew him personally. Unimpressed, she fired up another Pall Mall, "I reckon he's practicing on y'all. He's trying out his politician's image—serving the Lord as well as himself."

Lucinda and Mama giggled, but I told them patiently, "I pray for both of you every Sunday. My Sunday school teacher says Southside Baptist is a progressive church, so we should pray for everybody."

Daddy Phil and Priscilla were more like old friends than divorced parents. He stopped in several times a week to "take care of business" with her. Once, I bustled in from Mrs. Galloway's and found them scampering up from a pallet on the floor in the dining room. I smelled something in the room as strong as a block of hoop cheese. I could have cut it with a knife, but I couldn't see it. I sensed that there was something mellow—indestructible—in that room.

Priscilla made clucking sounds in her throat. Eyes shining, her mouth slid easily into a smile. Phil, however, was in a huff, straightening his tie with such force I thought he'd choke himself. He glared at me the way he always did these days, his blue eyes frozen like the Arctic pools I'd seen in my geography book. I shivered involuntarily, said, "Excuse me," in the quiet voice I assumed around him and went to my room as if I were being punished. I had come in with a vase of pansies for Priscilla, but I filled it with water and put it on my mother's bedside table instead.

When I heard the door slam and the sputtering of Phil's Studebaker, I crept down the squeaky stairs and tuned in *Howdy Doody*. I had missed half the show already. I didn't even laugh at Clarabell that day. I sat still, considering the mystery I had come close to.

Over the next few weeks, Katherine, Priscilla's daughter, became the center of everyone's attention, even though she had moved away. She was expecting Phil and Priscilla's first grandchild, but she had some sort of setback that left her bedridden. Priscilla hummed more hymns and smiled less while she waited for the outcome;

otherwise, we wouldn't have known how tense she was. At night, though, Lucinda and I eavesdropped when Mama talked to Priscilla after our bedtime.

"Priss, have you heard from Katherine?" Mama said when she went to the top of the stairwell and poked her head in the room that once was hers.

"Oh, Pearl, sometimes I don't know if I can stand it, being this far away from my daughter at a time like this," Priscilla sighed.

"Like they ain't got seminaries closer than California!" Mama sympathized. "You know, I can keep the boys in a heartbeat. Mr. Burnett told me I could have a few days off now . . ."

"I know, Pearl," Priscilla interrupted her, "but I'm saving that favor for emergency. Besides, I haven't been invited."

"You mean to Brother Know-it-All's royal palace?" Mama asked. They both laughed and then talked in voices so low we couldn't hear. Katherine had married a man who was full of serving the Lord. She had supported him working as a secretary until the new baby surprised everybody by showing up before they'd really thought about a family.

I still smarted because Lucinda had been Katherine's flower girl, and I wasn't even allowed to go to the wedding but had to stay home with Mama. Bill, the groom, and his family acted weird when Katherine chose Lucinda since she was part of Phil's "other family." I just didn't get it.

Most people liked Bill, but I didn't. He was handsome: tall, blonde, well-built. Lucinda said he ought to be a preacher because he looked so good in a suit. His tie always managed to hang the right length, always matched the shirt he wore. His blond, curly hair was already beginning to thin, but it framed his clear blue eyes well. His fair skin was smooth, almost like a girl's, and when he was embarrassed his cheeks turned rosy pink. Daddy Phil said blushing made him look sissy. Priscilla liked to get Bill flustered, I could tell. He was the only person she was unkind to.

Katherine survived the risky pregnancy, and as soon as the baby was a month old, they drove home. Everybody was excited about their first visit with a new baby. Everybody except me.

I didn't mind staying up late to wait for Katherine, though, because I got to watch Queen Elizabeth II's coronation. I was intrigued by the time difference: "Gollee, you mean it's really morning over there when it's night here?" I asked, riveted to the flickering screen, feeling connected to history through television for the first time. It made my brain sizzle to see a real queen instead of those in fairy tales.

Because the coverage of the coronation went on so long, we grew impatient for our own royal pair to arrive. Suddenly, we thought we heard them. Robby ran to the door and flung it open, banging the wall and making the chimes go haywire. Priscilla's face lit up, Mama put her sewing down, and Lucinda squealed. Nothing but a harsh gust of wind came in the door though. Robby ducked his head and admitted, "It was just a car passing by."

Priscilla said, "I may as well make some brownies to pass the time." She hummed while she turned the egg beater, and I tore myself away from the television long enough to whisper in her ear, "Could I lick the beaters this time?"

She never took her eyes off the beater, but mumbled, "I suppose so." When she waddled back in and sank into her wing chair, she was armed with beaters for me, a spoon for Robby to lick, and the bowl for Lucinda. Robby finished his fast and wanted to share with Lucinda, who slowly ran her finger around the smooth, gooey chocolate. She taunted Robby, licking goo from her finger and sticking her tongue out at him.

The brownies smelled better than Priscilla's cinnamon rolls, tempting us with the heavy, tantalizing aroma. Mama said, "I don't know which is worse, waitin' on Katherine or waiting to taste those brownies. I'm tempted to sample more than mixing bowls."

When Priscilla shot her an edgy look, Mama got engrossed in the hem she was stitching. Lucinda yawned and stretched out on the pallet where she and Robby watched the royal ceremony. Soon she was asleep, snoring gently. The swell of breasts, barely visible under the mint green gown, moved in the same rhythm as her snores. Hunger gnawed at me, emboldening me to ask, "Do we have to wait for them to eat a brownie? It's not like cutting a cake. How would they know?"

Priscilla poured tea from the enamel pot. "It's a matter of principle. Want some tea, Pearl?"

"Not right now," Mama said. I felt invisible. Priscilla never even looked at me, practically pretended I hadn't asked; besides, she ought to remember Mama didn't like hot tea. Most of the time I felt content with our new living arrangement, but moments like this made me long for the Youngstown kitchen in East Lake where my mother was in charge. I fixed myself a glass of water and drank it fast, thought maybe it would take away the hunger. When I saw the pan of brownies slathered with a thin coat of icing and topped with whole pecan halves, I realized it was more like a cake. I chewed on a fingernail and tried to think about the difference between craving and being truly hungry like Priscilla talked about when she was on a diet.

After midnight, I dozed off but was startled awake by the merry tooting of a horn. At first I thought it was Junior and his buddies who tooted in a secret-code rhythm for "Come out, come out, you sonofabitch." But this horn was more like coronation trumpets: a triumphant, *Toot toot tootoot TOOTTOOOOOOOT!* Priscilla's mouth puckered where I expected to see a smile, and tears flooded her cheeks as she ran toward the door. She hugged Katherine, laughing self-consciously about her tears.

The two women were frozen momentarily in a tableau I've remembered all my life. In their tight embrace, they became one, arms wrapped around each other so tight the bodies were inseparable. Then they pulled back to look at each other: profiles the same, hair in identical blonde twists pulled back from their faces, the only difference being the older woman's grey-streaked temple. The same mixture of sorrowful joy crossed each face.

Katherine's eyes brimmed, too, and her voice trembled, "Mama, meet your granddaughter, Priscilla Elizabeth."

"Elizabeth was my mama's name," another voice said to Bill, which caused Katherine to wheel around and grab Mama by the arm to enfold her in a warm embrace. "I know, Pearl, I know," she cried. Bill pulled the soft white blanket open for Mama to see, then handed the baby to Priscilla, who held her out for all to see. She pulled the baby to her loose, soft breast as if no time had passed since Robby had snuggled there a decade ago. She patted the baby's bottom while we gathered behind her to see the tiny red face full of blue eyes.

Bill shifted uneasily in his gleaming, carefully polished wing-tip shoes. "He's accustomed to being the center of attention, feels dethroned," Mama whispered to Lucinda, who smirked knowingly.

"Could we have a word of prayer?" Bill announced rather than asked. He strode stiffly toward his wife, took the baby from Priscilla, and everybody but me obediently bowed their heads and closed their eyes.

I peeped at the pair who excluded me from their wedding, both handsome, tall and blond, almost like brother and sister. The Reverend proceeded to perform: "Dear Heavenly Father, we give thee thanks for this blessed baby. We thank thee for this family . . . and the others . . . gathered here. We give thee special thanks for our safe arrival. Lead us to do your service. Amen."

We stood in awkward silence. I wondered if Mama and Lucinda were musing about the merits of being an "other," too. Priscilla moved in front of the pale, flickering screen and broke the silence, "I'm tired of watching stiff-lipped Brits crowd the street. Let that prayer serve as a blessing for the midnight snack I made." She served the brownies warm, topped with scoops of vanilla ice cream which ran lazily into puddles on the plates.

Katherine's face broke into radiance when she saw the treat, "Oh, Mother, my favorite! No wonder I've been so homesick! You are a wonderful cook, the best, and the hardest to live without!"

While we ate, the fat little baby with blonde curls was passed around as if it were baby Jesus. I was ready for bed even before Priscilla assured me that nothing important would happen in England before early in the morning. "Which morning?" I asked.

They all laughed, but Mama answered, "Our morning, baby. I'll wake you up. I promise."

Finally, Katherine held out her arms to me and smothered me with a genuine hug. Filled with religious fervor, she had an inner radiance that I envied, yet felt suspicious of.

For a week Priscilla hummed "When the Moon Comes over the Mountain" like Kate Smith in the kitchen, while the aroma of all Katherine's favorite foods permeated the air: fried chicken, dumplings, beef stew, curried fruit, cinnamon rolls, and apple pie. It was a happy time, especially for us "others" because Katherine had never resented us but had always loved us as much as the rest of her family. She especially loved my mother, who was more like a sister to her.

*How Can I Keep From Singing*

On the other hand, Bill did all he could to do her share of re-senting us. "Pick up those teacups, Bonita. Someone holding the baby might stumble over them!" he snapped. I had left them in a box outside the old playroom ever since we'd been here, and nobody else had even mentioned them. I scowled at him, carrying them upstairs and storing them under my bed. That was one room he could stay out of.

He was leery of Mama, too, resented Katherine's adoration of her. Mama was only 36 at the time—a beautiful, vibrant woman in her prime. She wore high heels to work where she stamped ciga-rettes like a mechanized version of herself for hours, leaving her tired when she came in. "Don't you think it's unhealthy for your feet to walk that far in those shoes?" Bill asked Mama.

"Nope," she answered, stalking upstairs and rolling her eyes to-ward Priscilla and Katherine who were decorating a bassinet with white satin roses. I was glad they were almost through because that meant Katherine would be leaving for the long drive back to Califor-nia with her baby nestled in the soft, padded basket under the cover where Mama had appliqued a quilted rabbit's bottom. When they did leave, the baby's head lay on a matching pillow with quilted ears that looked more like horns than rabbit's ears to me.

Mama had two bras and two pairs of panties and stockings, which she washed by hand every night and hung over the bath tub. No matter how exhausted she was by bedtime, she polished our shoes and rolled our hair in tight pin curls. Sometimes, I screamed out when she jabbed me with the pins—stressed, nearly crazy with fear of the unknown. While she endured that time of challenge one day at a time, Daddy Phil helped her out very little. She made house payments with the rent money; otherwise, we lived on her wages.

However, Mama rarely complained, took it all in stride, working hard to see that we had our basic needs covered. She transformed our hand-me-downs at the old sewing machine in our cramped room, sewing rick rack borders on faded dresses and embroidering flowers over moth holes. "Now, this navy dress is too little for you,' she told me one night, "but look how pretty the red trim's gonna be on this yellow pique!" She spent several evenings taking out the old stitches on the rick rack.

"Mama, you don't have to do that," I told her. "I like it fine just plain."

Lucinda piped in as usual, "Well, I don't! I want the red on my dress so you can't see the hem's been let out, and I don't want it to look like a baby's." The corners of Mama's mouth slid into her martyred expression, but her voice was cheerful, "I don't mind, darlin'. It gives me something to do, settles my nerves." She had a lot of pride about appearance and cleanliness.

One weekend, Mama and Lucinda talked in soft whispers after they thought I was asleep. Mama pointed to pictures in a tiny booklet she gave her oldest daughter. Her voice was soothing, but tinged with sadness. Soon I overheard Robby and Junior teasing Lucinda, snatching her booklet and hiding it so they could read it.

"Let me see it," Robby squealed. "That naked woman is something!" In reality, it was a sketch of a small breasted girl with wormy tubes running toward her privates.

"Give it here, Robby," Lucinda snapped, jerking the booklet out of his sweaty, freckled hand and stuffing it in her purse.

"Well, ain't you cranky today!" Junior mocked, holding his nose, "Must be on the rag."

That night, I told Mama, "Lucinda carries a picture of a naked lady in her purse. Did you know that?"

Mama's weary eyes fired up with indignant anger when she turned to face Lucinda, who simply rolled her eyes and pulled the booklet out. She held it up and sighed. She struggled to remain nonchalant when the zipper on her purse got stuck.

"Serves you right, smarty pants," I giggled. I asked Mama, "Why don't I need to know about the facts of life? The boys go on and on about how filthy menstrual periods are and how gross women smell."

Mama's mouth turned down at the corners, and the air seemed to leave her chest like a leaking balloon. "Do you know what a menstrual period is?"

"No ma'am, except that I've figured out only women have them even though the word starts with m-e-n."

"Come sit in my lap, baby," she said softly. Then in a less patient tone, she told Lucinda, "Give me that booklet. If you're gonna be showing it around so much, I might as well try to help your baby sister understand what's going on." Mama's shoulders sagged at the bathroom sink, her eyes in the mirror had dark circles under them like a raccoon's.

One sunny Saturday a letter from Rhett appeared in the mail box after months with no word from him at all. Mama's tension seemed to evaporate. Her smiling eyes were happy again, her step light and graceful as she hurried upstairs to read it.

Priscilla was not happy. Her face was tight, drawn. She didn't hum in the kitchen while she made a yucky rice pudding, which wasn't nearly as good as her bread pudding.

After the letter came and the news began to leak to us that Rhett wanted us back, there was no question in my mind. I wanted him back, too. I wanted to be happy and normal again. I forgot the problems as easily as my mother did when he promised it would be different now because he wasn't drinking and never would again. He was also involved in church, more than ever! I wanted to have our own house.

Priscilla's arms, folded over her chest, were tense now, the muscles in the forearms protruding from the clinched fists, like boxing bags fully packed. I didn't listen to the radio with her anymore, but I still went to church with her.

The rudeness and scathing remarks from the boys escalated, and Priscilla quit trying to stop them. Junior especially relished calling me a dirty little bastard in front of his tough-guy friends. They weren't mean to Lucinda though because she was on their side. She hated Rhett with a passion and told them our secrets, even sneaked Mama's letters out and read them to the boys.

Phil was the coldest of all. He didn't even try to catch Mama's eye anymore or say clever things when he was around. He pretended she was invisible, too, like me.

When Rhett came back to see us, the night was full of honeysuckle, hot pink azaleas in bloom everywhere, and the earliest lightning bugs of the year had begun to glow at dusk. I was delirious with the romance of it. The knight on the white horse was back. He took us to see *Pinocchio*, which I loved beyond measure, the pathos of Geppetto's voice crying out "Pinoooooooocchio" cutting into me like a knife. At the wise age of eight, I knew what being severed was about. I wanted another second chance.

When Rhett kissed us good night at the door, Mama said, "Y'all run on upstairs. Rhett and I might go for a little walk." I heard them talking softly downstairs for hours until I finally drifted into sleep, dreaming of white horses and knights and ladies. When I woke up crying in the night, Priscilla came to check on me. I couldn't remember what I had dreamed, but I couldn't stop crying even after I was awake. She pulled me to her soft bosom which reached almost to her waist and hummed that doe do doe lullabye. Just before I surrendered to the dark unknown of sleep, I realized Priscilla's clenched fists didn't match her soothing voice.

I don't think any of us, either family, had realized just how tense we were about having to survive together. Living in such close quarters could challenge even the most magnanimous spirits, and Priscilla's boys didn't take after their mother. She teetered between exasperation with them and defending their behavior.

Mama admitted defeat in renting out the house she had bought in defiance of maintaining rundown rental property. I heard her tell Priscilla the tenants were two months behind on their payments, adding, "I didn't realize I would have to take such a low-paying job merely to survive. This independence from Rhett cost more than I had bargained for."

Priscilla's response sounded detached, "Um hm."

On Sunday afternoon, Mama and Priscilla sat in the swing on the front porch talking in low tones and telling us to go play. I formed mud pies enough to feed an army, going close to the porch to get my dirt and straining to overhear them.

"Pearl," Priscilla said, "You always get whatever the kids need, but when you have to buy something for yourself, you seem like a flat tire. You have so little enthusiasm. It seems to get you down worse than it ought to. You never do anything just for yourself. Since Rhett left, where have you been but to work? Just name one time. That's why he can make you change overnight, turn into a different person. Maybe it's not him you want but just going to a movie or out to eat. I know it's not really my business, but I cannot bear the thought of you and the girls trusting Rhett."

Mama's rouge was too bright all of a sudden, but she didn't say anything. She lit a cigarette and blew smoke away from Priscilla, listening intently as Priscilla continued.

"After all, he conned Phil into giving him a huge sum of money and then disappeared without any explanation. In some ways, that money should have been mine; it was my daddy's money Phil started with originally, Pearl. You know I'd do anything for the girls, but Rhett is just another matter. Phil's bad enough. I can't tolerate two." Her words gave way to tears.

Mama's response was soothing, maternal. "Of course, Priss, so much that was yours has been messed with. That alone gives you the right to speak your mind." Then she blew her nose and started sniffling, too. They both laughed self-consciously. "Phil was a fool to leave you," Mama assured her.

"You know . . ." Priscilla started, but she stopped mid-sentence and put her finger to her lips, "Shh . . . I hear some kind of varmint scraping around in the yard."

"Reckon it's a squirrel?" Mama asked.

"More like a girl," Priscilla answered.

I knew I was caught, but I pretended I didn't know, just kept moving my spade further and further away from the swing and then went back to my oven and continued making meatloaf out of sticky red clay.

That was the only time I heard them talk about Rhett, but there were nights I heard them without being able to make out their words. They talked after all the kids were in bed, sometimes until later than Mama could afford to stay up, leaving her eyes scratchy the next morning when the alarm went off. She couldn't take a nap in the late morning like Priscilla could.

As spring teased the world into bloom, Rhett's letters became more and more frequent and Mama's delight in them greater. Priscilla laid them on Mama's pillow without comment. Lucinda said Priscilla told Phil about them, who made threats about getting his money back anytime Mama was within earshot. He claimed he had turned the address over to the police.

One night in May we had to raise all the windows and set ice in front of the fan to keep the house cool. Mama wore her slip to bed, perspiration glistening along her neck. She had seemed elated after reading her mail when she came in. She re-opened the letter at bedtime, handling the paper like a delicate treasure, and read over it several times. She smoothed the edges of the paper and ran her finger over the signature. Then she kissed us goodnight and went downstairs.

She and Priscilla played gin rummy at the table by the bay window, hoping for a breeze. At first their voices were muted, soft. As the volume escalated gradually, I could hear what they said. Lucinda stirred when she heard Mama's voice rise, "I know you're mad at me, and I don't blame you really, but he has become a preacher. I'm not changing my mind, Priss. I love Rhett . . ."

Lucinda groaned and rolled over, tossing the sheet aside. I pretended to be asleep so I wouldn't miss a word.

Priscilla sounded angry. "Hmmph! Don't talk to me about love. I'm too old to make important decisions based on emotion, and furthermore . . ."

"Stop it!" Mama screamed. "You can't put yourself in my place. He's not like Phil. He's been beaten down by a war Phil conveniently avoided. He's impulsive, but he's passionate. He's alive! Besides, I need a home for my children."

"They have a home here," Priss snapped.

"Oh, Priss, it's not the same and you know it. I really appreciate all you've done. I do. But we both know it's hard on the kids and on us. People talk."

"Well, they'll have plenty to talk about if you drag those children all over the county following a con man. I'm going to bed now. I can't concentrate on the cards anymore," Priscilla said with a tone of finality.

"It is late," Mama muttered. When she came to bed, she dipped a washcloth in the ice water pitcher and cooled her neck and the top of her breasts above the slip. I heard the match, smelled the sulphur, when she lit a cigarette, but I never opened my eyes to see the orange coal.

# Chapter Fifteen:
## Slings and Arrows

WE WORKED OUT A DEAL to get our house in East Lake back without a problem over the lease and have rent money, too. We moved into the small apartment and let the tenants rent the larger side of our vine-wrapped cottage, which had been such a dream before.

"We need the rental income until we get on our feet again," Mama reminded us often, lighting stubs of hand-rolled Bugler cigarettes. She kept smoking in private for awhile this time before she bought into Rhett's religious fervor.

I felt the same reluctance. I hated the way our tenant Laurie Ann left the shade up in the bathroom. She was only a first grader, so she didn't know any better. Every time I walked across the back porch I could see in their bathroom. She took a bubble bath at the same time every night. Spoiled brat!

I had to remind myself it was not Laurie Ann's fault she was in my tub because our family moved into the two-room apartment with only a sink and toilet.

The back porch smelled like White Rain shampoo. I even heard Laurie Ann screech that jingle: "Use new improved White Rain tonight and tomorrow your hair will be sunshine briiiiiiiight. White Rain! White Rain!" She kept a little umbrella propped between the tub and the window, so she could twirl it as she sang. One night after her bath, I took the screen off and cut a rip in the pink ruffled thing. I also rigged up a string and a stick so I could scratch on the screen and scare her without being detected.

Lucinda complained often. "It's really close quarters for four.

I need privacy; I'm not a baby," Her hair didn't shine like it used to, and her petulant smile had no trace of joy. Her lips were drawn downward in sullen parentheses, and she acted oversexed, wearing tight sweaters and lipstick.

"Buster's not the only boy at school! You don't have to smile and be nice to everybody when you have big boobs. Boys like you anyway," She snapped at me when I tried to talk about the change in her.

Mama and Rhett hogged the sofa bed, which she made up the instant her feet hit the floor in the morning. Shame seeped into Mama's shoulders when she thought nobody was looking. I was always awake, didn't sleep well anymore. Lucinda and I took turns sleeping on a pallet or the roll-away bed. At dawn, without breakfast, Rhett just slipped on his trousers, went in the bathroom and left from the back door. I hated his faded boxers and the dingy undershirt where Mama's careless darning showed. Sometimes she muttered to herself, "Damned old Indian could sneak right by St. Peter," when the door shut softly and he was gone.

Rhett didn't have a regular job, so he had time to work on his sermons while we were gone. I loved finding his Bible marked up where he'd been studying and making notes. He always brought in a good collection plate when he preached. He caddied some at the country club, drove cars at auctions, even sold a pint of blood now and then. It wasn't easy for us to strut like a preacher and his family.

I loved it that Rhett took up preaching. I heard Helen tell Mama if he preached long enough, he might convert himself, but he was serious. He heard the call, knew that he should be some kind of leader. I know because I've heard something like that too, have known all my life that I was born to deliver some sort of message. I was figuring out some things.

I first thought about hearing the call when we had a woman preacher from the Church of God at our revival. She was tough, mannish—wore no makeup. She reminded me of the suffragists I'd read about in the orange book about Susan B. Anthony. Her skirts swished when she made her way to the pulpit. She looked severe, braided hair pinned carefully to her shiny scalp, eyes peering into the faces of her listeners. Folks said her hair had never been cut, that nobody had ever seen it down.

I was tempted to follow her example that year, but I was terrified of hearing the call. I didn't want to answer it; I didn't want to be like this woman. I wanted, like most good girls in the 1950's, to be sweet and soft and pretty and have a man love me to death. Still, I knew that somehow I was meant to do something with my life: to spread the word, tell the story, something. So, I always felt empathic toward Rhett about his preaching spells, his need to instruct, to control others if not himself.

Mama's boss encouraged her at work. She repeated his compliment on the phone a thousand times: "We're proud of our girl Pearl, she made the highest score on that blame aptitude test ever been scored in this company!"

During sleepless nights, I knew just enough to wonder about aptitude scores and whether Rhett would need to sneak by St. Peter and why anybody wanted to say that rain was white. I worried that we would have to be the ones to rent from snooty Laurie Ann.

My first day back at Robinson Elementary was painful. "Class," the pleasant voice of my teacher announced, "we have a new student who is also an old student. Some of you will remember Bonita."

I shuffled my foot, examining the saddle oxfords Mama had polished to a shine last night. Like me, they were old but new—to me anyway—hand-me-downs from my cousin. None of the faces in the churning sea of students lit up like I wished they would. Mostly their mouths fell open and their eyes enlarged slightly as they examined me. "Linda, when classes change, I want you to show Bonita where to go," the teacher cooed in her soothing voice to a pert girl with curly blonde hair like coiled springs about to knock her Brownie beanie off. I wanted to knock it off myself because she still treated me as if I were invisible. I swallowed hard but kept my eyes dry, praying for true invisibility. I imagined myself the invisible heroine of a science fiction comic strip.

The teacher's mellow voice comforted me, however, as I made my way down the aisle and took my place at the empty desk, sliding my book satchel underneath. Mrs. Whitehead was the prettiest teacher I'd ever had, a voluptuous brunette with long, shapely legs. Her soft silk blouse was royal blue like the ink most pupils used. She wrote on the new blackboard, which was actually green, with yellow chalk, pointing out the difference between aaaa's and oooo's, looping each o as carefully as a chain stitch.

I filled my fountain pen from a bottle of Scripp's blue-grey ink, the color of a stormy sky. I worked hard to make my letters perfect, loving the feel of the pen in my hand moving smoothly across the paper.

Writing relaxed me as my body adjusted to the desk in the old/new school where the free-standing desks were made of blond wood attached to metal frames. In each row, tattered textbooks were stacked in the same order. Handwriting practice stimulated my imagination because I didn't have to think while I rhythmically copied letters from a lined yellow booklet. I knew I was good at cursive writing, exulted in it.

When Miss Elma Poore, from the Board of Education, came to examine our hand writing, I received a SUPERIOR sticker. No matter where I was enrolled in school, the ancient lady appeared. She sat in the back of the room poring through notebooks teachers thought were good enough to submit.

I cleared my throat when she called my name. Wondering if long ago her family's name was Poor without the e, I stood beside her as she flipped through my work. Maybe her family went hungry, lived through the potato famine in Ireland like Mama's. She was gaunt, her bones showing through the thin, freckled skin. Her grey hair, never a strand out of place, was drawn in a tight ponytail at her neck with a silk scarf. Miss Poore looked severe as she pored over the papers. My knees shook in her presence, but at the end she always looked up with a smile and said, "Yes, child, very good."

My teacher also praised me. She knew I was shy, felt out of place, so she made sure I found a partner or the right group for geography lessons. When we studied oat products and were asked to bring something from home, I brought Cheerios. Ms. Whitehead's warm, sunny smile assured me I'd pleased her even before she said, "What a great idea! CheeriO for OATS. I never realized before this moment that's why they're shaped in o's!"

It was my adoration for her that made my upcoming fall from grace a bitter disappointment. We had a contest to see who could read the most books, and I was one of those at the top of the chart. The sun glimmered across my row of gold stars at the same time every day—after lunch when we had silent reading period. I took the shimmering as a message for me to forge ahead. Every night I took home a new book, read it all the way through and exchanged it for a new one the next morning. One day I asked the school librarian, "May I check out two books, please?"

Her penciled eyebrows went up an inch, but then she said, "Sure, why not!"

The next day when I added two new titles to my list, the teacher frowned. I couldn't believe it. All night I had anticipated her praise for my doubled effort. Instead she took my hand in hers and looked straight into my eyes. "Bonita, are you sure you read both books in one night?" Her voice still sounded sugary, but the sweetness was missing.

My face reddened and my eyes filled with tears, which I knew only made me look guilty, as I muttered, "Yes ma'am." I was filled with shame, but I hadn't done anything to deserve it.

My enthusiasm for reading dwindled, and, of course, I didn't win the contest. I put my energy into church for awhile, helping prepare materials for Sunday school and training union. I was really proud of Rhett's preaching and wanted to do all I could to support his effort. He preached every Wednesday night at prayer meeting at the beginning of school. Nearly every week, I planned an art activity to go along with his text for that week. I figured I would get the kids and their parents thinking about what he was going to talk about ahead of time. We also had family talks at the dinner table about ideas running though his head every week. It made the sermons much more interesting to me. Sometimes, I was ashamed of how hard it was to understand him though. When he was excited, he talked so fast that he ran all his words together. Excitement was critical to him. He was always quoting that passage about being either hot or cold. I can see him now, rising on his toes, eyes ablaze in wonder, "If you are lukewarm, I'll spew you out of my mouth."

There was another kind of shame I felt at night hearing my parents' heavy breathing and squeaking springs. It was the first time we'd slept in the same room, and I hated the way their noises made me feel titillated and disgusted at the same time. It still made me feel confused, but I didn't cry now. I just made myself numb.

I lay awake, after they were snoring, and fantasized about eighth graders who seemed so cool, so worldly. I wanted to wear tight sweaters and makeup and bat my eyes at boys some day. Those girls, actually friends of the one who had become a real movie star, were even older than Lucinda but not as buxom.

When school was out for Christmas, I pretended I was as glad as my classmates. However, I knew I would miss the daily structure, the sense of accomplishment, the opportunity for praise. What I didn't know was just how miserable this Christmas would be. Mama and Rhett greeted the sun every morning bickering about money. I realize now they energized themselves sipping coffee and pumping adrenalin with anger as well as caffeine. This week the subject was Christmas; last week it was the sin of gambling because Rhett lost his butt in a poker game. It should have dawned on me by then he was secretly drinking again. We hadn't been to church since way before Thanksgiving.

"Ain't no sense in folks who ain't got money goin' in debt because department stores con them. You got to watch 'em; they'll take you ever where you turn!" Rhett pronounced, his chest puffed out with certainty.

"Yeah, well, ain't no sense in folks without money spending every dime on booze and cards either," Mama snapped, puffing on the half-cigarette she lit.

"Them cigarettes free these days?" he quipped, the sarcasm pulling the corners of his lips down.

"Second time around they are," she hissed at him, fire in her eyes.

The same fire blazed that afternoon as she chopped down our cedar shrub with a rusty ax. Those emerald eyes were greener than I ever saw them, filled with ferocity and determination. She brought the "tree" inside and stuck it in an old barrel with a bucket of water inside it.

"Oh, Mama, it's beautiful!" I exclaimed. Then we drug out the worn decorations and covered the tree with blue lights and big, round silver balls. As we threw the used tinsel on for the finishing touch, I could see the fire in her eyes turn to water. It reminded me of Granny dousing the fire, the tangerine coals turning gray. I hugged Mama close to me and wiped her tears. "It means more because you made it!"

"Really?" she answered, her eyes wrinkling in surprise and the brows moving up toward her curly bangs. "Let's go outside to see how our creation looks then." Her smile was softer than the hands she extended to us adding, "My sweet baby daughters."

Lucinda smirked, but she actually managed to keep her mouth shut. The lights really were beautiful shining through the sheers on the French doors, though the tree leaned. "Blamed if my kids are doing without a Christmas tree."

A few hours later, chilly under extra blankets, we heard the screech of tires and saw the yellow light on top of a car. We all three knew what a taxi meant: Rhett was drunk, a big spender taking a cab home from wherever he'd been. His indulgence set Mama off. Before he got in the door, she screamed, veins popping out across her forehead, "Who the hell you think you are riding around in a taxicab, Mr. Big Ike! Where'd you get money to drink when these children can't even have Christmas?"

"None of your business," he staggered toward the bathroom. She stuck her foot out and tripped him, making him fall flat on his face. She laughed hysterically at his puzzled, open mouth, the sound coming from her throat shrill, almost inhuman.

Fury was in his eyes and in the clenched fist he extended toward her. Suddenly, he changed his mind, spun around and knocked the tree over instead. "Ain't no need to have that depressing, pathetic thing in the way," he snarled.

Mama sprang out of that bed, gown flying behind her like a superman cape, and lit into him. They pushed and tugged and yelled until I closed my eyes and covered my ears. No use to plead with them to stop I knew by now. Under my muffled ears, I still heard her swear she was leaving him for good. Forever! *Yeah, right,* I thought. Then she was in my face, her voice urgent. "Kids, pack the suitcase. We're going to Helen's," she said between heaving, asthmatic breaths. Her breath came so hard I was surprised her chest allowed her air enough to talk. I worried that she would quit breathing.

Though I felt sorry for Rhett being left at Christmas, I was relieved to get away from their violence. Lucinda and I threw our green corduroy Christmas jumpers into the tattered suitcase along with our nightgowns. Dressing in the bathroom where Mama had lit the gas heater, Lucinda whispered sullenly, "I ain't cleanin' up that mess of a tree, and I mean it." Her breath was coming fast, too.

I didn't answer but went straight for the dust pan and swept up the shards of broken balls. The bright colors glittered in the pan like a rainbow. I put them in my jewelry box, a miniature cedar chest Priscilla sent me for Christmas.

By the time the taxi came, the warriors had already settled down. Rhett went to the car and told the driver, "There must be some mistake, buddy. We didn't call a cab."

Mama couldn't suppress the grin that crept across her face and into her eyes, peeping out the window at Rhett's convincing act of innocence. Rhett had convinced her to pour some whiskey in her water to settle her nerves. I didn't think it was one bit funny. "Why don't y'all play a game of checkers?" she suggested. She closed the door while my sullen sister and I spent the rest of Christmas Eve restoring the tree. I found some popsicle sticks, and we glued the broken ornaments, making some even prettier decorations. Then we played checkers at the kitchen table half-heartedly until our parents "made up."

Lucinda told me, "I worship Mama, the warmest, sweetest woman in the world, but she can be so dumb! Just remember, Bo, she would go to any lengths to provide for us, and we know we're loved. One day in Sunday school, that old crippled woman at Cheaha Mountaintop told me knowing your parents love you is the most important thing."

"Yeah," I swallowed hard. "Merry Christmas."

The next morning, we did go to Helen and Karl's to celebrate Christmas. They were in what Mama called a happy phase, expecting a baby. Helen's voice was tight at first until she had approval of her new home. "I never thought I would like living in a housing project, but if you mind your own business, it's not bad." Her voice rose on the last word as if it were a question. "I mean, this place is brand spanking new! They're still building units down the road," she added, her voice rising less this time.

Mama admired Helen's new apartment, especially the nursery curtains made with some old scraps of material Mama had given her. "Oh, they're just beautiful, like baby quilts!" Mama said, running her fingers along the lacy edges.

"And see in here, we've got a nice, big bedroom," Helen beamed. "We got a shower and a bathtub both in one," she said, swinging open the door to the bright yellow bathroom.

Helen made sweet potato casserole with marshmallows, and Mama baked a hen with dressing and giblet gravy. No matter how good her food was, Mama always found reason to apologize for it. I saw the triumph in her eyes when she took the glistening bronze hen out of the oven and lifted the hot dish of dressing. The scent of sage was overpowering, making the anticipation close to painful, but Mama apologized anyway, "This sure was a fat hen to have cooked down so. I hope we'll have plenty because we just couldn't afford a turkey this year."

Helen reassured her, "If that's not enough, we oughtta be whipped! Look at that bust line. Reckon that one's named Jayne Mansfield, heh heh." Mama knew it, of course. Fishing for compliments was a ritual that gave her comfort.

Rhett bought a real coconut for the ambrosia. Grinning, he declared, "I saw these things growing on trees overseas; all the soldiers loved to bust them open. Said they looked just like them ugly women over there."

It took him all morning to crack the brown scraggly thing. Finally he took a hammer to it, and we squealed as it exploded into small pieces. We bit into the pure white coldness of the inner fruit, thin milky juice running down our faces. "Y'all look like a couple of monkeys," he teased.

When he'd gone inside, Lucinda muttered, "And you look like a baboon! That thing probably cost as much as the difference in a turkey and a hen." We laughed, feeling wicked. More and more, he was becoming "the enemy."

I heard Rhett talk to Laurie Ann's daddy one night, kicking the tires on what they called "the big rig," the truck our tenant owned. I overheard his growling voice, "Yeah, Rhett, I think I had the right idea. You gotta go for the rig first, then the house. Hell, I'm in a position to buy this house if it was to be for sale now that I've done so well hauling that metal up to Detroit."

An hour or so later, I heard my parents whispering. Mama laughed. "I guarantee you he's just bragging about having that kind of money, but it gives me an idea. Instead of breaking our backs trying to pay for that new truck, you could get Moon to help you fix up one of those trucks down at that wrecker place. Then we could make ends meet, have some seed money again and save a little money ourselves. When you're not drinking, we could save a lot, just like other people do. That's how he's managed to pay for that big rig, one month at a time."

"Ol' Pearl, that's my girl," he said louder.

They did do better for awhile. He and Moon painted the truck a bright red, which you could see a mile away.

They even went in with some other parents to host an end-of-school party at East Lake Park: a wiener roast with baked beans, Mama's potato salad and ice cream cones. Some of the parents came and sat around talking. Linda, the girl who had led me around the first day, showed up with her dad who was a handsome, friendly salesman. He had to show Rhett how to cook out since he never used the brick pit in our back yard. He was always too drunk to barbecue.

We played on the gym bars and swings until dark; then we moved on to chase and freeze. I wished this whiff of normality, of belonging, had come at the beginning of school when I'd felt so alone instead of at the end.

When Mama wrapped the leftover potato salad and the smelly kraut, I noticed Rhett and Linda's daddy drinking a beer. It embarrassed me less since somebody else's daddy was drinking, too. Blonde curls coiled tight as if she'd stuck her finger in a socket, Linda didn't look any more surprised than usual. "Let's swing some more until they notice it's time to go," she whispered. I eagerly joined the conspiracy, knowing Rhett's beer meant we'd stay later. "I'm gonna miss you this summer, Bonita," she told the foggy night air in front of her. "You've been a lot of fun."

I looked straight ahead, too, grateful we weren't face to face. I wasn't used to open compliments. I barely heard my awkward muffled reply, "Thanks." I felt the glow of acceptance flood my whole being like a foreign element. I pumped higher and higher, making the rusty metal chains squeak. They were unaccustomed to this intensity just like me. We never had normal family get-togethers where dads drank a couple of beers and relaxed as the crickets and frogs overtook the night with their song.

When we got home, I couldn't keep the lump in my throat still. I was learning how to deny pain by daydreaming, but I wasn't an expert yet. Feeling good was so unfamiliar that it scared me. I couldn't trust it to last. I couldn't deny the sweet smell of flowers that had survived Rhett's massacre a few years ago.

The books I loved would say I had a sense of foreboding. I felt it in my bones.

# Chapter Sixteen:
# Climb Every Mountain

LATE IN THE AFTERNOON, Daddy Phil called Rhett. I panicked because it was the first time they had talked since Rhett ran off to Texas with Phil's money. My stepdad's tremulous voice was further warning to my pounding heart. Then I heard Daddy Rhett say, "Let's talk it over with a beer; I think I can explain a few things. You don't drink beer? Godamighty! I got something better 'n beer. I'll buy you a drink, man." His hollow laughter echoed like an omen, prickling my skin. "Besides, Phil," he said, his voice shaking, then stronger, "I owe you. You come on down here."

Mama never got up for supper, didn't even know Phil had called much less come over, but I lurked around as long as these two men I called Daddy allowed me. I did my homework on the back porch while they sat in the kitchen. Rhett tried so hard to be nice that I thought he was scheming another con job. He greeted Phil at the car, shaking his hand so hard I thought Phil would fall back into his Studebaker. Daddy Phil seemed shocked, but he quickly recovered and started acting snooty, tilting that long forehead as he followed Rhett around to the back door. "Pearl's taking a nap, getting her beauty rest," Rhett said, "as if she needs it." Both of them chuckled awkwardly. Daddy Phil never even looked at me, much less spoke.

Rhett had filled Mama's nice glasses with a few cubes of ice and set out a frosted bottle. "This is pure grain alcohol, made by a doctor friend of mine. We used to drink this in the Marine Corps. Smoothest thing in the world, no hangover . . ."

"No thank you," Phil said, his eyes colder than the ice he rattled, "just water for me."

Rhett's mustache fell, his mouth open in surprise. "You want it neat?"

"I don't want to drink that," Phil said. "Maybe I will have a beer."

Rhett grabbed a cold one from the fridge, "Pabst Blue Ribbon, good old red white and blue for the holiday!" He smiled amiably, his muscular arm sliding the can smoothly toward Daddy Phil, who opened it and sipped it occasionally. They made small talk about sports, the weather and Labor Day festivities until Phil moved on to the reason for his visit. "Rhett, there's a serious matter I need to talk to you about. There's a limit to the amount of inappropriate behavior I'll allow my daughters to witness. They know, of course, that you're indebted to me for the money you stole when you left for Texas. It was my understanding that you had quit drinking and that you had a job lined up with the Transit Company."

"I did quit drinking, Phil, and I do intend to pay you back every dime. I had a good job out there driving a city bus, saved up money to send for Pearl and the girls, but those nightmares came back." He gulped a drink. "You should have seen the Japs stuff your buddies' privates in their mouths. You'd know what I'm talking about. Or spend night after night being shot at. Or live through Okinawa. What do you know about it, man? You stayed home, making money off the war."

"I'm not here to listen to excuses. I want some explanation about why you aren't working! I've come to offer you an opportunity to make good money, enough to pay me back and support your family like a man."

"Watch your mouth, Phil. I'm on a waiting list at the Transit Company, and I've been taking every odd job I can find. What's this you're talking about?"

"You ever handle dynamite during the war?"

"No." Rhett spat the word.

"How 'bout in the mines?"

"Never."

"That lowers your value considerably," Phil said, eyeing Rhett as if he were cattle at an auction. "However, there's still money to be made in making deliveries without being detected." Daddy Phil looked crossly at me, finally noticed I existed long enough to tell me to go find Lucinda. The last morsel of information I overheard was from Phil's tight lowered voice, "This city is about to explode, man, and a guy like you could make a lot of money. No questions asked. Just do your job like a good soldier. Helps if you don't have much conscience," Daddy Phil added with a dry chuckle.

Rhett didn't sound amused. "Who the hell said I don't have a conscience?"

I tried to escape into my book, my concentration broken from time to time by the sound of male voices. Both voices began determined but progressed to furious pretty quickly. I heard Phil yell, "You can't afford not to!"

Followed by Rhett's deeper voice, "You're not a bank. You can't force me to do a damn thing."

Their anger woke Mama. Her mouth flew open, her eyes went crazy, but no sound came out of her mouth while her face struggled to get hold of itself. I had started to explain before we heard the commotion. When we heard what sounded like a kitchen chair crash through the window, we ran toward them at the same time. Phil lunged toward Rhett who shielded himself with another chair, and Mama and I tore out through the living room. Lucinda smirked at the doorway, a sense of disdain radiating from her erect posture, her lifted chin.

Mama's arms were covered with fierce red welts, her "nervous rash" on a rampage, which often happened over holidays. Her eyes sparkled with excitement as she attempted to pull the two men apart. When she saw she couldn't physically stop them, she lit up, her laughter shrill, chilling, "Well, look who's come down to the land of the lowly, Mr. High and Mighty tangling with the bad boy."

Phil bolted across the room like he wanted a handful of Mama's hair, but Rhett cried out, "Pearl, baby, this ain't really got a thing to do with you. Don't let that s.o.b. get to you."

Rhett's cautioning her set Phil off in a jealous rage. His voice chilled me to the bone, "You get decency and high and mighty mixed up, Pearl. Always did!" He ripped her housecoat, buttons flying across the curled linoleum. Phil's fury even brought a scream of terror from Lucinda. I wailed, pulling on Phil's trousers, "Please, Daddy Phil, stop it. Please."

We had managed to at least distract him long enough to give Rhett a chance to get steady on his feet and find a butcher knife, which he waved threateningly, his muscular chest heaving in the thin undershirt. Phil scuffled him to the floor and threw the knife toward the sink. "That's too good for you. I'm gonna beat that sorry streak out of you, set you straight this time." Phil, seated on top of Rhett, looked as if he'd flatten my drunk-as-usual stepfather. I couldn't think fast enough to identify what I felt, seeing Phil pound his fists into Rhett's chest. He had something iron on his fists I later learned were brass knuckles used by dirty fighters. I screamed—which shocked them—when I saw the blood-soaked undershirt. Then Phil stood, scowling at the defeated man a decade younger and potentially far stronger. Phil couldn't hide his elation over the triumph.

Mama seized the moment and lit into Phil with questions about his involvement in all this. While he explained to Mama what had happened, Rhett motioned to me. "Get me a nickel, baby," he whispered. We sneaked out of the living room to the pay phone on the corner. Rhett's hands shook as he put the coin in and dialed the police. He pretended to be a neighbor complaining about a disturbance of the peace. When we slipped back in, there was no indication that anybody had noticed our absence.

Phil sat at the kitchen table with a cup of tea, his chin in his hands, while—at the kitchen sink—Mama washed his bloody shirt. Finally I discovered another source of bleeding: Phil's nose hung flat on his face, blood still dribbling. I was entranced by the blood that was mine—Phil's. It seemed a different color from Rhett's on the undershirt.

When the Police drove up, Mama—at once—told me to go out to the back porch, assuring me that everything would be fine. Suddenly, I was not only invisible but needed to be protected from what I had just witnessed—even participated in by rescuing the underdog. "Bow wow," I muttered under my breath as I trudged past where Lucinda perched, twirling her hair and smiling that eerie way. I heard her footsteps but I ignored her.

I sobbed into a pillow, covering my head to muffle the sound. Only eight years old, my system was overloaded. The two men I loved and hated most in the world had just ripped into each other like animals, their blood going down the drain in the kitchen sink like those chickens Aunt Shannon plucked. How close to Judas, who was doomed to Hell forever, did it make me when I betrayed my own father? Hadn't Phil come there to set things straight, to take care of us in his own cold way? Did he want Daddy Rhett to work in the mines again or the steel mill? Wasn't dynamite dangerous like in the movies? It could blow your head off. Maybe that's what Daddy Phil wanted.

Mama looked worse than hacked, puffing Pall Malls like a defeated dragon, when she came to check on me. "Where's Rhett?" I asked.

"Them blame cops arrested him, tried to arrest Phil for trespassing, but he talked them out it. Turned right around and talked them into taking Rhett instead for disturbing the peace. He said Rhett started it all, but I don't believe him for one minute."

"He's the one who called Rhett . . ." I started, glad to have an ally in my defense of the loser.

"That's what he tried to tell them, but that young cop was a smart aleck, wanted to take somebody in real bad for some reason." Mama cried. She went back downstairs and, slamming pots and pans, made a loud supper. Afterward, she told us to go out and play.

"I don't want to," Lucinda announced.

"Then go read your book," Mama snapped, which sent Lucinda stalking to the porch.

It was nearly bedtime when Mama told us to get dressed. "We need to talk to Phil. He wants us to come up there."

"It's not too far to walk?" Lucinda whined.

"It depends on how desperate you are," our mother said, her face registering all the proof we needed that she was, indeed, desperate. She seemed to have aged a decade in the last month or so. Yet there was a flicker of toughness, of determination in those emerald eyes.

Phil met us at the edge of the path at Cascade Plunge, the pool, and led us up a trail toward his house at the top of the hill. We walked from our house on 82nd Street to 68th Street and then over several avenues and back, but it was an adventure. Soon, I lost my worry and focused on the novelty of night sounds in the woods: the hoot of an owl, occasional rustling in the foliage, and a hypnotic chorus of crickets.

It was the first time I'd been in the house since we lived there when I was five years old. The mellow light glowed through the shades. I was unprepared for the flood of poignant feelings as I entered the door and came face to face with the trapped deer mounted on the wall. I thought of Rudolph's nose and Phil's sore, red nose. I giggled nervously. "What's funny, Pumpkin Pie?" Phil asked, stooping toward me, smiling fondly.

"I don't know," I answered, not looking at him.

"Tell me," he said, a streak of impatience taking over his face, the blue eyes turning frozen, the condescending sneer twisting his lip crooked.

"I don't want to," I pouted.

"Why don't y'all go out and play?" Mama asked with that same insane tone suggesting this was a normal time to play.

Phil chimed in, "The boys have a basketball hoop lit up on the driveway. That ought to be fun."

"Sure," Lucinda sulked knowingly, a sinister grin ruling her face as we went outside.

"Whaaaaaaat?" We soon heard Phil scream, then a door slam.

"She must've asked him to get Mr. Jailbird out," Lucinda laughed, a cruel dry sound in her laughter. From the soft butterscotch light of Phil's office, the sound of Mama's sobbing replaced the loud talk, then subsided. We heard furniture being moved, then soft murmuring, then nothing.

"Wonder where Frances the Mule is?" Lucinda snarled. The boys called Frances Terez, Daddy Phil's big-toothed new wife, the Mule, after *Francis the Talking Mule* in the Donald O'Connor movie.

Later, when Phil walked us back through the night sounds on the trail, everything was quieter, softer somehow. He and Mama both seemed softer, too, as if that butterscotch mellow had transformed them. We stood at the clearing a long time, the damp cool of darkness making chill bumps on my thin arms and Lucinda's calves.

Mama put her arms around Phil's neck, and he buried his thinning blond head in her dark curls for just a second. He cleared his throat, lit his pipe and said, "I'll call you."

I was glad nobody seemed awake when we crept across the yard. Something about Mama's stealthy gait made me feel wicked, like three criminals in search of jewels from that Grace Kelly movie *To*

*Catch a Thief.*

Early the next morning, Mama raised the window in our bedroom to let the breeze in. Unnaturally cheery, she jabbered on and on about the fresh air. Then she made her point. "That hike we took last night makes me think y'all could climb Ruffner Mountain like you been begging to ever since we moved here."

"Reckon your asthma could take it, Mama?" I asked.

"Oh, no, baby, Pearl ain't climbin' no mountain," she laughed. "I'm way too old, and you're near about too young, but Lucinda could take care of you."

I anticipated a groan, but it didn't happen. Lucinda's face glowed with excitement, "Oh, Mama, I would. I swear I would. Everybody's been up that mountain but me. I know I pick at my baby sister, but you know I love her." She snuggled up close to me and coached, "Isn't that right, sis?"

I felt a warm tingle from the affection, which I rarely got from her these days. She snuggled close to me at night in her sleep but not in day light, and I hadn't heard anything about loving me for a long time. "Yes, ma'am," I lied. "We've been real close lately."

"I wish ol' Buster were in town," Mama said. "I haven't seen another boy I'd trust to go with y'all like I would him."

"We don't need boys, anyway," Lucinda said, already brushing her hair while I tied my shoes.

"You got to wear a cap, keep them ticks off," Mama said. "I'll fix y'all a Labor Day picnic to carry."

Lucinda smirked, "A cap! Sure," she mumbled to herself.

The air on the mountain was refreshing! That first hint of autumn stirred energy in my veins, filled me with anticipation. My fear began to disappear, replaced by exhilaration as soon as we stepped into the fern-filled, cool shade and climbed upward. Certainly there was no worn path to follow; only a few of the older kids had climbed the small mountain all summer.

Breathing hard, we scooted up the hillside, holding on to rocks most of the time and to each other some of the time. Lucinda and I called on our old teamwork as we approached the ridge. She went ahead of me along the rockiest hillside, shaking with the effort to keep a firm footing when the powdery gravel slipped beneath her tennis shoes. I was just close enough behind to get grit in my eye when the limestone and soft, crumbling sandstone gave beneath her foot. I grabbed hold of a small tree above me and pushed the upper branches inward toward her. Lucinda, flushed with terror, grabbed hold and moved up an inch or two, gaining a solid foothold again.

"Quick thinking, Bo!" she exclaimed, her full lips wrapped around her pearly teeth. "You're a good buddy to climb up this wild mountain with! I'd rather have you than anybody I know for my partner today."

Amazed at such an outburst of affection, I was dumbstruck. "Thanks," I said through a film of wetness that filled my eyes, a combination of grateful tears and sweat that poured down my face. Lucinda's face was covered with a thin coat of red dust. Her eyes crinkled into laughter as she cried out, "You look like a red zebra!"

"What?" I questioned, looking at my arms and legs, covered an even red like a deep sunburn. "All I see is red skin."

Lucinda interrupted her stream of giggles, "Like ol' Rhett's face when he's drunk! If Rhett was our real daddy I'd swear you were a Cherokee zebra with that striped face."

"Ok, ok," I sighed, "I get it."

"I'd be sweatin', too, if I had a cap on. I'd rather have ticks than Rhett's cooties and lice." She fanned herself with the green Birmingham Barons cap in her army bag. Mama had made us wear canteens around our necks and strap our lunches on our shoulders like knapsacks. "Mama said she couldn't remember whether these canteens were Rhett's or some Phil bought at the army surplus store, but surely anybody's germs are gone by now. Hope so, anyway." Lucinda guzzled the water from her upturned canteen.

"Whew, I'm hungry. Let's eat," I said and perched on a rock shaped like a pulpit. I said into my sister's enlarged eyes, "From up here, it's too beautiful down there to believe, so green everywhere. Look yonder, a few of those trees have started turning yellow already!"

"Really, Bo, you get so worked up!" she smiled. It was the second time she had used my old nickname. "Val de ri! Val de ra! My knapsack on my back!" she sang in a mocking voice, unstrapping her canvas bag and biting into her sandwich. Mama had cut the leftover steak up real fine and covered it with barbecue sauce and pickles. We were happy, carefree, above it all!

I hadn't anticipated downhill being worse than uphill, but it was! A thundercloud hovered over our descent and the rocks hurt my blistered feet. When I complained, Lucinda reminded me that this kind of fatigue was called "good tired." I wasn't so sure.

WHEN WE RETURNED we were shocked to see a black man at the wheel of Rhett's truck and two men heaping furniture on the back of it. "Want 'em to wrap that ol' mirror in a blanket, Miz Pearl?" Ida's husband called out.

"Yeah, Charlie, thanks. I ain't thinking straight at this point. I'm glad you're here to think for me. No wonder Ida brags on you," Mama smiled, taking the wet-lipped cigarette out and laying it, ash and all, along the top of the truck while she stuck groceries in the chinks between things. Her brow furrowed just before she buried her head in the clutter of quilts and curtains. She didn't see me charge into the yard, mouth open wide as a frog catching insects, eyes popped open even more than a frog's. I felt something die inside my heart, deep down in the core where we long for more warning that our world is about to change.

"Oh, Mama, what's happening?" I wailed. "I don't want to move again."

"You're too young to have a choice," she snapped. "I've got to do what I have to. Period. I knew you'd hate it, so I sent you off to have a good time."

"Lucinda, what you smirking about?" Mama jabbed, striking quick so she'd be first. "Y'all just do what I tell you. Don't ask questions. By the time you throw your clothes in those suitcases, we'll be ready to get outta this dump."

"Suits me. I hate this place," Lucinda said, scanning to see if any of her teenage friends were among the folks nosing around. She fairly flew inside, but I sat down to rub the blisters on my feet, tears flowing down my cheeks. "It's just a shock to be moving again," I assured Mama when she came to inspect my feet. I didn't mention that I worried about Rhett, still couldn't get that bloody undershirt out of my eyes.

Lucinda was throwing clothes wildly, making no attempt at order. "I, for one, cannot wait to get rid of Rhett and his sorry ways. Mama says Phil's giving us our own apartment this time, so things will be better, Bo. Come on. Cheer up."

"Rhett does cause all the trouble," I admitted. Still, I hate to think of him in jail. Reckon what he'll think when he comes home and we're gone?"

I mouthed the words that came out of my big sister's smart mouth, "Who cares?" I tried not to think of him anymore, tried instead to envision an apartment with pigeons that coo along windowsills wide enough to sit in. I'd pretend it was Rome, that we'd moved to Europe so Rhett could never find us and Phil would leave the Mule and come live with us again. Or maybe Dr. Paterson? Or a real prince since we'd be Europeans . . . .

These fantasies made packing go faster. I sat on the suitcase like Lucinda did to make it fasten, the bulge of school dresses that were once Lucinda's straining against the lock. Nobody came out to tell us bye.

Lucinda shook those boobies she adored and wiggled when she walked. "Lawdee," I heard one of Ida's sons say to the other. They were both big as grown men with rippling muscles. Charlie, Jr., picked up Mama's heavy Singer sewing machine without any help at all. I saw him cut his eyes toward Lucinda to see if she noticed, but she was busy wedging her suitcase between the dresser and Mama's sewing machine. "Lawdee is right," I told myself. She taunted little boys and grown men and colored boys with equal pleasure. There was no hope for her some days.

Just when we finished loading the old truck, I saw the yellow cab. The sight of it made my heart race. Rhett, drunk as a coot. His lips trembled, "What the hell's going on here?" he yelled.

Charlie never looked directly at Rhett, but his voice was soft with empathy like a preacher's when somebody dies, "Miz Pearl says it's time to move on. I'm just drivin' the truck, captain."

"I was a sergeant, not a captain," Rhett slurred.

"Um hm," Charlie answered to the shoulders headed toward the back door. Charlie shuffled toward the truck, dragging the leg that wouldn't bend behind him. He'd been injured in the war, but it didn't seem to slow him down.

We heard Mama scream, "Heeeeeeellllllll no!"

Then Rhett pleaded. Faces gathered at the screens of every window for this round. Mama made it short, flying up on top of the precariously piled furniture faster than the screen door could slam. Sure-footed, strong as a man, she threw Rhett's suitcase at him, barely missing his head.

Defeated, Rhett slumped to the ground, his body turning into a flimsy bag of disappointment. Eyes fiery as the eerie magenta sunset, Mama slammed the door of the truck and yelled, "Gun it, Charlie!"

Rhett sprawled in front of Lucinda and me on our way to the truck, "Ain't you gonna give your poor ol' daddy a farewell hug?" he begged. I focused on the intense crimson of the princess feathers Aunt Mary Alma had given me on Friday. Lucinda prissed right on to the truck and crawled up on the tailgate between the two movers, their glistening mahogany shoulders taut as they helped her with the bird cage. Charlie called softly to them, "Y'all walk on back to the house and get Mr. Logan to bring you to Miz Priscilla's." He grinned and added, "Tell Asa I said no nipping until the driving is done."

His sons slid gracefully off the truck and disappeared around the corner in an instant. I felt sorrier for Rhett than anybody else did. Grieving over his misery, I stopped just long enough to give him a strained hug and one of my flowers, then crawled up on the tailgate with my sister. No matter how hard I tried to fight them, tears slid down my sunburned cheeks.

Just as we rounded the corner, the chairs piled on top teetering slightly, Rhett made a guttural sound like a war cry and jumped on the truck, causing Lucinda to scamper up toward the unsteady chairs. Mama's incredulous face was focused on Rhett. He turned his handsome profile toward the red sky, the prominent nose unmistakable. Yet, for a few seconds, the profile could have been Jeffrey Hunter's, the white actor who played many Indian roles. I wanted the sky to be a movie screen, prayed this was not reality. Rhett cried, begged, would not give up. I felt like a hostage. When Rhett reached for my hand, I pretended I didn't see him and held on tight to the rope Charlie had tied around me. I faked concern about the old chest of drawers that teetered, pressing against the weathered rope that secured it to the cab of the truck. I held the bird cage and talked in a soothing voice to the terrified creatures.

Finally, Mama sighed, "Oh, hell, Charlie, let's go on. Figure it out when we get there. Phil said I could have the apartment. It's not my fault Rhett got out of jail early."

Lucinda glared down at both of us, contempt so strong we could have cut it with a knife. I tried to focus my attention on the bright lights of the Magic City against the blood-red sky.

Once the furniture was unloaded, Rhett disappeared but came back with beer and barbecue. He convinced Mama to swill a few while they took the newspaper off dishes and stacked them in the kitchen cabinet.

When we arrived, Priscilla never even waved to us, just stood solidly on the front porch of her apartment, glaring. Every time she came out, her arms were folded over her soft chest so hard it looked as if she were straining fiercely to hold her arms down. It made me giddy imagining her a wronged angel about to fly away. I entertained myself by humming the tune about flying away to God's celestial shore.

I did all I could to dull the throbbing contradiction of emotions growing in my throat as if I'd swallowed razor blades. Perched in the kitchen window overlooking the valley, I allowed strings of street lights, sparkling like diamond necklaces, to hypnotize me into a false sense of satisfaction.

Later, the warm water in the claw-footed tub soothed my tattered heart as well as my blistered feet. We wound up using the dining room for mine and Lucinda's bedroom, and Mama and Rhett took the one with privacy.

"When will I ever have a room of my own?" Lucinda sighed wearily, taking off her padded bra. As if she needed padding! She turned her back to me when she saw my dull stare. She looked like a goddess from behind, her tiny waist swelling into round, shapely buttocks. Her soft curves resembled the Greek statues in the Encyclopedia Britannica in every school library. No matter how many times we moved, the school encyclopedias were a constant.

I tried not to look at the soft private curves but focused on Lucinda's hair blazing golden in the lamp's mellow light. I could have sworn I saw a halo when she pulled the thick blonde mane up and pinned it off her neck.

When Lucinda reached to turn the lamp off, the swell of her breast was visible through the thin, cotton gown—rounded like the dipper in Granny Youngblood's drinking-water bucket. I closed my eyes, pretended I hadn't heard my sister repeat the complaint about sharing a room. Glad the light was off when tears slid down my face, I was too tired to sob, much less talk about it. I didn't make a sound, purged by the private release. I thought of Priscilla's folded arms like some warrior watching from a mountain crest before the battle began. I knew she would have called Phil by now, and I dreaded his reaction to Rhett's spoiling Mama's latest attempt to leave him, this time by surprise. I finally fell asleep amidst the shadows of boxes filled with dusty photos, useless curtains, and worn towels in our latest setting for "starting over."

# Chapter Seventeen:
# Summer Pastimes

AT DAWN, LIGHT WASHED over the walls of my new "home." First, the walls were bruised purple, then rosy. Finally, sun rays filled the back wall with a golden glow the color of Lucinda's hair. Strands fell softly around her neck as she snored slightly, curled into the fetal position like the diagrams of babies in her "facts of life" pamphlet.

Lucinda seemed ten feet tall, growing daily—in every way. Her rounded curves reminded me more and more of the sculpture of Aphrodite at the East Lake Library. I touched a golden curl that glistened in the morning sun to be sure it was real. I tried not to disturb her, but she stretched like a cat and yawned at me.

"I always think God is sending a message when a ray juts out from a puffy gray cloud like that," I whispered, pointing. "Maybe this place won't be so bad after all."

She looked through me, didn't answer, crawling across our mattress, which swallowed space in the tiny dining room we'd been demoted to. She made her way across the large, awkwardly arranged room, "We might have known Mama would claim the larger room when Rhett came along for the ride. She said she'd sleep on the sofa so we could have our own room."

Her voice turned bitter when she mocked Mama's sales pitch: "A nice big room with bay windows where you can sit and see the lights of the city at night!" She knew I didn't want to move back here with Priscilla and her brats.

I listened to her gripe but tried to hold on to my hard-won hope that things could work out until, at last, I heard Mama say, in a sugary voice much too cheerful, "Rise and shine, girls." I prayed she hadn't heard Lucinda's meanness.

Mama fidgeted with a wrinkle in the white-collared trim on the navy shirtwaist she wore to work at least once a week. She applied her lipstick, blotting it on toilet paper, fluffed her hair and peered into the mirror for confirmation. The reflection's weary eyes looked heavy over the mouth that struggled to avoid the martyr's resignation. She turned to us. "I guess I'm a little embarrassed about taking the old drunk fool back, girls, but . . . but . . ."

I wanted to make her feel better, but I was still mad at her for giving in. When I stared at her without saying a word, trying to poison her instead of myself with my sadness, she looked away quickly and rummaged through her purse. "Here's some pennies; get you something when the peddler comes. And by the way, when the ice man comes, you don't have to do anything, don't even have to talk to him. He's colored. Stay in here and let him put the block of ice in that ice box down the hall just outside my room."

"We'll tell him," Lucinda mumbled. I couldn't stay mean like her. I got up to hug Mama goodbye.

"I get off at 4:30; see y'all then." She sighed as she kissed my sweaty forehead and added, "Rhett will probably sleep all day," as she went out the door.

"Like we care," Lucinda groaned.

When the old black man trudged up the stairs, calling ahead of himself, "Here come the ice man this mawning," he woke Rhett up.

"What?" Rhett hollered like a scalded dog. "What's going on?" he called from his room.

"It's the ice man," I answered, then told the man where to put the ice. Rhett looked sheepish when he peeped in our room stretching his muscular arms and rubbing the stubble on his cheek. He almost acknowledged that I was awake, grumbled some sort of greeting in my direction. Then his eyes lingered on Lucinda who had turned over toward the wall, her fanny shaped like a valentine.

He lit a cigarette and blew smoke rings in Lucinda's direction, but she ignored them. Then he croaked to me, "Sweetie Pie, run down to that store on the corner and get me some tomato juice; my stomach's kinda queasy."

"Want some buttermilk, too?" I was familiar with his cure procedure.

"Let me see if I've got enough money," he said, pulling out a handful of change, mostly pennies and nickels.

"How about I get Lucinda and me some cocoa and marshmallows for breakfast?" I tried to negotiate a delivery fee.

"Naw," he snapped too quickly, then handed me two pennies, "ain't enough money there. Get you some blow gum."

I trotted to the corner grocery store instead of running, not sure if he really meant for me to run. I tiptoed back up the stairs, the cold package pleasant against my flat chest. I smelled the vodka before I saw it. He waited at the top of the stairs with the vodka already poured. He sloshed the tomato juice, then downed it, telling me, "It's medicine, baby."

"You sounded like a dragon screaming in the night," I scolded, but the jab didn't seem to register.

He chuckled, "I saw a few dragons after midnight." After that, Rhett was zonked for the day. Lucinda said he and Mama had worked out a plan where he wouldn't really be living with us but just visiting sometimes late at night so Priscilla wouldn't have to know. Mama was really worried about how angry Priscilla was. No wonder. Rhett was planning to stay with his folks and work out of town some, too.

When Robby showed up at our apartment with a deck of cards, Lucinda and I were still unloading boxes. He examined the sketches of naked women the previous tenant had penciled on the wall. "That fella lived here before called himself an artist, but he didn't say he was a pervert," Robby said. He eyed Lucinda's full breasts, which swayed as she bent to unwrap the newspaper around each bowl. "Let me help y'all, then we can play a little Black Jack." Lucinda's eyes flickered for a second when she saw his glance, then her perfect ivory teeth stretched the pout right out of her lip. She was, as always, getting on my last nerve, but at least he seemed glad to see us. Nobody ever looked at another blooming thing when Lucinda was in the room. She crossed her long, shapely legs, rared back in the chair poking her chest out and said in her sweetest voice, "Oh, Robby, that would be so sweeeeeeet."

I hated them when we started to play cards, both of them acting like I wasn't even in the game. He explained everything to her, not me. "I'm the littlest one, Robby; you should help me learn the stupid game."

He squirmed, then tousled my hair, punching me on the shoulder, "Here's the key, Bonita: The ace can go either way. It can save you as a one or bust you as 11. Oh, you need some more copper, don't you," he added, piling pennies in front of my place. "Let's give her a little extra," he told my sister, the goddess. She winked. I groaned.

Once I caught on, I whipped their butts! I couldn't believe the smile that sneaked across my face, the charge I felt inside my tummy or the voice that got stronger each time I said, "I'll stay," or "Hit me." By the time we quit, I had twice as many pennies as either of them. "Do we get to keep them for real?" I asked.

"Nope. They're for cards only," Robby ordered, raking the circles of power up and shoving them in his pockets. I turned away to hide my disappointment. "Hey, come on, Bonita, tell you what. We'll have one penny for the winner when the peddler comes, ok?"

Lucinda dug baloney out of the old ice box and smelled it, "I don't think it's spoiled. Mama worried about not having ice last night, but here, Bo, you sniff," she demanded.

"She might get boogers on it," Robby said, which set the two of them into giggles.

"I'll have mustard on mine," is all I said.

Lucinda turned on the radio, insisting we listen to *The Loves and Life of Helen Trent*. I liked the suspenseful love story more than I let on, transported into the familiar world of make-believe by the dramatic footsteps and the sound of doors closing. We ate our lunch on the sofa after the program, envisioning Helen and her lover. Robby said, "If their looks go with their voices, they must be pretty fancy folks."

"I think he's tall, dark and handsome, maybe has a scar above his eyebrow to add to his mystery," Lucinda observed.

"I bet Helen's got big titties," Robby giggled, eyeing Lucinda's.

"Y'all bore me to death," I snapped, chewing the stale bread crust. My mind drifted away from them. I looked across the street at Mrs. Shaw's huge Tudor house, its dark wood trim and tan stucco exterior like pictures of houses in England. For some reason, Mrs. Shaw had adopted Vicki's little sister, Tiny Thatcher (now Tiny Shaw), after we moved to Lakeview. When her husband died, Mrs. Shaw converted their private home into a boarding house.

I envied Tiny for living out my adoption fantasy right there in the neighborhood for all the world to witness. This escape fantasy surpassed my noble death fantasy, the one where all my wrong-doers filed by my coffin—remorseful and longing for one more chance. However, in Tiny's fantasy, wrong-doers had to be sorry and kiss her now-royal butt, too.

After the radio program, Robby insisted we play another round of cards, "Give me a chance to win all that money back," he grinned, piling up the pennies. He demonstrated a good poker face, got serious about the game and played aggressively, going way too fast for me. Of course, he won.

Robby's pants always threatened to slip off his skinny butt, but when he scooped in his winnings, his pockets sagged more. The weight of his victory threatened to reveal even more of the crevice above his useless belt. When he jumped up and down on the bed in glee, I saw it coming, but not in time to warn him. His pants slid down around his skinny, freckled knees! His dingy undershorts slipped down in the back, but remained intact in the front where he quickly cupped his hand.

Lucinda quipped, "Look at the card shark, blushing dark as a plum!"

Robby squirmed off the bed with his back to us while he unloaded the pennies to the cigar box he'd brought them in and pulled his britches up. We cackled hysterically, Lucinda's hand over her mouth to stop the giddiness. I almost lost my breath laughing at the sight of Robby's pale buttocks, smooth as a baby's—the fragile image, frozen forever, like a dusty photo, in my head.

"It serves you right for winning every time," Lucinda said, eliciting a sheepish grin from Robby.

"Ah hell . . ." he started, but the sound of our howling drowned his words. Eventually, he surrendered to being ridiculous and joined our hysterical giggling. The promise of Robby's pants falling, with the crack of his butt always visible, may be what started the trouble with the stranger.

# Chapter Eighteen:
# Daring the Devil

WE WERE SPRAWLED INNOCENTLY on the rug another afternoon—engrossed in cards—when I first felt the chills crawl up my neck, raising the downy hair on my arms. "Y'all," I whispered, "somebody's watching us."

"Silly," Lucinda teased. Robby kept dealing cards as if I hadn't said anything. I tried to ignore it, but the weird suspicion wouldn't go away. Finally I froze, couldn't think anymore.

"She wants us to think she's psychic like Granny Creeps," Robby suggested. That's what the boys called Grandmother Byrnes.

"I'm not playing cards with y'all anymore," I declared, throwing in my cards and pennies. I looked out at the Thatchers' house with its gabled windows, envying Tiny.

"I wonder if I'll ever see Vicki again. She was my best friend for a long time," I muttered as much to myself as to them.

Robby said impatiently, "I told you, Bo. Vicki and her mother moved, but the old man still lives there."

"She might come back to visit." I scanned the well-kept lawn for Vicki, craning my neck to see around the rose bushes. That's when I saw him out of the corner of my eye. Then, my eyes drawn—as if by a magnet—back to the sight on Mrs. Shaw's top floor, my hand flew to my mouth to stifle the terrified "EEEEEK!" in my throat. "There he is. Look," I pointed.

Robby and Lucinda both jumped up and came to the window, eyes wide. Their mouths were even wider when they saw the man standing on the window sill, naked as a jaybird. Bushy hair sprouted on top of his head, around his ears and between his thin legs. Lucinda's flawless face registered a flicker of fascination, but then she tried to act as grossed out as I was. Robby let out a nervous titter when she shrieked, "I can see his thing! Puke."

When we looked again, the guy was gone, and we weren't even sure which window it was. Once the scare was over, we got tickled. Robby said seriously, "We better not tell anybody, or he'll tell on us for gambling."

"Yeah," Lucinda said, a daring look darkening her eyes.

Absorbed in gin rummy, even I forgot about the man. We played cards on the living room rug until we finally heard the peddler's horn toot and saw the old black wagon coming down the street. He had built a neat roof, tall enough for him to stand inside, over the back of a truck. Always punctual, the peddler was amiable, quick to offer his twinkling smile. Not much taller than us, he looked soft and pudgy like Santa Claus.

Remembering me, he greeted us warmly. "Well, lookie here, little Miss Bonita's back! Still readin' all those books?"

"Yessir, Mr. Tuohy," I told the clear turquoise eyes smiling down at me under the soft, white eyebrows. I tried hard to conceal my pleasure in his remembering my name, given all the kids he saw every day on his route. He glanced at Lucinda, then looked away, busy stacking candy bars. He may be the only man from my childhood whose eyes lit up for me instead of lingering on that golden hair, the smooth face, the voluptuous body. He may, in fact, have been the one consistently virtuous adult male in our lives.

The peddler opened a box of penny candy and pulled my ear like he used to. Lucinda bought sticky, bright yellow banana pops—little rectangular blocks of taffy that stuck to our teeth, and Robby went for Bits-O-Honey. Feeling a need for more nutrition, I bought a peanut butter log. The bar of silvery sweetness had ribbons of brown that I always thought must be the peanut butter. I didn't even wonder about artificial flavoring. When Mr. Tuohy waved as he drove off with his magical sweetness, I glanced at Ms. Shaw's top floor, relieved by the absence of evil that had loomed from that window and grateful for the presence of the peddler's goodness.

We played blackjack again on the lumpy mattress, the wide window spilling sunlight on us, until the late afternoon. Maybe it wasn't so bad to be living here again. Except for the creepy neighbor. If he was crazy enough to stand in a window buck naked in broad daylight, what might he be capable of?

The sunlight created heat quicker the next morning, beating down on the panes above the open windows. "It's gonna be a scorcher," Lucinda proclaimed, poking at her cereal. She wore an old slip of Mama's—its ivory lace, so lovely for the honeymoon, now dingy. My sister mopped the sweat underneath her hair at the nape of her neck and fanned herself more than she needed to. I knew she wanted an excuse to parade around in Mama's slip.

"Aren't you going to wear some clothes? Robby's bound to be here pretty soon."

"Robby is family," she sighed disdainfully. "You're such a worry wart." She absently ran her finger, which rose and fell with the curves, along the lacy edge at the top of the slip. A strange shiver crept up my spine.

I found Mama's ivory robe and tossed it to her. "You better wear this, or I'm telling Mama you wear her stuff when she's not here."

We were still picking at each other when we heard the sound of sneakers pounding the stairs accompanied by a thin jingle of change. Robby thought our spat was funny, started doing a parody of the music that heralded Helen Trent. Robby's radio voice was deep, unreal: "Lucinda, born to love," he whispered, "and Bonita, born to boss. Where will it end, my friends in radio land?"

"Shut up, stupid," Lucinda laughed. "I'll tell you where it'll end. We'll all be in school this time next week. Can you believe it?" She told us, "I figure Jaybird is a boarder who comes home for lunch every day. Let's watch and see if he appears two days in a row between twelve and one o'clock. I watched for him yesterday but never saw him again."

"I did, too, but I never saw him again either. I still think we ought to tell on him," I said. I didn't like this conspiracy, felt an intuitive resistance to its danger.

Robby smirked toward Lucinda. "Let's play cards," was all he said as he dealt the cards. Entranced, we played until lunchtime, then piled on the mattress and stretched out in the sun. Lucinda positioned herself in the exact center of Jaybird's vision while we listened to the radio program. "That sun is hot as fire," she mumbled as she slipped off the robe and propped on her elbows. Pushing her milky, white breasts closer together, she created a crevice that matched the one peeping out the back of Robby's pants. He closed his eyes like he always did when he listened to the radio drama.

My heart beat fast, sweat drenching my underarms. I didn't know whether it was from the sweltering noonday sun or fear as we waited to see what the lunch hour would bring. A mix of emotions churned inside me, making my insides feel like clabbered milk. This time I felt more than goose bumps when Jaybird suddenly stood in his window naked—dark and hairy—watching us. I felt frozen, speechless. Lucinda crawled out of bed and stood at our window looking straight toward the strange man, her chest swollen with something between defiance and showing off.

Then Jaybird no longer stood still, but began grinding his pale, thin hips toward us. I was horrified when Lucinda began to grind her hips back at the man. A shrill scream came out of my mouth all the way from my toes. "What on earth are you doing?" I screamed at her, but she ignored me. Robby sat on the edge of the bed, mesmerized until we saw Jaybird's hand reach down into the bush of kinky hair at his crotch. I shrieked at my sister, "Now, look what you've done. He's shaking his 'thing' at us. Gross!"

Lucinda's face turned from a shocked girl's into a woman's smugness for an instant before her lips opened as far as they could, filling up the room with shrill laughter. I was terrified, puzzled at her reaction. She and Robby both howled hysterically. "What?" I asked. No answer. Then Jaybird disappeared as suddenly as he had appeared.

We collapsed on the bed, Lucinda allowing me to huddle together with her, trying to make some order of it. Robby and Lucinda laughed until they both rolled off the bed. I tried to laugh, too, but it was frightening to me. I sat frozen in the corner, imagining I was a block of ice keeping food fresh—not feeling a ripple of anything. I wanted to escape, but wouldn't leave the safety of the corner, which wasn't visible from the Shaw's house. Robby and Lucinda tried to make me tell them what was wrong, but the more I tried to tell them how I felt, the more they derided me.

"Don't be such a baby," Lucinda sulked.

"Don't make a big deal of it," Robby warned.

Their derision planted the seed that burst forth, half-grown, in my head of ice. As soon as Mama came in, the sun came out inside my brain, bringing my idea into full bloom.

"Mama," I ventured, picking round bones out of canned salmon for her, "How big a sin is gambling?"

She rummaged through the cabinets for her canister set, which had been stuck under the sink. "Of all places," she sighed. "Not near as bad as most of the sins I know up close. Why?"

I continued. "Remember how you made Priscilla send somebody to paint as soon as we moved here because of all those naked women drawn on the walls?"

"Yeah," she answered absently, organizing the flour and eggs for salmon patties. Just mentioning the day we moved here seemed to make her tired. The air in the vinyl kitchen chair sighed as Mama plopped down, her own air seeming to disappear like the chair's. Her shoulders slumped, and her voice went flat, "Um hm, naturally I wanted that filth covered up."

"I figure it would make you pretty mad if a grown up showed us real naked stuff, wouldn't it?" I began.

"What you mean?" She asked. As she lit a cigarette, her eyes squinted, then enlarged into orbs of anger trying to get hold of itself. She snapped, "Come on, baby, what you driving at? Don't torture Mama."

I blurted, "Robby said Jaybird would tell on us for gambling, but we were just playing blackjack and the money wasn't for keeps. He took it all back."

"Who's Jaybird, baby? What money? Slow down now. Let's get this straight."

"Lucinda said he might hurt all of us if we told on him, Mama, but I wanted to tell you the first day."

Her face fell, the jaw going slack like an old tired dog's cheeks. Then like a slow fire, the air came back to her body. Her chest swelled. Eyes flaming, she asked, "Who are you talking about, Bo. Get on with it!"

"I'm trying to, Mama. It's this man who lives at Mrs. Shaw's. There's never a light on in his room at night."

"My God, Bonita, how do you know which room belongs to this stranger?"

"I been watching him back 'cause he watches us."

"Watches you?"

"Come on to our room. I'll show you," The charcoal strokes on the magenta canvas of sky filled the unlit hallway with an eerie timelessness. Mama's dress rustled behind me, her thighs rubbing silk stockings against each other, moving fast. "See that one, second from the end. You watch it until bedtime. Every other window on that floor will be lit, but not Jaybird's."

"Who's this Jaybird?" Mama screamed, shaking my shoulders, her eyes gone from fire to tornado. "I'll kill the fool. Tell me!"

My heart sped up, and so did my story. I told her everything except about the slip and Lucinda's grinding hips. "I agreed to let it go until today when he shook his old thing at us. I don't care whether Robby and Lucinda like me anymore. I figure it's time to tell on that old creep!"

Mama and Priscilla didn't like it that the police said we had to set him up again, catch Jaybird in the act of exposing himself, but Robby and Lucinda thought it was an adventure. I pictured myself in a mystery novel and got into the spirit of intrigue myself. Just as we were coached, we played cards and listened to the radio as usual. Lucinda, of course, wasn't "in costume," but Jaybird nibbled the bait nonetheless. I felt the creepy tingling again, could see him before I looked. No sooner than I looked up, he stood on the window sill. Two blue shirts appeared behind him and Jaybird fell backwards. Pointing, I could only muster, "Ahhhhh." Robby and Lucinda jumped up and practically crawled out the window to see. Mama and Priscilla came in from the hallway, one face a raging fire, the other placid, calm. They stood behind us, protective arms on our shoulders. When the police took Jaybird away, we watched from the window as the two hats who led the prisoner glistened in the blazing sun. The pale thin stranger looked so harmless with his hands cuffed behind him. I felt a stab of guilt for having told on him, for not telling on my sister, for destroying our daily adventure. We went on with the cards and Helen Trent on Friday, but our other adventure—racing out to see who could meet the peddler first—was not quite the same.

# Chapter Nineteen:
## Childhood Plays

I WAS RELIEVED WHEN SCHOOL STARTED and my teacher wasn't so bad after all. Every year I promised myself I wouldn't listen next year to older kids who wanted to dread school. Except for some problems with long division, I reveled in making E's for excellence from Miss Nanette Dacord, a very particular, petite woman who wore navy suits every day. In her sensible, medium-high, navy heels, she took baby steps like in Mother-May-I. Wrinkles battled for dominance across her puffy face, topped by a bright red wig set in stiff waves like doll's hair. In retrospect, I've often wondered if Miss Dacord might have been a cross-dresser. Her pale, soft skin seemed as ancient as the aged man who sat behind the principal's desk, her body as genderless.

Unlike her, he didn't seem to do anything all day but sign passes to use the rest room, signing R.T. Horton with great flourish on the yellow slips that were immediately discarded. I never understood why he took such pains with his signature. Lots of smaller children would rather wet their pants than invade his territory. He barricaded himself with self-importance—raising his thick, unruly eyebrows when interrupted. He always had a stack of papers on the huge wooden desk, but they never seemed to change. The teachers revered him, said that he was a prominent citizen who had devoted his life to education, but he didn't impress me.

South Highland was set in a better section of town than my previous school, and Mama said that's why the class work was more demanding. "Rich folks don't take no crap, don't let their kids either," she told me. "No need for you to be embarrassed your last school was behind in math, still doing short division."

Miss Dacord's perfectly-made-up mask of a face smiled at me when she called me to her desk for individual work on long division. I was afraid the other students resented my preferential treatment, but I soon saw they didn't.

I was grateful to be back here where intelligence mattered. If we spelled all our words correctly, we got to write our names on the chalkboard, and we got stars by our names for every E. It was at least a month before I felt settled in, accepted by my classmates, but it was worth it. Ms. Dacord's world was a cocoon of order. Her gentle encouragement brought me up to the level of the others quickly and promoted a sense of harmony in the classroom as well. Everyone, it seemed, was still eager to please the teacher that year, afraid not to cooperate in our pact to keep life orderly like interchangeable navy blue suits. I loved the dependability of fifth grade, its innocence and trust.

I found a few friends, but I never invited any of them home because Rhett might be there drunk. Pauline, a quiet girl, invited me to her house. We walked what seemed miles up the hilly streets along the ridge around the Highlands to an old stone house that overlooked the city. It was cold inside the house, damp. I never saw her mother, but waited in the vestibule while Pauline checked in with her and brought us a snack of some sort before we played outside in the cold biting wind of autumn. I assumed her mother was a rich snob who didn't want to meet me because I was poor, which made me peep self-consciously around at the antiques and family portraits. One portrait of a rosy-cheeked, cherubic girl intrigued me because the head was too large for the plain silk dress and pearls the child wore.

When Pauline quit coming to school one day, I learned that her mother had died after a long illness. I cried myself to sleep, ashamed I had assumed the lady was snubbing me. "Why wouldn't Pauline have told me?" I asked Lucinda's tear-soaked shoulder.

"Sometimes, people are hard to understand. Some things hurt too much to talk about, baby," my sister answered, her voice trailing off somewhere into the depth of mystery we had learned from the blues singers at The Club Rose. Her silky voice was soothing, maternal. I didn't mind her calling me baby this time. My shudders came

*How Can I Keep From Singing*

further apart until I finally fell asleep trying to visualize the woman in that grand house permeated by chill. I had seen her turban, the cigarette holder. They weren't about me. She probably had no hair. Was her head too big for her body? I never knew, never again heard from Pauline, yet another best friend.

After that, I stayed closer to home for play time. It seemed safer than venturing out into the world. The boys had rusty old trucks and army tanks filled with military rations and canteens. We played out big battles from the war, fed by the tales from Robby's uncle, who brought back slides of lush German countryside and a beautiful sad-eyed girl. He swore he was going back for her and their child, but he never did.

Lucinda groaned, "He told me in gory detail about the loss of her virginity." We were washing cement mix from our hands because we weren't supposed to play with the mixer or plastering equipment, but of course we did since the boys did. We built the sturdiest tree house in the neighborhood.

"What's that?" I asked.

"You know, like the Virgin Mary was a virgin."

"Oh, yeah. I get it," I lied.

The gray November sky had turned dark already when Mama came home. Rubbing her feet, she slumped at the kitchen table and drank a cup of coffee before she started supper. "I knew that footprint on the stairway had cement stuck to it before I ever saw your shoes, Bonita. I'm telling Phil to clean up that trash heap. Somebody's gonna step on a rusty nail and get blood poisoning."

This threat sent a shiver up my spine.

"Just like I warned Phil about that ol' dog. Everybody else had to wait until Junior got rabies after the mad dog bit him."

"How'd you know the dog was mad, Mama?"

"'Cause the dog slobbered and staggered like he was dizzy, but those shots in the belly cured Junior. I was the only one who would take him to get them. He hated going. But you're getting me off the subject of cement, Bo. I strictly forbid you to go near that equipment in the back field. Do you understand? It's too close to the alley and the colored quarter anyway."

Phil straightened up the back field, took most of our war toys and everything else Mama considered dangerous, but he pouted about it. He was more aloof than ever, which was saying something. His nose tilted when he saw me, sweat running down thin blond hair into his eyes from the effort of cleaning the back yard. I wanted to laugh, but I didn't. I was beginning to hate him, all puffed up and full of himself like a banty rooster. White starched shirt rolled up to the elbow, dripping wet from unaccustomed physical exertion, he glared at me commanding, "Move that pile of junk into the trash fire."

As I stooped to pick up the army-green satchels containing our food rations, Robby shot me a look that said *traitor*. With Phil impatiently breathing down my neck, my shoulder muscles tensed, creating a crick in my neck. I managed to sneak the canteens out; otherwise, the war was over again. "Lazy old jerk, he's just mad because he has to do something instead of boss other people, so he recruits his own children," I mumbled to Robby when Phil cranked up the cement mixer.

Ironically, it was Phil's cleaning up that led us to even more dangerous equipment. We thought we'd found a goldmine when we discovered the doctor's trash pile. Across the alley, the small brick office building looked squatty, box-like, next to the enlarged hospital. The rundown condition of the building and the unkempt lawn had pricked our curiosity. Eventually, we heard the news of Dr. Taylor's death from the women who cleaned out his office.

At dusk, we filled paper sacks with samples of medicine on cardboard advertisements, as well as pamphlets explaining every inch of female anatomy and the birth process. I was too mad at Phil to play office. I didn't want to pretend to take construction orders for a company anymore, but I quickened when I saw the medical office's colored paper forms, index card files, gem clips, etc. Robby held up a picture of Dr. Taylor with his grandchildren and a box of old pipes and loose tobacco that pierced my nostrils with a sharp, pungent odor. He bit a long, full-bent pipe and said between clenched teeth, "I'm glad that old coot died."

Lucinda feigned disapproval of Robby's remark, "Oh, hush your mouth, boy, or the Lord will strike you dead." She pored through the pamphlets on menopause making intermittent responses like, "Yuck. Gross."

Repulsed by the freakish pictures of babies in the early months of their development, I was also fascinated. I read them but didn't understand altogether. Most of the pamphlets I skimmed quickly, setting up my "office."

Robby moved all our junk into a vacant basement apartment, fully furnished, perfect for our games. He flattered me, "Bonita, you're so good in school. You'd make a fine supply clerk and receptionist, but you'll have to dress up in high heels."

I nibbled, eager to play dress-up. Lucinda hobbled up to my desk in a faded dress of Priscilla's, "Is this Dr. Taylor's office?" She croaked in a country voice so authentic I doubted her real identity myself. "I got a terrible belly ache," she wailed.

"Yes, ma'am," I told her. "Dr. Taylor will see you in just a minute." Then I prissed back with a "chart" I made from the mildewed forms we'd found. Robby's ragged white jacket came down to his knees, and his gloves were stained with purple ink from the mimeograph machine, but he was ready, authentic.

He held up an X-ray and peered into it. "I believe that girl had the same problem the last time I saw her." I ignored their giggles. It was easy at first to tune them out while I busied myself with the dilapidated filing cabinet, making folders for various patients, sorting through the medicines and color coding them.

It wasn't a full week before Robby "hired" Junior as an X-ray technician. "I can't believe Junior's gonna deign to play with us," Lucinda cooed, trying not to show her delight. That extra puff in her hair and the dancing eyes betrayed her. Robby spoke in a tone I hadn't heard from him before; he assumed his doctor's voice, very efficient, "We'd better get our office open and get to work, right Lu?"

"Right," my sister, the puppet, beamed. She had on red high heels and a low-cut blouse of Mama's. "Are these seams straight?" she asked me, lifting her taffeta skirt a hem's length.

"Who cares?" I asked, then put it together and added, "Do you have Mama's garter belt on? She's gonna kill you!"

"No she ain't cause she ain't gonna know," Lucinda warned me. Our altercation stopped when Junior appeared at the door. He took a handkerchief out of his back pocket and wiped his face, leaving the perpetual adolescent smirk behind. He was good looking—tall and broad-shouldered, a natural athlete. His red-blonde hair, always neatly combed, and his freckled face gave him an all-American look in spite of his habitual sneer. "Bony Bonita!" he greeted me.

"Hey," I muttered from my card file. My enthusiasm for the day's drama had waned. He wasn't fun like Robby. Soon, though, Junior settled into his office in the back, and Robby came out with a stack of X-rays for me to file. I studied the appointment calendar.

"Miss McIntyre," I called out efficiently, and Lucinda clomped in, heavily made-up with exaggerated moles drawn above her left breast, which looked as if it might jump out of her bra. She swished toward me, then signed her name.

"What kind of problem are you having today?" I asked—folder open, pencil poised.

Lucinda's voice was sultry, rhythmical, "I got a mole here on my chest," she showed me, "that rubbed against my bazeeer." The husky voice, the mascara-caked, twinkling eyes and the embellishment of the mispronunciation seduced even me into laughter.

Robby slumped in a chair across from me while the technician talked to the patient. I struggled with the corners of my mouth, suppressing a smug smirk. Let him see how it felt to be left out, I told myself.

We heard nervous laughter from the next room. Elated to have company in my outsider's role, I whispered, "Wanna help me type this card? You call out the information I wrote on the sheet, and I'll type it in."

"You don't know nothing, kiddo," Robby mumbled, then moved closer to me, brushed my hair out of my eyes. I hit the keys that still worked as hard as I could with my forefingers, feeling proud of my office savvy. Robby couldn't keep his mind on the information for straining to hear the sounds from the next room above the clacking of the typewriter. Muffled conversation about schedules now floated out to us. We couldn't tell what they were saying, but Lucinda's tone was coquettish. I typed faster, not trying to make words anymore, hitting random keys.

Emboldened by our rare moment of closeness, Robby slipped his arm over my chair and leaned toward me. He grinned like he was proud of being the boss.

I went to the filing cabinet, keeping my back toward him so that he couldn't see my face.

"Bony butt," he muttered, already retreating. As soon as Junior left, Robby forgot my presence. He rushed in to Lucinda spouting suggestions for tomorrow's appointment. When they finally came out, he announced, "Junior's bringing Bailey in here to clean this place up and teach us acting lessons, too."

Bailey, the janitor who lived in the other basement apartment, was in his early twenties, not much older than Junior. He was a nice-looking man, with a gentle smile and soft hands the color of cocoa, who gave us bandaids if we skinned our knees. Sweet and soft spoken, Bailey always listened to anything we had on our mind, but we were told to avoid him because he was colored.

Since he kept the fires stoked in the furnaces for all the apartments, the older kids swore he was the devil. We hid in the basement to spy on him. When I first saw his dark, handsome frame against the blazing furnace, I trembled with fear. When he opened the creaky, heavy door and poked the white-hot flames, I was convinced that he was the Prince of Darkness.

Now that I was older I knew better. "I thought Priscilla told Junior not to hang around with Bailey anymore," I said.

"Who asked you, squirt?" Robby grumbled. "Besides," he eyed the cobwebs, wiped mildew from the dank, low ceiling. "He's gonna clean this place." Lucinda beamed at him, the smooth full lips wrapping around her face. She was pleased with her fan club.

Really, we were all thrilled that Junior and Bailey were interested in our hangout. Junior had been in *Our Town* at his high school, and Bailey studied acting at Miles College. They both thought I wrote good skits and Lucinda was a strong actress. It made us all feel grown up to have our own place! Bailey taught us about blocking and pacing and costumes, and Robby could build a set out of nothing. Bailey had spent a summer in California, where he learned something called theater games.

He taught us how to do games like mirrors, where we chose a partner, then mirrored their every move, including facial expressions. Then we moved on to situations where each character would come to the stage with an idea, the next would respond, then the next and, finally, when we heard the command stage picture, we would all freeze into a human sculpture of cooperation where nobody was left out and nobody was allowed to hog the stage. If you were in front of somebody you had to slide over, etc. I loved that part. It made me feel like a beatnik when we did these games.

Once Bailey cleaned up the apartment regularly, our hideout was discovered. We came home from school one day in a freezing rain to discover we'd been "evicted," all our supplies dumped by someone's tornadic fury. Dissolved vitamins streamed down the red-clay bank into the scrub grass like a weird rainbow. All my files were rain-soaked, useless now forever. Tears flowed from my eyes, heavy as the colored streams of medicinal rain.

Robby found a note on the dented filing cabinet shoved up under the eaves out of the rain. We could see the anger in the penciled scribbling, the pressure on the pencil so intense the paper was perforated in spots. "Put this back where it BELONGS!!!" the note read, and an arrow pointed inside a drawer where the typewriter had been stashed, with another note reading, "Ditto!"

We knew Phil's handwriting, saw his apparent rage when he discovered we'd been playing in the abandoned apartment. We never knew why it upset him so, just that Priscilla sat on us like a brooding hen for weeks after that. "Phil doesn't have time to discipline a hoard of wild young 'uns," she snapped when Junior questioned Phil's outrage. "You do what I tell you as long as you live under my roof. Period," she added, calmer. Then she was humming in the kitchen, making rice pudding with old hard, otherwise useless, raisins.

"She hates it when he beats us," Robby said, his finger tracing the pale, thin scar on his bony arm, which he swore was from Phil's belt buckle. "She's being mean so we won't get our punishment from him."

"Junior says you're still a baby," Robby taunted.

"And a tattle-tale," Lucinda whined. "We never should've let you in the drama club."

I didn't want Daddy Phil to leave buckle marks on Robby's fair skin, so like mine with freckles and light blond hairs on his arms and legs.

"Robby hits me on the shoulder, plays like he's kidding but it hurts. Look!" I finally confided on Saturday afternoon as Mama and I walked home from Hill's Grocery, carrying brown paper sacks stuffed with next week's rations. I pushed my blouse open with the sack and pointed to the various stages of bruises: purple from yesterday, yellow from last weekend.

I saw fury run across Mama's face before she covered it with that mask of neutrality adults muster. Her eyes went from wide open fire to slits of mossy fishpond. Mama said Robby picked on me because he was desperate to be older than somebody.

A few weeks after I mentioned the bruises and the drama club to Mama, Bailey moved out of his basement apartment and Phil posted signs saying KEEP OUT on the basement doors and padlocked them. When Phil's punishment of the boys was over, Robby and Junior had red, puffy welts all over their bodies for a week. We could hear the commotion all the way from our apartment, but we didn't know then what it was about. Junior's hoarse voice pleaded with Phil to stop, but all we heard from Phil was the fierce pop of leather followed by croaking howls from the boys. We never mentioned it to them. I promised myself I'd never forget what makes boys mean. No matter what they'd done, I knew children shouldn't be punished in that humiliating way. Mama said Phil had gone berserk like this a few years ago when Bailey was teaching the boys basketball moves. He was really good, too, but Phil said he wasn't supposed to socialize with the boys. It seemed to enrage him that Bailey knew more than they did. Mama added that he knew more than Phil did about a lot of things, which is what really bothered him. She said Doc teased Phil about having a college boy as a janitor. "Doc is the meanest father-in-law in the world." Mama laughed. "He and Phil deserve each other."

We weren't allowed to play together for the rest of the winter. Junior began dating soon after that and seemed to disappear from everyone's life. Bailey went to Chicago to study theater with Viola Spolin some more. Lu and I went to Girls Club after school until Mama came home from work, and Lucinda began to notice boys around the neighborhood more and more.

I met a new friend at Girls Club named Nina McMillan, who walked home down my street—my first pal since Paulette's mother died. Nina was beautiful with thick blonde hair and green eyes, and at ten, she still had enough baby fat to make her skin smooth and soft. Her dad was a red-nosed Irishman who was worse about drinking than Rhett, parading to the bathroom naked throughout the night. I discovered that, in this house full of children, being naked didn't seem to be very important. It was merely funny that Mr. McMillan did it and nobody paid attention to him. It embarrassed me, and I avoided him, but I didn't really care.

Nina lived in a huge, sagging house where the upstairs windows reached from the high ceiling to the floor. The faded yellow house was around the corner from the Salvation Army, where we bought doll dresses for a penny. I spent the night almost every weekend since she only lived a few houses down the street.

Mama said, "I reckon it's all right since I can hear and see if anything happens to you. I've seen him coming in from the store on Friday nights with every one of those tow-headed boys totin' groceries. Plenty of booze in those bags, too, I know."

"Mr. McMillan doesn't drink any more than Rhett does," I replied. I never told her about his naked wandering to the toilet at night. Nina and I giggled about our crazy dads and drinking and sat out on her roof in our nightgowns and counted stars, talking for hours about everything in our lives. We had no secrets but confided all our hurts and fears. She was, and is today, one of the great treasures of my life. Though we've grown apart over the years, it only takes a glance or a phone call to re-connect to that unconditional love that young girls are sometimes capable of experiencing.

By that time, Lucinda was preoccupied with her first real boyfriend, Jimmy. They were always sending me away, like a scolded puppy, on stupid errands.

In some mysterious way, however, Jimmy brought us closer. Lucinda treated me more and more like a little sister than a baby. She confided in me, "It's so weird the way my tummy tightens when I see Jimmy walking toward our apartment. Look!" she squealed into the dark fog outside our window, "I get goose bumps just thinking about it." Then she giggled that stupid, uneven laugh she had developed. "Huhhh Huh uhhhhhh." The soft fog made a halo around the streetlight, which offered too little illumination to see the arm she extended across the pillow. I blindly ran my fingertips along the soft, downy hair on her forearm, the moist skin topped with a prickly patch of goose bumps. "So that's how love feels!" I laughed.

Of course, I had a crush on Jimmy, too, with thick sandy hair falling across his pale blue eyes. I loved being included in the secret of their relationship. Mama didn't know anything about Jimmy; he came to see us after school before she was home from work. At first

Lucinda and Jimmy sat on the steps and talked, then they moved to the front porch. When they disappeared repeatedly into the hallway, I switched into my trance of denial. It was far more entertaining to look for black-capped chickadees or a tufted titmouse than to worry about the sins of the flesh I had no intention of committing. "Oh, y'all, look! It's a Baltimore Oriole," I might cry out, but more often than not they never even heard.

Once the greenness of summer took over the fragrant grass beneath us and the trees above us, we gathered on the back field to play scrub with all the neighborhood kids, even the Asian kids up the street Mama had warned us had strange ways. "They're Buddhists from the medical center." I figured that was synonymous with strange. The boys were just too good at softball to be left out, and they were smart and fun. I was no better at softball than most sports, but I tried. I loved the thrill of a good hit and running the bases when I didn't strike out. Playing outfield, I often missed a ball while riveted to a violet popping out of the grass only to be smudged out by a racing sneaker. Or I might be transported by the silver streak an airplane left across the aquamarine sky when a pop-up came toward me.

I loved the hilly sidewalk, the rat-a-tat-tat of constant jackhammers expanding the medical center. I admired the slight curve of sidewalk toward 20th Street and a thousand other marvels my playmates never noticed.

One day after playing ball, I curled up with a book on the front porch that used to be ours but now belonged to Priscilla. I heard the chilling screech of brakes and the shrill yelp of Robby's dog Suzy. Pregnant, she had waddled around, stretched and bulging so much we had thought the puppies were coming a month ago. I jumped up and ran to the street just in time to see her last waddling—into the path of a car that raced over the hill. Crushed, Suzy lay lifeless in a pool of blood, the puppies we had waited so long for slung all over the street without a chance of life.

Robby ran after the driver, screaming and cussing. I ran toward him, held his sobbing head against my chest and cried with him. "Why didn't you get that driver's tag number?" Junior sneered at us as he dragged the bloody heap toward the curb. Robby and I stared mutely at him until he stormed inside, slamming the door in our faces. Then we found an old pillow case and put Suzy and her puppies inside it.

We sat in the swing in silence. I had never realized how much we looked alike, his profile exactly like mine. Our freckles even splotched our faces in the same pattern. Most of all, his hazel eyes were like mine. That afternoon, his eyes were like a cool stream as the tears ran gently down his cheeks. Robby and I planned Suzy's funeral so well that none of the older kids taunted us but, instead, joined hands and said the Lord's Prayer and sang along with us, "Swing Low, Sweet Chariot."

There was a tenderness, a real sweetness between us as brothers and sisters that day that transcended the pecking order we typically used to hurt each other and the sexism we were all victims of. Burying Suzy and her puppies struck a chord in us that made us glimpse, without understanding, our own mortality, our own random existence as we piled the dry, rusty dust over that sweet, loving dachshund and her litter of unborn puppies. After that, we drifted apart more, were never as close as that year, especially that day.

# Chapter Twenty:
# Blending, Gluing, and Independence

RHETT DISAPPEARED AGAIN, but I was never told anything except that he was gone. The mailbox never produced that hoped-for letter like the one that had come from Texas.

On humid afternoons, I lay on the cool marble porch at Priscilla's and pretended to be asleep. She and Phil had tea before he went home to his wife, Frances Terez, for his version of a highball: a straight Scotch. I memorized the sound of their voices, delighting in the contrast of her musical murmuring and his crisp pronouncements, usually these days about the problems with colored people. After several days of my snooping, they came to the subject of Mama and Rhett.

Snuggling a faded pillow from the wicker sofa, I was glad I had turned my face away from them. My heart accelerated and tears stung my flaming cheeks as I heard Phil spit the words, "Why the hell did she ask me to try to find him when he wandered off like a stray Tom cat? I've a mind not to tell her, but I found out he's renting a cheap efficiency from some widow in Cherokee, North Carolina."

Even though she thought I was asleep, I heard Priscilla scold Phil for talking within my earshot. Then their voices whispered so low I couldn't make out their words. I surrendered, allowed the sound to lull me into the sleep my body and soul demanded in order to bear the latest sorrow in my see-saw life.

The air felt lighter as we adjusted to Rhett's absence. Lucinda's bounce was back, the Vaseline-slick smile wrapped around her face again. She was often affectionate toward me and Mama with Rhett gone.

One early morning, her hair sweat-darkened at the roots, she woke me up early. "Come help me," she said, breathing hard. "I want to surprise Mama." We scrubbed our weekly laundry, which Mama usually did on Saturday afternoon. The cold, soapy water smelled fresh as the morning. We'd been awake since dawn. The rhythm of the grunts from the metal washboard soothed me like Lucinda's soft eyes.

"Won't Mama be surprised?" I sang happily, rinsing the print blouse in the pan of clear water I'd set on the toilet. I wrung it hard, then threw it in the basket to be hung out as soon as the sun came up and changed the pink sky to yellow. Lucinda said, "I'll be glad when Mama gets over this depression."

"Do you think it's 'cause she misses Rhett?" I asked. "I heard Phil tell Priscilla that Rhett has a place in North Carolina, something called an efficiency."

She scrubbed a white organdy blouse hard. As a lone cloud passed overhead, the soft fluffy clouds of soap suds seemed to turn grey in her hands like her eyes, suddenly shadowed. "I dunno," is all she whispered.

"Look!" I squealed when a nickel fell out of a skirt pocket like a silver porpoise flipping through the early morning sunlight. Afterward, we grabbed some RC Cola bottles and headed to the store for the deposit, coming up with enough to buy some day-old breakfast rolls—sticky buns glazed with pecans and cinnamon.

The bald man's eyes creased at the corners while he croaked his usual encouragement of our thrift. "Yesterday afternoon when the shop closed, these rolls were top of the line!" Winking, he tossed in an extra, "Gives y'all two apiece," he said. He noticed Lucinda, his eyes following her around the bakery, but she seemed unaware of him.

"Thanks," I beamed. Lucinda studied the floor.

We walked fast, the concrete sidewalk already scorching our feet. Mama heard the door open, looked at us through puffy slits, then rolled over. "Mama's so tired," she mumbled, "need to sleep a little longer."

We crept quietly to the kitchen where Lucinda put the rolls on Mama's best tray, and I put the Queen Anne's lace we had picked in a milk bottle. Lucinda tickled Mama's nose with a cinnamon crumb. "What's this?" she yawned and stretched her arms overhead, pearlescent breasts rising in the dingy gown.

Mama laughed from her belly when I told her we bought the rolls with RC Cola money. "Lordy mercy, what girls I've raised!" She rolled the cinnamon bun around in her mouth, savoring the flavor. "Umm Um," she hummed, eyes brimming.

When she padded toward the bathroom and saw the mess we'd left, she cried out, "What is this mess in here, young ladies?"

"Look on the clothesline," we shrieked in unison. Then she did cry, pulling us toward her.

"I don't know what I'd do without y'all," Mama told us. "It's such a relief to sleep late and then not to have to wash those bloomin' clothes! My babies are too good for this world."

"Now that school's out, we can wash 'em while you're at work if you like the way we did it," Lucinda offered.

Mama buried her face in Lucinda's golden hair for a long, silent time, finally murmuring, "Thanks." She busied herself with the coffee pot while Lucinda set up a starch pot and the ironing board beside the window, hoping to capture the occasional breeze. Mama's underarms made purple half-moons on her lavender blouse.

In the afternoon, Mama announced, "Phil's taking me to Shanghai Lowe's for supper, so I need that front porch spic and span." We scrubbed the smooth floor on the porch—the chips of pressed marble cool to our bare feet. Phil had experimented with a new finish for porches on ours first, then made a big deal of the "pouring" on Priscilla's porch.

A shudder of pride ran through me when we saw Phil's Studebaker park—not at Priscilla's—but at our place. He ignored the clean porch as well as us, bounding up the stairs toward Mama. His blue Nordic eyes were icy, erasing the offspring his heart had no apparent interest in. I stirred ice-cubes into my own heart, imagining it iced strawberry Kool-Aid. "Open up, Pearl," he yelled to the bolted door. "I have some news for you."

It didn't take long to tell her whatever news he had, which I suspected was about Rhett. She chattered as she clomped down the stairs in high heels polished to a frenzied shine. "I can't wait to taste that Chicken Chow Mein and Chop Suey; that canned stuff does not compare. Rhett wouldn't eat it, said he'd had enough of China during the war."

"That fool doesn't know what he's missing," Phil said, his eyes scanning Mama's body.

"I'll be back before dark," she assured us, her eyes ambivalent. When the green lizard of a car disappeared over the hill, Lucinda and I invited Nina, our new friend down the street, to come over. We decided to form a trio, practicing our singing so we could perform for Mama when she came home.

"This porch makes a perfect stage," Lucinda said, dressed in one of Mama's glittery dresses, belting out "Hey, Good Looking" as if she intended to draw a crowd.

Nina and I chimed in on the "hot-rod Ford and a two-dollar bill" verse, our voices lilting like Lucinda's. We sang our hearts out, but even Lucinda couldn't draw an audience. Desperate for one, she insisted Daddy Phil stay long enough to hear the concert when they came back.

"Just one song," he agreed, glancing at the pocket watch that had been his father's.

"I know a spot just over the hill . . ." we crooned, but the lilt was gone. Suddenly tired, I couldn't summon the energy to imagine the place in Hank Williams' song where soda pop and the dancing's free. I hated Daddy Phil's power over me, how he could douse the tiniest spark.

Mama's eyes were peaceful, her lips curled upward instead of the constant downward turn we'd seen lately. She hummed while she set the table for us and opened soup and egg rolls from small cardboard boxes. With patience we were unaccustomed to, she showed us how to use chop sticks. She laughed at my awkward, uncoordinated attempt. "Just use your fork, baby, once you've been polite enough to try. Phil wanted y'all to have them with your take-out." She sat down with her cards while we ate, stringing out a hand of Solitaire.

She tried to make the news casual, "Thought y'all might want to know Phil located Rhett. He's fine, has a job and a nice place to live."

Neither of us said a word, shoveling the foreign, tasty food into our mouths like two robotic puppies. I liked it better now when Rhett wasn't with us, but I could tell it was just a matter of time. In a few weeks Mama claimed she got a raise, and we found a house of our own to rent. This time we, at least, didn't have to change schools. "We're only moving from Ninth Avenue to Tenth and on the same street. We'll be just around the corner from Priscilla and the kids," Mama assured us as if we all wanted that. During our last week, Lucinda and I packed boxes, this time carefully labeling everything.

Mama helped herself to some grapefruit in Priscilla's freezer while she was at Southside Baptist Sunday morning. Her defiant, thin eyebrows raised in triumph, "I can't believe Phil brought all that fruit back from Florida and never offered us any. They had so much they couldn't eat it all. I even helped peel some for freezin', and they didn't ask if we wanted any. I'm tired of seein' them eat better than us. It ain't fair!"

"But Rhett was living with us then," I observed, my ears red enough with guilt for not going to church, much less stealing.

Mama ignored my observation, "You gonna love Mr. Wilson, honey. He's sweet and serious like you. He listened to my plan when I told him all I needed was a three-room apartment and we could rent out the rest to boarders and split the money. Then he answered in that tee-nineny, soft voice, 'I believe Mrs. Wilson, God rest her soul, would agree that you can have the downstairs as a three-room apartment. I'll charge you for that, but you can use the upstairs all you want, too. I believe the Lord would agree that those sweet little girls don't need any boarders around. Besides, I don't need money where I'm headed.'"

Mr. Wilson, silver-haired and still elegant, was saddened to leave the stained-glass windows that covered the front door. He ran his slender fingers over them, "My wife was so proud of these years ago." The sweet-gum tree that filled the summer afternoon with a fragrance he called "distilled sweetness," brought tears to his already watery blue eyes. He was moving into a "home" after the death of his wife.

I admired the brass clock on the mantle, rubbing the smooth haunches of the dog sculpted beside Grover Cleveland, my mouth open in awe of its realistic detail. Mr. Wilson was affectionate, "St. Mary's didn't even want it for a white-elephant sale. Keep it, dar-lin'." He smiled, patting my head.

"Oh, thank you, sir," I squealed, wrapping my arms around his waist and hugging him.

That night, her razor blade efficiently trimming the new linoleum in the kitchen, Mama warned. "Don't let that man put his hands on you if he ever comes around when I'm not here, you understand?"

"Yes ma'am," I whispered, a strange mysterious shame climbing up my spine because I had touched the lonely man. Tears sprang to my eyes. I dreaded the responsibility of being unfriendly to him since we lived in his home, and he'd only moved to "a home."

I focused instead on taking good care of his enchanting Victorian house, my favorite in a long line of rented houses. I had lots of space to explore and a secret hideaway on the roof where I could escape to calm down or sunbathe without being seen.

I read sometimes all day on the porch in the sagging, but comfortable, rockers. There was also a good reading lamp on the landing of the staircase with a floor-to-ceiling window where I could read night or day with proper light over my left shoulder, the way all Birmingham children were taught they should read. The fluffy, lace-trimmed pillows on the window seat matched the faded curtains. Dust motes floated in the afternoon sunlight when you rustled them.

The walnut bannister, Mama's pride, required almost daily polishing until we discovered a better way to keep it shining. Lucinda always made her entrance in our plays by sliding down it. We had to focus entire episodes around the grand entrance, but, as playwright, I was willing to abide by that constraining rule since Nina and Lucinda were good company in my world of make-believe.

One sweltering summer day, Nina endured being dressed in Mama's winter clothes. Covered by a veil underneath a small velvet hat, Nina's smooth face twisted into the sneer of an old friend who had come to visit the recently famous "Carolyn." Nina's hands, covered with wrist-length gloves, could never be still, so I had to keep making up things for her to do with her hands. Mama's Pall Malls were a natural inspiration.

Dressed in Mama's best suit, I played Carolyn's roommate from London, who had the pleasure of telling the old friend what a fine life Carolyn was living now. "In fact," I said, "old girl, you're just in time to see! Carolyn is performing."

On cue, Lucinda, with great fanfare and operatic screeching, slid down the slick bannister; however, it crashed, throwing her headlong into Mr. Wilson's Tiffany lamp. Swaddled in petticoats, Lucinda was unharmed by the shards of glass and splintered wood. We laughed hysterically for half an hour before we tried in vain to repair the lamp so Mama would never know. We were fairly successful with the bannister, so we never mentioned it, but the lamp was a disaster.

Mama spent the weekend gluing it back together one piece at a time, making us hold the jeweled pieces of glass while the glue stuck. All I had to say for several years to break up the gloomiest cloud of Lucinda's adolescence was, "Carolyn is performing." Automatically, she would be transformed into a giggling child.

I relished this power, this women's world filled with creativity and laughter. Mama cooked fresh vegetables every night because our aunt sent us the surplus from her garden. We shelled peas until our fingers turned purple, rocking on the porch and people-watching.

RHETT SLITHERED BACK into our paradise in stages, just phone calls at first, then for dinner. "I'm helping my mother with Moon for awhile. His drinking is bad," he said sadly, reaching for Mama's hand and slipping a turquoise ring on her finger. I concentrated on the grease her fried chicken left on their hands.

Lucinda wouldn't talk about it. I was ambivalent, but not as easily taken in as the last time. Neither were Daddy Phil and Priscilla pleased apparently. It was more and more clear we had moved because they told Mama if she ever took Rhett back, we'd have to leave.

I heard Mama tell Rhett, "I told those two smart alecks it wasn't any of their business what I did. I was in my own place within a week."

Rhett slid back in so gradually I didn't know if Mr. Wilson ever knew about him. He had learned to make his own silver jewelry in North Carolina. "It's a side line," he explained, gluing stones on a pair of earrings. "I went up there looking for some of Mama's folks, but I never found them. I learned a lot though while I was up there. Beautiful country." He now wore a headband and beaded moccasins as a work uniform. "Folks believe silverplate's sterling quicker 'n anything!"

As part of Mama and Rhett's, "trial basis," while Mama tried to see if she and Rhett could live together in peace, Lucinda and I were to spend a couple of nights with Daddy Phil and Frances Terez each week. I overheard Phil wisecrack to Frances Terez, "Wonder how they spell peace. Crazy fools."

On our first "visit," Frances Terez picked us up and took us shopping at Pizitz Bargain Basement for bathing suits. Right away, I found a pale pink flowered suit made of shiny polished cotton. Lucinda tried on ten thousand, but wouldn't settle on one until Frances Terez took her upstairs to the more expensive departments. Frances Terez's gentle brown eyes remained patient, glowing from her smooth, shiny face. She knew she had met her match.

Phil's new wife didn't look like a home breaker to me, the skin on her plump arms shaky like Jell-O. Her frizzy curls were sprinkled with gray, her thick legs always covered with matronly shorts or slacks.

Frances Terez worked all day in her garden and cooked all night. They didn't eat until after our bed time. Most of the time Phil worked out of town (to avoid us, I supposed), but Frances Terez seemed to like me. Lucinda wouldn't give her a chance, spent most of her time down the street with Grandmother Byrnes, who had moved back South. I felt guilty, weird, confused. I never told a soul that I couldn't stand my grandmother, even though I looked just like her.

We had to eat at Grandmother's on Sunday while Frances Terez went off to the Catholic church with a rosary around her neck. I wanted to go, too, but I never asked to because I knew Mama and Rhett wouldn't like it. Southside Baptist with Priscilla was one thing; this was another.

When Frances Terez let us out at the curb on Sunday, she sang out to me over the half-rolled window, "You must come over and swim at Cascade Plunge soon!"

"Sure!" I grinned shyly. "Thanks for the suit." Lucinda slammed her door and stamped up the steps past Mama and Rhett in the porch rockers. He stayed the night.

On Monday morning, Lucinda opened the door to Mama's room with a skeleton key and peeped in to find a few of Rhett's shirts hanging in her closet and a pair of leopard skin panties on the closet floor. "How disgusting," Lucinda said, slamming the door. "Let's get going. I feel about as welcome in here as Cinderella."

Mama had made us fresh lemonade and a bowl of tuna salad

for sandwiches. She had taped a note to the bowl: "Welcome home, girls! Love, Mom." Rhett had scrawled his name underneath hers.

Lucinda hissed, "Ugh!," then added, "Frances Terez's fatso Sonny said he wasn't going to Cascade Plunge with pale faces. I'll show him. I'm gonna have the best tan on Southside!" She dressed in a flash and spread a quilt on the front lawn where she plopped her royal fanny down and basked in the glory of her two-piece suit. I put on my suit, too, came out and used some of the baby oil and iodine, telling my sister, "If I were going to the Emerald City, I'd ask for a brain, a heart and courage."

"So?" she responded. I went upstairs to sun privately on the roof with *The Wizard of Oz*.

It was no time until Lucinda had a new boyfriend who came by to check on her tan every day. She'd sigh when she pulled the straps to show him the milky white skin against her golden tan.

I began to warm to Rhett again when, at dusk, he burned what he called a smoke bomb to kill off the mosquitoes. He made a circular burner out of wire and we gathered leaves to create smoke, which poured out with a force equal to the molten iron's smoke at the viaduct. I thought about Rhett burning in hell forever, reached for his hand that had walked me to first grade. He squeezed my sweaty hand, but we both looked straight ahead into the smoke, which got in his eyes, too.

Until the smoke bomb, we'd just slapped at mosquitos and ignored them the way we did roaches or rats. We expected them, were told they always infested rented homes. I wondered if there might not be room in our lives for a man again when I saw Rhett set out mousetraps with crumbs of cheese, prepared to dispose of the bloody corpses.

Christmas was lean that year, but we cut a tree in the woods at Granny Youngblood's house and actually decorated as a family. Mama told me she had a suitcase for Lucinda when I caught her wrapping presents. When I tried to warn Lucinda to reduce her disappointment, she laughed at me, "Stupid. We got a 45 rpm record player for Christmas just as sure as this world. That was the only thing on my list. The trouble is I'll have to share it with you."

"Ahn un," I warned her, but when she opened it Lucinda shrieked with joy and hugged Mama and Rhett both. She unsnapped the grey, square case and spun the turntable.

"Just like the one on Priscilla's mahogany console," I squealed, amazed that a record player could be so portable. The free 45 rpm that came with the player was a gospel tune by some black quartet. Lucinda slipped the shiny record on the turntable and "Christmas giiiihiift, won't you hand it heah!" rang out so loud we all jumped.

I opened my smaller packages and jumped gleefully to find a pair of pastel panties for each day of the week. They weren't the ones I had asked for, but less expensive cotton ones Mama had embroidered the days of the week on. I tried to keep them out of Rhett's view, but told Mama quietly, "These are gonna keep me organized!"

That record player changed my life in some mysterious, imperceptible way. My pre-frontal cortex was stimulated by music as well as my adolescent longing was being fulfilled. It was more satisfying than listening to those quartets sing about "Moments to Remember" on the radio when I had to wait for the DJ to read my mind and play what I wanted. I could listen to "The Wayward Wind" as many times as I wanted to, imagining trains with passengers headed out of town to places like Hollywood and New York where everything seemed more real, more valid somehow.

Lucinda and I both saved our lunch money to buy Elvis's records. "Blue Suede Shoes" filled many a rainy afternoon, but my heart stood still as Blueberry Hill when I heard the sultry pain in "Heartbreak Hotel." Something intense in my throat was released when mid 50's early rock 'n' roll ushered in my adolescence. In Elvis, I found a friend who truly understood. "Blue Moon" could convince me quicker than any person that my blues would someday turn to gold. I thanked God I was no longer alone but had Elvis to take the place of earlier imaginary friends. The voices from The Club Rose evolved into a sultry white face I could fantasize about. I could even buy magazines instead of comic books and read about his life.

Sometimes, Nina and I slept on the roof at her house, dragging our blankets out the long windows at the foot of her bed. On a moonless night, the stars overhead seemed so big, so bright I imagined I could touch the sky. I told Nina, "I understand the song about getting stars in your eyes when you fall in love. I wonder if the farmers' daughters ever fell in love with traveling salesmen."

"I dunno," she answered absently. She gazed at the shimmering orbs over the rooftop for a second before turning back to the blouses in the window of the Salvation Army store across the street. Instead of doll clothes, Nina and I had begun to buy our own clothes there. "Look!" she pointed, "I love that Spanish off-the-shoulder blouse!"

"That red one?" I asked. "Yeah, cool."

Maybe it was guilt that made us avoid Nina's weird Nazarene church, run by an old blind preacher who seemed to think he was Jesus; maybe it was good sense. I worried about worshiping the statue of a pagan god when we walked to Vulcan instead of Sunday school, but I felt purged trudging up the hilly streets and then climbing the clanging stairs inside the iron man. Vulcan, with his urine stench and deformed leg, was a favorite of mine, like the ugly duckling. We understood each other.

The view of the city from his vantage point was as awe-inspiring as any church experience I'd ever had. Spring had splattered pastels across the trees: dogwoods and redbuds burst open everywhere like the new city underneath our feet. Compared to older cities, I had read, the Magic City of Birmingham was still budding.

At Vulcan Park, the clouds of smoke from the steel mills seemed far away. We fed the goldfish in the pond and admired the profusion of landscaped flowers—bold reds and yellows—along the flagstone steps.

Our uplifting Sunday ritual of worshiping the Greek god was always concluded with a cherry Coke at the drug store. We used our last nickel to play Little Richard's "Tutti Frutti," the music's intensity touching a chord in me, setting me free somehow. I'd much rather put that nickel in the jukebox than in the alms plate passed toward me by Brother Mead's pale, puffy hands. I knew I was headed to hell for choosing a wild colored man to give my nickel to over that boring old Nazarene, but I didn't care. I figured it must be puberty and hoped it would pass like all the magazines said.

"In spring," my stout sixth grade teacher told us with dull eyes that seemed unimpressed, "a young man's fancy turns to love." It sounded so sweet, but it didn't always come out as love or in a sweet way. It was true, I had begun to suspect, that male hormones raged more when buds—warmed by the intense, bright sun—burst open all around us. However, I observed, it was young girls who fancied love, listing names of boys who were firsts at anything. They chattered about first valentines, first kisses, first vanilla Cokes after school, and first boys who carried their books.

On the last day of school, Dud Martin, a tough, unfriendly guy provided me with a shocking first. Headed to watch the final track relays Dud, talking to me mostly, walked through the tunnel with a cluster of girls. I saw him eye the swells like marbles on my chest that hurt sometimes in the night, and suddenly a streak of warmth shot through my chest, hotter than the sun that bore down on my neck. I felt awkward and shy, too small for a bra, too big not to have one. Dud stuck his hand in my shirt pocket and touched one of my breasts, grinning at me as if I'd appreciate it. I wanted to spit in his face for the gruffness, but I clenched my fists and walked away, head down with shame. He never touched me again or ever spoke to me before or after.

During the first week of summer, Nina and I extended our heresy by skipping vacation Bible school, pooling our collection coins to make strips of photos together in the booth at the drug store. One night, while Lucinda turned into a bath tub for an hour with the door locked, I took a strip of photos out of my jewelry box and studied hard the new person I was becoming. I admired my tough expression, the way I'd learned to turn my grin into a crooked smirk.

Same freckles, same drab hair, same eyes mostly, but meaner. Mainly, it was the lopsided smirk that told the world I didn't care. I read awhile in *Call Me Duke*, a paperback novel about a tough guy in New York who only allowed his friends to call him by his nickname: Duke. I stuck a Pall Mall in my mouth and whispered with gravel in my throat to the mirror, "Call me Bo."

I heard the first beer popped before nine o'clock on the Fourth of July, when Daddy Rhett announced to Mama's friend Helen, "The only rule in this house about drinking in the mornin' is you have to open your eyes first."

She twirled her thick hair and told him in a cigarette-husky voice, "If I had eyes as handsome as yours, I never would close 'em."

His face relaxed into a smile that stretched all the way to his gold tooth in the back, as he looked her up and down. Her flimsy bathrobe made his eyes smolder like molten steel. I expected a smoke bomb to go off between them any minute. I wished he wouldn't slick his hair back like Clark Gable, couldn't understand why women carried on over that old man in the movies. Slick hair made Rhett's eyebrows too bushy, made him look out of style. Ladies like Helen and Mama swooned over Rhett's looks though, talked about his rippling muscles.

Rhett had been drinking "just a little" for about a week. When Helen arrived late that night with a puffy lip and a long story about how Karl had kicked her out, that's all the excuse Rhett needed to extend a little beer to a lot.

"Just wait until he cleans a few smelly diapers; he'll come begging," Mama had assured Helen.

"Worth begging for," Rhett had reassured Mama's long-legged buddy. That smoky squint from Mama's eyes was barely noticeable; I was probably the only one who saw it.

"I can smell trouble today," I told Lucinda when I went back to bed, "Looks like he could smell it coming, too."

A shrill weird laugh erupted from her throat. I thought she'd forgotten me until she rolled over and scratched my back, "Don't worry, baby, he can smell it coming."

I concentrated on the rhythmic scratching of her hot pink fingernails against my dry skin and tried not to understand what she meant. "Put some lotion on my back," I pleaded. She did. We heard Mama banging pans in the kitchen and asking herself, too loud, "Where's that waffle iron?"

Then we heard her call us, "Come and get it, girls! Soon as we cut this fruit, we'll be ready for waffles."

While Lucinda carved the watermelon, Rhett, shirtless at the table, watched her every move. She halved the ruby melon and licked the juice running down the green rind before it soaked the newspaper, looking up to be sure Rhett still watched. Then she ran her hand along the blade of the knife with a strange, mean cloud crossing her face before she plunged it into the soft, crisp redness. Her eyes locked with his as she pressed hard on the sides of the melon and ripped it into quarters. Then she turned her back and went to the sink to wash her hands.

"Who's that boy been hanging around here on that motorSICKle with his tongue wagging ever' day?" Rhett asked.

"What boy?" Mama quizzed, her mouth open.

Lucinda answered neither of them but smirked toward Helen, "His name's Bubba Tolliver, and he drives a motor-sigh-cle; ain't nothin' sick about it. He's got long sideburns like Elvis, and he wears a red silk jacket like James Dean, but he wears his brother's leather jacket when he borrows the motor."

Helen kept her eyes on the potato salad she was mixing, the mustard taking over like a jar of water yellows when you dip your paint brush in it.

Mama lit a cigarette, "I've told you no boys are allowed in this house when I'm not here. And if I ever catch you on any motor-SICKle, I'll kill you before you have a chance to die in a wreck. I mean it, girl."

"He's never come inside this house, not once," Lucinda shrieked. She glared at Rhett who smiled slyly and sipped his beer.

Helen, reaching for another Pabst Blue Ribbon, attempted to change the subject, "Gotta do my patriotic duty on Independence Day. Here's to red white and blue!" She lifted the beer to toast, but her joke fell flat. "Well, maybe to my own independence whether I asked for it or not." She lifted her glass to the light bulb with exaggerated self-pity.

Mama snapped, "Give me one of them beers."

"We got enough to go around," Rhett declared, eyeing Helen's breasts as she stooped to get Mama's beer. "They's plenty more where that come from."

"What you gonna use for money?" Mama snorted.

By the time we finished lunch, they were all beery and sleepy. Rhett stretched and yawned, all the cue Mama needed. "I think everybody at this table needs a nap."

"I'm not sleepy," Lucinda groaned defiantly.

"Me neither," I tried to echo in Call-Me-Bo's gravelly voice.

Of course, we all lay down. The fan with the ragged cord whirred, turning round and round. As I drifted off, I wondered if the clogged dust around the blades added to the noise. Before I knew it I was sound asleep, exhausted.

I was awakened by muffled, soft laughter, heavy breathing and a male voice in our room mumbling, "Godamighty!" Alert, I froze for a second before I heard Mama's feet hit the floor.

Like lightning, Mama was in our room, dragging Rhett off my bed where Helen was sleeping for the weekend.

"Get outta that baby's bed," Mama screamed, lightning in her eyes then, instead of her feet. She beat Rhett's shoulders with her fists clenched hard as rocks, but she couldn't make a dent in him because he was drunk, feeling no pain. He just grinned at her, amused like an elephant attacked by a flea.

Helen's eyes had turned into flying saucers, circling around the room in terror while she sat frozen on the edge of my bed. Her long, slender arms crossed over her mouth, trying to protect that swollen lip of hers.

Mama turned on her, "You fool, I'll slap you cross-eyed. I mighta known better than to take pity on you. No wonder Karl's divorcing such a worthless hussy. Get your sleazy butt out of my house now!"

"Now, Pearl, let's talk this over . . ." Helen began, but Mama threw her flimsy suitcase at her. Helen's mouth quivered.

"I'm giving you three minutes to throw all your junk in this travelin' independence case and get out of my house, or there'll be hell to pay. Do you understand me? Phil always said you were evil to the core. I don't need any more proof."

"Better move it, like she says," Rhett boomed like John Wayne. I tried to figure out how he could get on Mama's side so quickly, but he glared at Helen so convincingly even I trusted his loyalty to Mama.

I decided maybe I was getting tough, too. I didn't feel an ounce of pity for Mama's sorry friend whose fanny jiggled when she ran toward the door, still buttoning her red striped blouse.

Mama slammed the door so hard behind her, the chimes fell and the stained glass rattled. Rhett moved toward her, his arms up as if she'd told him to reach for the sky. "Don't come near me. Don't you say a word to me," she spat at him. He looked toward me, but I picked up the chimes as if I didn't see his plea. Lucinda stalked toward her room without a word.

Mama stuck her nose in a magazine. When Rhett nagged her about reading trash, she snapped, "Ain't near as trashy as what we saw here today. Besides, I like knowing some folks have it worse than me. Believe it or not."

By the time I got the chimes working, Rhett snored from their bedroom. Mama was asleep on the sofa, with *True Confessions* still in her hand and reading glasses on her nose.

Nina had invited me to her new house up on 16th Avenue to watch the annual fireworks display, so I headed out at dusk. I declared to my friend that I was Vulcanian more than Christian. I felt no fear this time when the glittering colors burst into the air, splitting my eardrum and sending a pleasant thrill up my spine. Some sparks fell so close I tried to catch them. Nina's house was on the edge of the hillside where we saw rich ladies dressed in glittering dresses like human fireworks dancing across the ballroom in the private club atop Red Mountain.

"I want to be one of them," I announced, promising Nina, "I will be one day."

I offered a fervent prayer to Vulcan. I asked to float away from my tainted parents and my sister. I connected to the iron god's lofty distance high above Earth's fracas as I prayed to be released from my prison of misery. I was ready for independence day!

I never dreamed the situation could be worse when Nina's mother walked with us to see that I got home safely. I was relieved they had watched from the corner, waved gaily to them even though I heard Mama's shrill voice from the porch. Thank God there was no sign of Rhett, only the sound of his snoring. Mama had a cigarette in her mouth and the telephone receiver in her hand. It seemed to grow out of her frazzled hair, which had not been combed all day. I figured out she was calling Phil, a beer in her hand, her eyes wild. She didn't drink much; every beer told on her.

The cigarette bobbed as she mimicked Phil. "Oh, Pearl, do this. Pearl, do that. What do you ever do? Maybe I need to let my hair down some time," she squawked, then ran her hand through the tangled mess.

"What?" she asked, incredulous. "Right now? All right, Mr. Know-it-All, you've got yourself a deal. Twenty minutes? Yeah, we can do it."

She slammed the phone down, exulting in her triumph. "Your daddy wants y'all to spend some time with them this weekend," she announced trying to sound casual. "Let's get your clothes packed. Sonny wants to take y'all swimming."

"I'll bet," Lucinda sulked, throwing things in her bag. "Wait until Bubba hears about it."

My mood plummeting after the exhilaration of fireworks, I packed my clothes like a robot, didn't allow myself to look at Mama. When Phil arrived in his pajama top with crumpled slacks, he was colder than usual, especially to Mama. "Pearl," he nodded to her. "Let's go, girls. It's late."

We didn't say a word in the car. Lucinda sat in the front like she thought she was Frances Terez. When we passed Sloss Furnace, she turned around and silently held her nose. She winked, squeezing a small tear from the eye that moved, then turned quickly around and stared straight ahead into the unknown dark night.

She strutted through the house in her swimsuit the next day, flaunting her tan until Sonny noticed. Finally, he couldn't be quiet about it. "Great tan, Lucinda. Let's go down to Cascade and take the plunge."

She yawned, "I don't usually go to the pool with fat boys." His eyebrows jumped an inch, and Frances Terez's angry eyes popped open over her morning paper, making her frizzy hair seem to stand on end. "That isn't a nice thing to say, Lucinda."

"No worse than what he said about pale people last time we were here." Lucinda's chest swelled in triumph.

Frances Terez shot a look of disapproval toward her son. "I thought they'd teach you some manners at that fancy boarding school."

"You get your money's worth. It gets me out of your way so you can play humble obedient servant to His Royal Highness." Sonny tried to cover the pain that throbbed above his eyebrow.

Frances Terez told her newspaper, "Some things you're too young to understand."

"Sonny's a half-breed. That's why he tans so easily," Lucinda purred, pretending innocence.

Sonny looked at Lucinda with new respect instead of fury. If I'd said that, he'd be mad. Still, we all three bonded over the weekend, competing to see who felt the most unwanted. I chimed in, went along with the contest. He had a 1949 Mercury like James Dean's in *Rebel Without a Cause*, and we drove up to Pinecrest at night and rode down the hill to a dead end as fast as the car would go. It may have been the most dangerous thing I've ever done, but I loved the thrill of it, the wonttheybesorry self-pity of it.

However, I was keenly aware that Mama rarely threw in the towel and sent us away, but rejection was a way of life for Sonny. Frances Terez had made her choice, was willing to give Daddy Phil the child-free existence he wanted. I had heard Mama tell Aunt Mary Alma that's what he had wanted from her, that he'd never meant for us to be born.

Sonny was chubby, but he had nice smooth skin and a deep tan. That morning, my stepbrother couldn't take his sad, dark eyes off Lucinda's two-piece suit and all that popped out of it, which nauseated me. I decided to ignore them before they excluded me. I lay on the top bleacher and cooked my skin to rival my sister's tan.

I didn't realize I had a fever since I'd been so hot all day, and nobody thought to check on me for sunburn. Mama met us at the doctor's office once Frances Terez discovered, when we got home, that I had a high temperature. Mama was pale when Dr. Paterson—who'd agreed to meet us at his office on Sunday—said, "She has diphtheria."

The only sign of Mama's fear was that brief lack of color in her face. Otherwise, she turned to granite, made me believe she could make me well with the sheer force of her determination.

Lucinda whined, "I want to stay with Grandmother. I don't want to catch Bonita's disease."

Mama was decisive, "Suit yourself." I heard Mama, through the fog of my fever, whisper to Daddy Phil, "I don't care if I do lose my job." Guilt surged through my veins, but I continued to catch phrases about counting on Lucinda for help since cigarette stampers don't get sick leave.

Phil's voice cracked with emotion as he told her, "Pearl, you need that job. Call the temporary nurse's aid number and get someone trained to look after our baby while you're at work. She needs professional care, not a teenage sister's help. I'll pay for the nurse."

"We'll all feel safer," he added with a gravity that frightened me. He touched Mama's elbow. He had called me his.

Miss Hubbard, the stocky old nurse wore a hair net all day, but not one of those stiff little caps. She wore white nurses's hose and sturdy white shoes, but a regular house dress. Even in my febrile haze, she struck me as the perfect example of two and two not making four. Too sick to read, I listened to the radio all day when I wasn't asleep. The nurse told me all children called her Mother Hubbard and insisted I do it, but I tried not to call her anything. Smelling like Granny Connor's talcum powder, Nurse Hubbard read in the rocking chair beside my bed. I pretended she was Granny Connor, which I was convinced made my fever break.

I paid just enough attention to her prattle to buy into what I wanted to. She witnessed to me in a frenzy about being Seventh Day Adventist. "You can make yourself well if you believe. We can make a world of difference in our bodies! You must listen to the wisdom of your body," she wagged her head and pointed her fat finger toward me like the witch in Snow White.

It made sense at first, but the more frenzied she got the more frightened I was. She began hobbling around, dancing and speaking in a language I'd never heard, her cheeks rosy. Her eyes were dreamy, her breath rapid, her voice shrill—out of control. Then as suddenly as her "spell" started, it stopped. She became peaceful, explaining to me she'd just had "the Holy Ghost."

I told Mama, "She reminded me of that old woman who lives down the street with all the cats. Her cheeks turned rosy like that. Folks swear that cat lady's a witch, and Mother Hubbard was talking in that same strange language. Neither one of 'ems a foreigner either."

Mama stroked my hair, smiled, "The cat lady's just a pitiful old widow who wears too much rouge." That night, when we heard the cat lady's mournful chant and her old-fashioned thick-heeled boots clop clop clop down the sidewalk and the cats' screeching welcome, Mama woke up and held me to soothe my fear.

"She's walking home from Jimmy Hale's Mission, baby. She marches five miles and back to get her dinner free and then stays for the singing. Now that weird talking is probably speaking in unknown tongues, a mystery beyond me," Mama sighed.

Mama scratched my back as she continued, "Maybe she's Irish, using that old-fashioned Gaelic language or maybe she nips a little with those winos at the mission. All I know is the cat lady's harmless, has been for years. I don't know about this Mother Hubbard though. Lord have mercy."

The next day Lucinda came back home, and we never saw Nurse Hubbard again. My sister brought me cold drinks every hour but didn't sit in the room with me. She acted as if I had leprosy, but I could tell she was concerned, too. She was always right there on the porch or in the living room while I was sick.

Rhett stood over my bed rattling his change every morning before he left and every night when he came in, but he never said much. I pretended to be asleep, I couldn't look at the pain in his eyes under the sleek black hair he'd let grow out. He was beginning to look like Indians in the movies. After a week or so, we were all back to normal, and I had to summon my strength to fend off Lucinda's escalating meanness. I measured my recovery from diphtheria by the bristle of her insults.

Soon, however, we were both absorbed, like all the other girls, by the shock that hit our neighborhood when Bubba's 27-year old brother eloped with a fifteen year old girl named Lacey Wickware. She told us about her wedding night with great fanfare, made it sound like something I was supposed to be longing for, but I wasn't sure about that. The most daring sexual fantasy I allowed myself to have at 11 was that Rex Morgan, M. D., would finally marry his nurse, June. Therefore, I wasn't prepared for all Lacey's details.

I changed the subject a dozen times asking questions like, "Is it true Bubba's mama poisoned her three husbands?"

Lucinda shook me hard in the bathroom, whispering, "I told you not to ever tell a living soul that poisoning story."

Wondering if she made it up to scare me, I explained, "I only mentioned the poison because I was curious."

"Well, there's more interesting stories to be curious about this morning than that stuff," Lucinda huffed, hurrying back to news of the great elopement.

Lacey, gat-toothed, with curly hair heaped on her shoulders, looked like a dance-hall girl in the western movies we saw every Saturday. The elastic, off-the shoulder blouse barely covered her breasts. It was a mustard yellow, which was not the only thing that made me want to puke that morning. And yet, to tell the truth, her story also made me tingle, made me want to race out to the older boy who zoomed around the neighborhood, his legs straddling a loud, throbbing motorcycle. He wore black leather all summer and smelled like a horse. He also smelled like Vitalis, his hair slicked back in an oily duck tail. That slight tingling was the first step in my wandering off the path like Little Red Riding Hood.

# Chapter Twenty-one:
## Breaking Away

BUBBA'S LEATHER JACKET—together with Lacey's wedding night stories—inspired me to break away from my fierce attachment to Mama. If Mama was gonna keep taking Rhett back and wearing those leopard skin panties like a wild animal, I figured I might as well go a little wild, too. While Ida said Rev. Shuttlesworth was busy fighting for civil rights, lots of my teachers said he was making headlines and teaching colored people not to follow the rules.

Bubba and his friends were busy forming a gang. Looking back, I imagine it was modeled loosely on the Klan. Instead of white sheets, however, these high school boys wore black leather. They frightened me when they'd appear at the picture show or hang out in clumps at the bowling alley across the street. However, once at a safe distance, they tantalized the rebel in me.

Instead of getting into serious trouble, I formed a club of my own: The Black Cats. Mary Ellen Harris, our president, became my best friend and Mama's worst nightmare. Flattered by Mary Ellen's attention, I began to see the world differently that summer, and Mama knew it instinctively. Our friendship brought on one of my first serious clashes with Mama, who didn't want me to "run around" with a girl she said was "too fast."

"I can't stand that smart alecky look on her face," Mama hissed, "and that peroxided hair looks cheap and common! Listen to me, baby, I know what I'm talking about," she pleaded. It was no use. The more she protested, the more I was drawn to the girl. I had to beg Mama for a week to let me spend the night with Mary Ellen.

Since her mom was a cocktail waitress and didn't come in until late, we felt free—very grown up. We went to the picture show for the last feature around nine o'clock, smoking at least ten cigarettes before we got to the movie. Mary Ellen was fast, kissing some boy before we were even seated. The boy's friend didn't seem to mind being stuck with me. "You look familiar. You go to South Highland?" I asked.

"Lakeview."

"What's your name?"

"I'm Smoky Arrington."

"I can't believe it! I knew you," I said as if one of us were dead. "In first grade. I'm Bonita Byrnes."

"I usually go to movies at the Avon in Lakeview," he said, "but I'm with my cousin tonight. He lives in Five Points." Awkward pause. I could tell he didn't remember me. "I like John Wayne movies myself. How 'bout you?" he asked, trying to sit in his seat the way John Wayne sat on his horse in the previews, shoulders rared back and bow-legged.

"Well, I like Randolph Scott," I looked straight ahead. I knew he wanted to kiss me, but I felt dumb because I didn't know how. I thought if I never turned toward him, he'd give up. He was more aggressive than that though. He kept making remarks about the Tarzan movie and Jane's skimpy costume. Eventually he started leaning forward and twisting around when he talked to me. I could see it coming, felt the strain of saying no rising in my throat. Suddenly I heard my voice erupting, "Want something from the concession stand? I need to be excused." I tried to look confident like Virginia Mayo as I climbed awkwardly over his bony legs, trying to ignore Mary Ellen and the much cuter boy who had his arm around her.

Just for security, I bought a Tootsie Pop so that I could keep something in my mouth and avert Smoky's attempts. He seemed relieved that I thought of such a good excuse. We worked hard to be cool, laughing at the movie in the wrong places when Tarzan and Jane swung from the vines with Cheetah following. We were more relaxed after the movie, feeling wild because it was near midnight. I could never have stayed out that late on a hot July night if I were going home.

The boys walked us down the dark streets to Mary Ellen's home.

When we all stopped at the front door, the others seemed expectant. I said I had to go to the bathroom as soon as Mary Ellen's key unlocked the door. "I had lots of fun tonight, Smoky. See you later."

It took Mary Ellen a long time to come in, so I crept back toward the front door to peep: the boy's hand inside her blouse was busy and Smoky, lost in gaping, let his tongue hang out. It made me tingle and filled my heart with fury simultaneously when I saw Mary Ellen let Smoky feel too, even kissed him. Then she buttoned up her blouse, and devilish laughter erupted from all three of them as both boys groped for a breast outside her blouse. "Let's save something for next time," she said, licking her chops like Brer Fox.

I rushed to the hall bathroom and ran water. When she came in, we giggled and compared notes until we heard her mother come in downstairs. We smelled the liquor on her breath when she came to see if we were in bed for the night.

"Y'all stay in here. Don't be up, wandering around. I brought a friend home tonight," she said, then made a sinister chuckling sound which Mary Ellen echoed. It sounded like "heh heh" from the comic books. Her friend was dark and handsome, with thick hair and eyes burning with mystery. He was dressed in a flashy dark silk shirt with a lighter tie and shoes whose soft leather gleamed in the moon light. Mary Ellen's mother and the guy, whose eyes had exuded the forbidden, made groans that seared through the thin walls.

"My mother says he's in the Mafia," Mary Ellen whispered into the dark. "I think he's real sexy, don't you?"

"Well, yeah, I guess." I was not used to thinking of grown men as sexy.

"Ummm, you ought to sit in his lap sometimes. He knows how to do some things that drive me crazy." She giggled huskily. "Have you ever felt sexy?" she asked me.

"Not exactly," I say, remembering the night noises in East Lake. "I don't even know how to kiss a boy."

"Pretend my Coke bottle is a mouth, and I'll show you how," she said. She ran her lips around the circle of smooth glass, then stuck her tongue inside. It looked like fun, so I tried my bottle.

"If you want to French kiss, you put your tongue in," Mary Ellen said, her voice really husky then. It was the first time I had ever stayed up all night. We practiced kissing with Coke bottles a long time. Then Mary Ellen showed me how herself. "Let's pretend I'm a boy," she murmured, "so you can really see how to kiss Smoky next time, ok?"

I was surprised to hear my own voice, barely audible, whisper, "All right." Her lips were full and soft, which made her look pouty most of the time, but they felt much more inviting than the bottle. One thing led to another, starting with French kissing. Mary Ellen's hands felt silky on my breasts, then I felt silky all over and moist and evil, loving the sensation. By the time she explored the tingle in my crotch, I reciprocated.

Mary Ellen wanted to be the boy, of course. I never realized how bossy she was. We drifted off into a deep, peaceful sleep near dawn. Her mother's schedule was perfect for the night life I'd just experienced. We slept until noon, had breakfast and then went to the shop around the corner, where we swapped comic books we'd read for other used ones. We traded in *Little Lulu*s for *Archie and Friends*. We both acted as if nothing had happened the previous night, never referred to it, in fact. It was all too fast for me, and I didn't beg to spend the night with her again.

Not long after that, Smoky became my boyfriend. He was a short boy with curly hair, sparkling eyes and freckles. I was ready for him, the practice had helped. Mary Ellen and I were best friends for the rest of the summer while she went through Smoky's friends like a tornado. The most I did was play spin the bottle and go for long walks holding hands with Smoky. It was a truly affectionate relationship, evoking memories in my carefully controlled senses of the redbud tree and the sweet, curly-haired boy next door in East Lake. Smoky's kisses were pleasant, tentative, not filled with searing darkness like the practice ones had been. His lips were full and soft, and his young body was athletic, muscular.

One afternoon, after visiting his mom in the hospital on Highland Avenue, we walked down the hilly street by St. Mary's, holding hands. His mother was Italian, beautiful with long dark hair and eyes that laughed. She had hugged me when Smoky introduced me as his girl, but I jerked my hand from his abruptly when I realized my folks were on the porch. They craned their necks to get a better look at us.

I introduced Smoky to Mama and Rhett, shuffled my feet awkwardly and told him goodbye. He hadn't even made it to the corner before Rhett asked, "What's this hand-holding business?"

Lucinda and Mama laughed loud. I blushed, felt tears spring to my eyes. My throat constricted with a combination of anger and shame. This time, knowing the shame was unwarranted, I rejected it. I held my head high, "Nice girls hold hands with their boyfriends."

"Boyfriend?" Rhett asked eyebrows working with concern.

"Yes," I answered imperiously and closed the screen door behind me.

Lucinda said, toward my retreating back, "Smoky's a great dancer, but Bonita won't even try. She doesn't even go to the Pickwick Club for the Saturday afternoon sock hops." I knew the gesture so well I could see her eyes roll without looking back. Then I heard the soft, patronizing chuckles in response to Lucinda's assurance that I was weird. I took the stairs two at a time and locked my door before I cried. Half the time, I didn't even know why I cried anymore. Mama said it was puberty. Rhett said it might be all the trouble colored folks were stirring up. "They say they're gonna integrate places like the Pickwick Club."

I collapsed on my bed. Later, when Lucinda knocked softly and apologized, I let her in. She told me about James Dean's wreck, and we felt close again. She was mournful over the news: "He was driving a Porsche—going way too fast—and smashed it all to pieces."

I crawled to the bathtub and soaked until I looked like a prune. Mama even let me shave my legs for the first time. I cut more chunks of skin than hair, which left pink swirls in the water and a sting in my calves.

Lucinda confided, "I was a fan before his death, but the intensity of my fascination has accelerated now." I knew she didn't come up with that way of describing it by herself. I resisted telling her she sounded like a magazine because I felt a strange, dramatic response as well.

A new force took root in me. I wanted to be sped out, mangled in metal, buried with my hero. His sad eyes and baby pout shredded my heart.

The Black Cats offered me a safer, but still daring, chance to break away from my family, my childhood. Toward the end of summer, we played hookers in Mama's party dresses, Mary Ellen being the madam of course. I felt wicked enough strutting around in high heels in a black and red lace dress, but the black voile topper to the dress Mary Ellen chose was worse than wicked. The older girls each had an empty room upstairs, but Nina and I had to share. Relieved, we sat on the roof and talked while the others did God knows what. I loved the eye makeup, the sexy clothes, but that was all I was up to in broad daylight.

That same week, I finally knew in my heart—beyond doubt— what I'd always suspected about myself. I was too chicken to fight, just a loud mouth pretending to be tough. All summer, we had taunted a slender little black girl who passed our house alone in the afternoon. We hid in the bushes and called out hateful names like jungle bunny and worse.

Then she began to pass by earlier before we'd had a chance to hide. Next, she was accompanied by three older girls every day. Mary Ellen wanted to fight them. "We could take them, Bo. You get the little one, and Lucinda the big one. Nina and I can handle the other two."

"I don't know," I stalled. "Mama would die."

"Mama! How would she know about it?" Lucinda asked, lighting a cigarette butt. The thin blue Pall Mall scripted on the end reminded me on a daily basis that we betrayed Mama. I wanted to cry, bust and run, but I said softly, "O. K."

We hid early and jumped out of the bushes when the girls came by. "Where you goin', little tattle-tale?" I asked my victim.

"I'm goin' home after helping my mama clean up for some lazy white lady like yo mama, but it ain't none of yo' business, girl."

The anger in my gut astonished me, gave me a rush that emboldened me. "Don't you talk about my mama like that, you sorry slut," I yelled after her.

They walked faster, but she yelled back, "Shut yo mouth, you freckle-faced fool!" Her friends laughed loud, a deep, rich chocolate laughter like I'd heard from The Club Rose. Stunned, I knew the smaller girl had the best of me already. I couldn't think fast enough to fuss, much less fight. My mind filed away my amazement that she thought being white and freckled was not a good thing to be, my stupefied mouth hanging open. Then my friends pounded past me, chasing the black girls up the street. My heart froze, but my feet moved forward on their own.

By the time I reached the corner, an older girl beat Mary Ellen with her fists, yanking the peroxided orange hair and pulling Mary Ellen back so far I thought her neck would break. Mary Ellen's eyes were open wide, rolling back in her head. All our pale cohorts made a circle of gaping mouths, exposed tonsils. We smelled like fear.

The black girls' chorus cheered Mary Ellen's conqueror on, "Stamp that smarty-pants!"

"Hit her in the belly, honey!"

"Do it for yo' mama, baby. Pull that dyed hair right outta her ugly old head!"

The remark about their mama struck a chord of fear in Lucinda, too. "Somebody better call the police," she wailed toward me.

"I'll do it!" I yelled, all too eager, and made a dash to Little Key Creamery, where I often bought loose cigarettes for 2 cents apiece from Mr. Lee, who always seemed amused. The same smile took over his lips as he followed the drama outside, his blue eyes twinkling. "Help us, please!" I cried. "Call the police on those colored girls!"After he picked up the phone and merely reported a bunch of little girls squabbling, I didn't go back to the scene of the crime. I hid behind the ice-cream freezer until the fight fizzled with the threat of police. The Black Cats paraded in, rummaging through the icy water in the cooler to find Nehi's and RC's. Lucinda's breasts heaved with her heavy breathing. Mr. Lee couldn't take his eyes off her while he listened to all of them brag. "We really gave 'em hell, didn't we?" Mary Ellen crowed.

"You might say that," he said, then shot me a knowing look. I was mortified. He was going to tell them I hid. CLUCK CLUCK CLUCK went off in my head like in *Rebel Without a Cause*. I thought I might stop breathing. The bemused smile came back to Mr. Lee's face as he brushed the blonde-grey hair from his eyes, "Yeah, girls, you could say that."

It hurt me to the core to see he had our number, especially mine. We never taunted the little girl again, never even went to the front of the house when it was time for the little girl to pass by. The incident cured me.

It was New Year's Eve. Mama and Rhett toasted with midnight drinks and kicked off their shoes for dancing. Lu and I ran wild through the house to ring in the New Year our own way. She was dragging me on an old quilt and singing "Auld Lang Syne" at the top of her lungs, running as fast as she could. I was squealing louder when I bumped over a threshold, fell out of the quilt and broke my leg. What a way to change a moment. An evening. A year!

Next day when Granny Conner came to stay with me, my resolutions were enormous. First, no more smoking. I would be better to my parents, etc., etc. Staying with Granny always brought on reform anyway, but I meant it this time.

It wasn't a week until we moved. I tried not to cry when Mama warned us because her eyes were red and swollen already. "Your Aunt Mary Alma says Granny can't stay here any longer, and I can't make ends meet in this big, drafty house. Rhett has found a job driving a bus in Montgomery, but we're not moving down there with him. He'll come home when he has weekends off. I found us an apartment just six blocks from my job, so I can walk to work, and if you need something, I could get home quick. It's a nice brick home, a low-income apartment with good heat and everything we need."

"Oh, no," Lucinda whined, "a housing project. Right?"

"Yes, it will be our first time to live in the western section of town, near Birmingham-Southern College and the Fairgrounds."

"That's supposed to be good?"

Mama shook her head, lit a hand-rolled Bugler cigarette, and finally answered, "It's the best I can do, girls. The best I can do."

I swung my crutches around and crawled toward the warmth of Mama's chest. We didn't say a word, just held each other tight when Lucinda stalked down the hall and slammed her door.

# Chapter Twenty-two:
# Changing

THE TEACHERS AT MY NEW elementary school conferred with those from my previous school and sent me a packet of instructions for continuing my school work at home. I lay on the sofa, crutches propped against the bare yellow wall in our newest new apartment, and watched the shades of spring take over the barren playground. The irises, prematurely swollen, led the way for pastel greens to deepen into darker foliage. Young mothers, only a year or two older than me, pushed babies in rattling, metal strollers. Hips sagging already with the weight of their fate, the teenage mothers had an air of defeat. During my retreat, I had time to wonder if they, like the buds, weren't prematurely swollen. I developed a fear of pregnancy, as I watched the soft, little hands reaching out to the soul-dead eyes of weary mothers, still children themselves.

The striking difference here is that so many more people could be stacked together efficiently in a housing project, and even though we had a small fenced back yard we had no feeling of privacy. We all shared the front courtyard that must have included 200 families, and within a week I knew the regular comings and goings of most of them though I didn't know their names or their stories yet.

Sitting in silence, after Mama and Lucinda's now-daily ritual of snapping at each other over breakfast, I exalted in the sound of birds heralding spring's promise. They twitted and trolled, touching something deep in the core of me. I sketched a few birds on my cast under Granny's name where she had written *Pretty is as pretty does*.

Lucinda plopped down beside me and lit a Pall Mall. She ran the cigarette under my nose to tempt me, but I smirked, "Smells putrid to me." Lucinda stopped in the middle of a sneer, her pouty lips dropping open to marvel at the bird I had sketched. Her mouth opened in awe as if she'd just discovered I could breathe. I felt like a bicycle tire getting pumped, could feel myself expanding, and fought hard not to show the unfamiliar pride. "It's just a bird."

"Mama, look at this," Lucinda praised, "Bo's been hiding her talent under a bushel. Just look at this art work on her cast, really." Lucinda traced the bird with her long ruby fingernail.

"Skip the talent, just give me the bushel," Mama quipped. "I wish I'd canned those peas Rhett brought home last summer. I didn't have time to shell a whole bushel . . ." She flicked the inch-long ash of her cigarette, dried the waffle iron, and came to see my creations. "Um hm, that's real nice," she said, patting my shoulder.

"I can't believe you're wearing those heels, Mama. That style heel just isn't in this year, and two-toned shoes are out, too." Lucinda instructed.

"Spectator pumps are classic style, thank you, Miss-Know-it-All." Mama retaliated, far more engaged by fashion than my impractical artistic creations. I didn't even bother to tell them Rhett had taught me that's not the kind of talent the Bible means in that passage. Lucinda forgot as well, energized by her new role as co-bickerer. For a fleeting moment, I regretted that my leg had healed enough to have the cast removed and that I'd be free of the cast, thus my creations, in just a few hours. I traced the birds to my notebook and entertained myself by filling in the final touches, feathering with sharp pencils while I waited for Mama to dress. I liked sketching almost as much as the word pictures in my notebook.

I was elated, anxious to be "normal" again, to have my body back. Mama took the whole morning off from work, primping more than she had in weeks. "You're tickled to have an excuse to see Dr. Paterson," I teased. She held the tiny rouge puff in midair as if caught like a thief, the natural color diminishing the need for cosmetics. My own color rising, I stammered, "I mean . . . I mean . . ."

"I know what you mean," she said gently, busy now with the eyebrows. "Maybe I'm sensitive about that now that . . . he is a nice person," she added.

"He's handsome, too, so I'm glad you washed this rag mop of

mine last night," I pronounced as I unpinned the curls and brushed my hair around my shoulders. "Dishwater blonde is the most disgusting shade."

"I think it's nice," Mama mumbled, fluffing her own lustrous hair over the lonely eyes that glanced toward me from the mirror. When I opened the curtains and cracked the window, the morning sun set the red highlights in her hair on fire. My eyes widened in the shimmer of it, my heart igniting with love for her. I vowed to make her life better someday.

As soon as the nurse hammered the last blow and my plaster of Paris birds exploded like a piñata, I saw my hideous withered leg. I felt the balloon of disappointment in my throat like the fragile pink bubble a lizard blows. Rather than candy in a piñata balloon, my prize was a deformed leg—shriveled and hairy—like a newborn squirrel. I recoiled as I ran my finger over the hard knot of pus encircled by a puffy red mound, the largest of the sickly pimples that had formed. In a flash, I saw myself running away with the fat lady and the Siamese twins in the pickle jar at the Fair before I heard the nurse assure Mama, "Those pimples will be gone in a day or two now that the skin will get air. Does she shave her legs yet?"

"Yes!" I answered proudly, elated to think I could shave the long, dark hairs that covered my leg. Mama and the nurse locked eyes, but I ignored them. "When can I start to school?"

"Oh, any time, as long as somebody can take you and pick you up. Even with crutches, it'll be another week or so before you can walk to . . ." the nurse halted, aware of our silence.

"I have to be at work at seven o'clock," Mama said, omitting the detail of not having a car or a driver's license. Her eyes were drawn to her hand, which fidgeted with the buckle on her purse. I was preoccupied with the blank white ceiling. The nurse wrote on the clipboard, then smiled—a vacant, perfunctory gesture—and shut the door behind her wide rear end.

Dr. Paterson's eyes took in Mama's breasts, then her legs as he asked her, "How are we?"

I might as well have been air in the room, "I'm better, much better," I announced, demanding full attention. "I'm starting to a new school. I drew pictures on my cast. Lucinda said they were great."

He pulled a crumbling bird out of the trash can. "That's nice work, Bonita. May I keep this one?"

"Sure," I tossed out, wishing I could get the others out of the trash can, but I knew better. Mama would worry about germs. I grasped for hold on the conversation again, "I've been cooking supper every night."

"You should see her, Dr. Paterson, hobbling around on those crutches to make biscuits that smell like Heaven when I open the door at supper time. My baby is such a good cook these days, such a sweet girl."

"Wonder where she gets that?" he smiled, first at me, then toward Mama, his gaze lingering. "Pearl, you've done a fine job with your girls, fine."

He didn't seem to notice how hideous my leg was, touched a few places with a flat mirror, looked at one pimple with his magnifier, then pronounced me well. "No need to come back," he told my chart, "unless you have a problem." He massaged his temple, the small silver hairs glistening in the sunlight as he gazed for a moment out the window. His stiffly starched coat turned a dazzling white in the shimmering sunlight, and for a moment I thought I could make out a steaming white stallion come to take us all away right there before my eyes. The radiance caused leaves outside the window to flash diamonds of dew at the sun.

Dr. Paterson broke the trance, "Feel free to call me any time, Pearl, any time." He flashed the even ivory teeth inside the beard that Mama called salt-and-pepper and closed the door softly behind him.

Mama was touched by the magic, too. Transformed by the doctor's presence, her face was radiant, relaxed. The polka dots on her dress even seemed brighter, and the spectator pumps took on a shimmer that wasn't there before. The sweet opium Southern women experience when a man finds them attractive can be deadly or it can be a lifesaver. That whiff gave Mama a rush that lasted the weekend.

It wasn't until Sunday I realized she'd been talking to Daddy Phil on the phone. For all I knew, he died about a year ago when Cascade Plunge, "the babysitter," closed. We didn't even hear from him during Christmas, and since he had too many children to remember birthdays, we'd never been "spoiled" by that kind of attention. I heard Mama's light laughter, followed by, "Oh, Phil, silly . . ."

The flash of anger I felt frightened me. I had never felt such a surge straight from the gut, quick as a trigger. I beat my pillow to a pulp the way those actresses with pencil-thin eyebrows did on *Hollywood Hit Parade*, a daily run of movies from the 40's. Feathers flying around me, I finally surrendered to the tears that welled up from years of anger and disappointment. Still, I hid the tears from Mama. I knew it was strange to be so guarded toward my father when I was open to the flirtation with our knight in medical armor. And, too, there was this confused voice in my head that still felt loyal to Rhett.

Monday morning, I made a list of all the things I wanted to do during my last week at home before going back to school. I sent my bird sketches along with a copied sketch of a woman's head in a DRAW ME ad for correspondence art school. (Later, when they discovered I had enormous potential if I could produce an enormous check to tap my talent, I never even asked Mama.)

I finished all the poems I had started in the notebook that had been my "teacher" and put them in my folder. Back to the grind, with math and science thrown in to frustrate me.

Starting to a new school as a seventh grader was rough as a cheerful cripple when I entered Tremont Elementary at mid-semester. That spring, I learned isolation from the inside out in a deep and lasting sense. People responded to me as if my limp were permanent. With the cast replaced by a shriveled, underdeveloped limb, I joined the "lepers' colony" of the disabled. I promised myself I'd never forget what people do to those whose challenge is difficult enough without stares and taunts.

Eyes dismissed me, refused to look once they saw the crutches. Faces under swishing ponytails and crewcuts that rushed past me that first morning worked hard not to meet my eyes.

Red corduroy jacket zipped against the chilly morning wind, I struggled to keep up with the mass of housing project children flowing toward the elementary school. The universal unwritten rule dictated that upperclassmen took over the front flank, with the smaller children bringing up the rear. At this school, I learned that disabled seventh graders finished last.

A dark woman rocked in a creaky metal chair on her porch. Patting kinky silver hairs sprouting out of the braid that ran across her head like a crown, she smiled sadly at me. I glimpsed a golden tooth inside the smile beneath ebony cheeks. Though her eyes were the only source of compassion I had seen during the long trek, I looked away because her recognition of my sorrow brought tears to my eyes. I fought hard to forget the limp, to think of something else.

Soon Johnny Ray's hit song about the game of love was in my head. Maybe that's all Phil and Mama were doing, playing a game like the song said. Visions of Pearl and Rhett, their long, Hollywood-style kisses filled my head as memory of the singer's voice spurred me on. Then the memory of . . . Ah yes, Dr. Paterson! That's the fantasy I wanted. Maybe someday it would be me instead of Mama. I'd find a man just like that who would love me, take me dancing, buy me diamonds, take me to Sardi's to propose! And some day our daughter (who would look like Shirley Temple) would shake her ringlets and crawl in his lap, pleading like a well-trained coquette, "Daddy, take me to Sardi's."

I had come to the end of the first row of houses, with their dilapidated, unpainted wood exterior, to the tar paper house with rag dolls and broken glass stuck everywhere. A short, apple-shaped first-grader with thin legs, which made him look like a bumblebee, dropped back long enough to whisper, "That's where the hoodoo lives." Chills took over my arms, but I tried not to stare at the glimmering hubcaps fastened to the roof's edge like a necklace.

The block closest to school had nicer houses, some with brick siding and flower pots along the steps. When I heard rich laughter muffled behind the screen door of the last house I passed, I assumed someone was amused by my limp. Maybe I was trying to toughen my skin, pretend I didn't care if they laughed to prepare for the greater pain of facing a new class with my disability externalized.

# Chapter Twenty-three:
## *Out of the Cast, Into a New Class*

ONCE INSIDE THE RED BRICK SCHOOL BUILDING, I felt a familiarity that provided safety, protection: the oily smell of sweeping compound, the swish of teachers' stockings and the metallic taste of cool water from the fountain. These were constants, no matter what school I found myself going to. My seventh-grade teachers at Tremont all had the same canned response. They weren't overtly unkind, but they gave me the treatment we reserve for those who are physically challenged: polite condescension.

As always, the teacher appointed a friend for me to tag along with when classes changed. June sized me up, "Hi, Bonita," she said in a friendly voice. She compared my oily, pimpled skin to her flawless complexion, saw that she had won the competition, and scurried down the hall toward our next class, unaware of my hobbling after her. Once she twisted her pale, swan-like neck and saw I wasn't there, she apologized, "I'm sorry." Her tone told me she was the one with power.

During library period, I whispered to June about Edgar Allan Poe's scary stories, enticed by the wickedness of breaking the rule of SILENCE, lettered neatly under the librarian's name plate. June's face turned pink when she caught herself staring at my leg. I ignored her embarrassment, smoothed it over for her by rattling on about Poe. "Have you read the one about the Usher family?"

"No. Just the one about the vat of wine and the man with the weird heart," she answered, her whisper animated. "I love to read!"

"Me, too," I confided. I flipped through the book I had checked out and pointed to the illustration for "The Fall of the House of Usher." In the dark sketch of a castle with a moat around it, the narrow windows were barely visible. "Poe says the eyes are the mirror of the soul. That sounds like it ought to be a poem."

"Yeah," June's eyes widened with admiration. Our eyes connected as secret book-lovers, in a world that called us bookworms. I liked June, but by the end of the day, I knew I couldn't be really close to her. Her father taught at the snooty college nearby. We were worlds apart, yet bonded in important ways. When June left school half an hour early in a black leotard and tights, she disappeared at the end of the hall like a shadow, her pink ballet slippers like Dorothy's red shoes on the yellow brick road. I promised myself that I would find the wizard someday, too, and have him teach me ballet.

Boys didn't look at me. Period. Once they saw the crutches, it was over. The girls might allow themselves one glimpse to see what else came with the crutches, but the only time boys noticed me was during art class when we were all seated at a table, legs equal, out of sight. They delighted in bringing color to my face by molding penis shapes when we worked in clay, but I intrigued them with the swirls I made in the water jar after each shade of tempera.

My water art was better than my paper art, but they sabotaged that, too, jabbing our water until the jars became muddy or mauve or sick purples. Their foolishness annoyed me, but less than their waste of good paint. They splashed thick globs on their paper, making it crack when it dried. I had no way of knowing yet that they rode adolescence like a bronco, trying to find their own way through.

One frightened, nervous girl with darting eyes befriended me during the first few weeks of school. She stuttered when she was called to read aloud, which caused the cruelest of our classmates to titter, but Clara was spared most of the time because we silently read short passages and took quizzes for comprehension at the end. If you loved reading, it was a snap, but if you hated reading aloud like Clara did, it was torture.

"P. E. is like that for me," I told Clara, walking home one day. "I can hit balls when we practice, but when it's my turn and the team counts on me and everybody watches, I strike out every time." I shivered with the recollection of the tight throat, the sweaty palms, the terror in my gut.

Clara touched my arm, "I l-l-l-ike you."

"Yeah, me, too," I said without the same fervor. My limp was temporary. I was in charge of the power in this configuration—and just as cruel as others were to me. I enjoyed the taste of superiority on my tongue like salty blood.

It wasn't long until I had formed a cadre of buddies who were bright enough but not part of the college faculty kids. All six of us, fairly attractive, lived in or near the project and came from working class backgrounds.

My closest friend, Lanni Lollar, lived three doors down. Her mother, a lawyer's receptionist, had to struggle to make her salary stretch enough to support two children. Mrs. Lollar was tall, statuesque. A handsome woman who had forgotten such luxuries as beauty, she dressed well in clothes her sister handed down regularly. Mrs. Lollar's apartment was always neat, sensibly furnished. "One of these days, I'm gonna buy a new sofa, get rid of that one filled with unpleasant memories," she told us.

Lanni explained that her father, who had died of cancer the previous year, had slept there day and night the last weeks of his life because he was unable to go upstairs anymore. Then he'd left them with what Lanni called "the disgrace of project life."

Mrs. Lollar told the suds in her dishwater, "One morning, Louis asked for a cigarette, lit it, went into a coughing spasm, and died . . . just like that." She then dried the corner of her eye with the dishtowel she pinned around her waist like an apron. She'd blurt things like that, as if talking to herself, in an attempt to believe the horror of watching a husband not yet 40 die. The honey-voiced lawyer Mrs. Lollar worked for took $10 a week from her salary for over a year to help her save for a new sofa.

The glimpse of radiance on her face when the sofa was delivered convinced me that the tangled vine of grief whose grip threatened to smother widows had lost this round. Her mouth was usually drawn tight, but that Saturday morning, her lips relaxed into a smile that reduced her age by a decade. Her eyes sparkled in the way some women reserve only for men. Lanni squealed with joy, jumping up and down on the concrete floor so high her mother scolded, "Lanni, you're gonna have a concussion if you hit that concrete ceiling! Settle down, darlin'.'"

Even scolding couldn't erase the joy in Mrs. Lollar's face. She polished end tables and ironed curtains all weekend when she wasn't sitting on that sofa sipping iced tea and rubbing the soft tweed arm rest.

Lanni told me, "Our living room looks so much better than yours." She brushed her curly ponytail and checked her teeth in the bathroom mirror, speaking through bobby pins. "I mean our place looks more like College Hills . . ." Peering at me under the sun-streaked bangs, Lanni's deep blue eyes registered recognition of my hurt. "I mean, the couch is so new, ya know? Come on, let's get some sun." She tugged at the swimsuit that struggled to conceal her rapidly developing breasts.

"Don't you think if we get Curtis and Jimbo to come over and watch TV one night we should invite them to my place?"

"I guess so, if you can talk your mother into it. She's so strict," I jabbed.

I was engrossed in my book as soon as we spread the plaid blanket on the ground, a fuchsia and chartreuse color Lanni described as "pukey." We hadn't been there ten minutes until the drunk who lived in the apartment between Lanni's and ours appeared at his window like clockwork in his dirty undershirt. "I swear you'd think from that cocky smile he thinks we should be thrilled by his presence," I quipped, behind my teeth.

"Yep. I hadn't noticed him, but there he is, sure as the world. You'd make a great ventriloquist," Lanni said. "That would be a good talent in the Miss Alabama contest."

I groaned and rolled over on my stomach, keeping my small breasts to myself. I tried to ignore the man's stubbled face at the window, but I couldn't ignore him like Lanni. I hated him for the shame I felt and the gnawing titillation I couldn't admit to myself. That night, we heard his wife scream, a high-pitched sound of terror like an animal caught in the jungle. I lay awake imagining the dirty old man had murdered his wife. The next day, whispers went around the courtyard about a huge black man who had leapt from the coal bin into our neighbor's kitchen. Supposedly, he gagged her, tied her up and raped her.

When I told Mama, all she said was, "That slut? I doubt it. She don't need a stranger to rape her." We'd been initiated. The tough skin had begun to dull our senses to the routine pain of our neighbors.

I spent all Sunday afternoon escaping in the cavernous library downtown next to the courthouse, researching a career in law like *Perry Mason*. The cold marble floors echoed my steps. The chill of the stone walls made me shiver, made me promise myself to come back all summer without an assignment so I could pore through the musty documents like digging in a treasure chest. I felt important in the room with serious, intent, note-taking adults. Mrs. Lollar had shown me exactly where to find the documents I needed.

I enjoyed struggling with the antiquated language in the dusty records of the heavy, leather-bound books. When I tried to explain it to Lucinda, she was intrigued, too. She had that same light in her eyes she used to have when she was interested in art. She seemed to force herself out of the enthusiasm, tilted her head in disdain and advised, "Maybe a woman should aim for Della Street's job, not Perry Mason's. Look at Mrs. Lollar."

On Wednesday afternoon, Lanni and I worked hard to finish our note cards for Thursday's deadline. We moved on from munching popcorn to making fudge. "I'm not getting that greasy stuff on my note cards!" I exclaimed, trying to help Lanni get her cards organized. "I'll die if I have to start over when I haven't even finished yet," I said, in exaggerated frustration. In truth, I loved the smell of ink, the round shape of the Scripp's bottle, and the bright blue color that streamed from my hand as I wrote.

"Blue-black ink is a requirement. I know it is," Lanni warned from the kitchen where she stirred the bubbling chocolate concoction, its aroma intoxicating.

"I asked Ms. Watson if I could use blue, told her we only had this color at home. She felt sorry for me and said it was alright," I grinned.

"Here's a reward for being such a con," Lanni teased, popping the small square of fudge in my mouth. The buttery fudge melted on my tongue, the sweetness of chocolate exploding my taste buds. However, it was almost as messy as the popcorn. I rubbed my napkin hard across the edge of my palm. Suddenly the ink I had set so carefully on the arm of the sofa was everywhere. "Oh, no!" I screamed, sweeping the whole bottle off the arm of the grey sofa onto the concrete floor where it shattered, making an even worse mess.

Lanni shrieked, "No, Bonita, no. Not Mama's new sofa! What'll we do? What'll we do?" Her hysterical voice became that of a much younger child.

"Get to work for now," I yelled, grabbing the roll of toilet paper we used for tissues and sopping up as much as I could from the sofa. It was hopeless. The white wads of tissue paper only left blue lint behind. I rushed to the kitchen, found a sponge and Ajax, came back shaking the cleanser everywhere and rubbed the sofa as if I could rid it of my curse. I sobbed as hard as I rubbed, knowing there was no way to undo this.

We were still scrubbing and sobbing when Mrs. Lollar came in from work. Her eyes opened wide in horror as if she'd seen blood, not ink. Then she clenched her teeth in anger, closed her eyes and let the droop of disappointment overtake her. She slumped into the sofa's matching chair, put her head in her hands and cried. Then, with the coolness of Hamilton Burger when he had Perry Mason trapped, Mrs. Lollar said, "Lanni, you'll pay for this from your allowance if it takes forever."

"Oh, Mrs. Lollar, it was my fault, not Lanni's. It was an accident. I had the ink propped between two books so it wouldn't spill, but then I . . . was . . . using my napkin and my elbow just . . . please don't hate me."

Mrs. Lollar looked away from my contorted face and snarled, instead, at her daughter. "Lanni, you promised you'd do your homework this afternoon."

Lanni, not about to help me out, pouted because she was accused as an accomplice. She frowned at me, "I didn't do anything, Mama."

I broke in, "I came to help Lanni with her note cards, and we did homework together since we were only copying over stuff, didn't have to think."

"It's apparent nobody was thinking," Mrs. Lollar snapped, her eyes fiery, teeth clinched like an alligator's. "Let's get some dinner started."

On cue, I made my way to the door, still pleading, "There's no point in pretending I can pay for the sofa. I don't get an allowance, but I would do anything to repay you. I'd wash your dishes for a whole year, iron for you, anything." I turned back to face her straight in the eye and said, "I mean it."

"I know you do, Bonita. I know you do, darling. I don't want you to pay for it. Things happen. We'll see," she said touching my shoulder lightly as she shut the door, a weary sigh just audible behind it.

The last week of school, we brought current events for discussion so the teacher could get her book inventory out of the way. "Don't the colored people realize they're keeping white people who have to ride the bus away from their jobs if the bus quits running?" I protested when June read a clip about the bus boycott in Montgomery.

"How do you think they get to work?" June asked, her fair cheeks flaming a deep rose, her normally lithe body tensed as if for battle. Under the golden hair that glistened like a halo, her eyes beseeched me.

Before I could respond, a small, freckled arm went up in front of me. A boy's voice croaked with metamorphosis, "Just cause niggers have friends and preachers to ride 'em around don't mean white folks can do the same." His observation was met with titters.

That was my concern, but he had spoiled our concentration with his mean talk. It was true that white people who needed transportation suffered even if they never mistreated colored people.

A tall boy with a thick bristle of hair countered. "I saw an angry bus driver move that little green sign that divides the colored section from the white all the way to the back of the bus last week when there were plenty of seats up front, made those colored people jam into the back and stand up, right here in Birmingham. Now, I don't think that's right."

I tried to recount the discussion that night at supper, but when I repeated the boy's point about making the colored section of the bus too small, Mama growled, "His daddy's a foreman at the coal and pipe foundry, so he probably comes home talking that stuff his Yankee bosses tell him. That little squirt of his just wants to be like them college professors' boys."

I winced, certain that last jab was intended for me. I liked the faculty kids, agreed with them far more often than my neighbors. Lucinda glared at Mama, winding spaghetti around her fork thoughtfully and stuffing a huge coil of it in her mouth as if to stifle all she wanted to retort.

I tried to talk to Lucinda at bedtime, "You know, it's hard to decide what I really think about colored folks riding in the front of the bus. There's no rule that everybody has to think alike, but people assume you agree with whatever they're spouting, ya know?"

"It's hard to think period in this stifling heat, but any fool could see how wrong it is to jam people in the back of the bus with empty seats up front. It's wrong to treat people that way because of the color of their skin; it's what's inside that matters." She fanned her flushed face with the floppy hat, then sighed, "I've got my own problems. I'm not wasting worry on colored people."

Rhett called from Montgomery occasionally, but Mama never passed his reports along to us. Their talks didn't last long.

The semester over, I had time to regroup, figure out how to mesh my spring retreat of art and reading and ideas with the real world of Tremont School. I began to see a connection between the history books I loved and the current city bus drama. I missed my school friends from College Hills, like June the ballerina with her strange ideas about racial unrest. She had even shown me poems she wrote about Rosa Parks and bus trouble.

That summer seemed one long continuous "threat of thunderstorms," like the announcer predicted each afternoon on the radio. The ominous heaviness in the humid air underscored the portentous racial tension around us that I had just begun to realize was history in the making.

I lay on the sofa, listening for the birds who'd been there in the spring, tried to remember the feather-light strokes of my pencil as I sketched them. However, the spell was broken. I thought more and more about my friends, old and new, not just the birds. Thinking about the strange new creature that struggled to be me, I gazed at the huge oak tree outside my window, its tangled roots choking the sidewalk. Had those limbs ever wondered which way to stretch? Did those leaves never tire of "looking at God all day"? Did the leafy arms ever rebel and refuse to pray?

It shocked me to think of the tough guy I had been the previous summer, less than a year ago. I looked at snapshots from camp to be sure I was truly the same person. Now a reformed juvenile delinquent in a ragged, but ruffled, cast-off nightie of Lucinda's, I decided the reformation seemed to work better with the faculty kids I wanted to emulate. They had an air of generosity about them—an air that stems from waking up each morning without worrying about things like a "roof over their heads." An air of having enough to share. It was a luxury Mrs. Lollar might have known if her husband hadn't died young. It was an air Mama didn't have time to dream of.

I needed a hit of fantasy. I went upstairs and sneaked a cigarette from the crumpled pack Mama left on her dresser. The large round mirror over the small drawers looked like the waterhead babies at the fair. I sat on the vanity and puffed a cigarette, studied my reflection for traces of Duke. Instead, I found Miss Kitty from *Gunsmoke* looking back at me with a world-weary smile.

I also tried on different personas by devouring a box of books Priscilla sent from her mother's attic, mysteries from the early 1900's, many of them about a woman named Stella Dallas. I treasured them more because they were mildewed and dusty, quaint relics from another time, like going back in a time warp.

Rhett had finally managed to get a job as a bus driver in Birmingham, just so he could strut in that uniform I figured. "Yeah, they need a Marine in charge like a captain of a ship," he told us proudly, "after those snipers in Montgomery and the trouble with Shuttlesworth."

"I can't believe they bombed his house and he rose up out of it just like Jesus," I said.

"He's a trouble maker, but that bombing ain't right. The Lord showed us that much right then and there," Mama said.

"You tell 'em, Mama," Rhett said, patting her rear right in front of me. The more we worshiped and heard Brother Baggett preach about how important men were and how much we needed one, the more I began to soften toward Rhett again. I told Lucinda, "We might as well like him more, Lu. She's going to."

"Hmph!" was all Lucinda said from the thick book. Even as hot as it was, Lucinda had on her hat along with her sullen mask.

Rhett hired me to do his ironing for 10 cents a shirt. I clipped recipes from *The Birmingham News* and articles about how to freeze linen to keep from scorching it. I put the clipped newspaper in my hope chest, waiting for the day I'd press my own husband's shirts instead of Rhett's and feel the same warm glow when the smell of Old

Spice deodorant drifted to my nostrils through the steaming iron. The starchy smell was clean, simple. I was happy being domestic, content. I ironed blouses for Mrs. Lollar, too, and paid a little of my earnings toward damages on the sofa whenever she would let me.

Lanni had lunch almost every day during the summer with her aunt, who lived in an elegant house near the college campus. Occasionally I was invited to the learning-to-be-a-lady exercise where she used floral china and crystal that chimed when you tapped it. She always made centerpieces from her rose garden, made her linen napkins blossom in silver napkin rings, and set what seemed like a dozen different eating utensils for us.

"It's like an extension of Home Ec.," I told the soft, fluffy hostess whose mouth—puckered in pleats—puzzled momentarily over whether I had passed a compliment. The sparkling blue eyes recovered composure quickly, her lips relaxed into a smile, "Why, thank you, dahlin'."

Aunt Mary smiled at me often the way teachers did. She was warm, gracious, and encouraging to both of us, talking about literature with me each visit. She often loaned me books. She talked fashion with Lanni, giving her copies of *Seventeen, Mademoiselle* and *Vogue.*

She was eager to hear about Rhett's experiences as a bus driver, what he thought of "all the changes." Lanni and I told her about how rude white people were to the Negroes who had to cram into the rear of the bus. I told her, "There's one lady who's hard of hearing who shouts mean things about 'niggers' trying to take over. But others talk loud just so the folks in the back can hear them. It makes me nervous."

"I'm sure it does, dahlin'," Aunt Mary comforted. "Just trust in the Lord."

About half way through the summer, Aunt Mary sent Lanni to modeling school. On Lanni's first day, Lucinda and I peeped behind the organdy curtains in Mama's bedroom at the strange thirteen-year-old under the navy and white hat perched on her head like a pill box. Waving a white-gloved hand toward us, she prissed by in her navy suit, the clop clop of her high heels echoing throughout the courtyard. "Look at that feather on the back of her hat!" Lucinda howled. We were both jealous.

Lanni rode the bus downtown and transferred to some snooty neighborhood over the mountain where she learned to walk like she had a quarter stuck up her butt. We giggled and mocked her, but—secretly envious—I practiced holding my butt tight and walking with a book balanced on my head.

At the same time every afternoon, Lu locked the door to the bedroom and talked on the phone, whispering and purring. When I asked who it was on the phone, she wouldn't tell me a thing. However, I heard her muffled sobs and worried about her as if I were the older sister. It sounded like Lu couldn't make up her mind about breaking up with somebody.

I also worried about someone else older, thus presumably wiser than me: our weird new neighbor in the apartment on our right. Madeline, a small, muscular woman—once pretty—listened when I witnessed about the Lord. She'd do anything to have company. Her pale blue eyes sprang open as if she'd seen a ghost so terrifying her eyes had stayed that way, so it was hard to read her response to my explanations of The Scripture. She kept her dark curls wrapped in a turban above her pale luminescent face most of the time, giving her frizzy hair a "beauty treatment." When Rhett swore Madeline was passing the color line, Mama gave him a look that silenced him.

I wasn't even sure what that meant, but it wouldn't have mattered to me because Madeline was my friend, someone who treated me like the grownup I longed to be. Her voice was silky, sweet as honey one day and shrill the next. On the silky days, she was a great storyteller, and she listened intently to mine. She said I was good at making up stories. She even gave me a pink vinyl diary for my birthday to match my autograph book. "Write your own story; tell all. Diaries don't talk back," she screeched, her eyes explosive. It was one of her nervous days.

We stood at the back door, watching her son Timothy's knobby knees make their way toward his daddy's sky blue Mercury convertible. "You think Jack likes to flaunt that car?" I asked Madeline, whose hands clutched the door knob till her knuckles turned white.

"Yeah. I do," Madeline whispered, the frightened eyes fixed on the blonde ponytail of Jack's new wife who demanded a hug from the trembling, pale seven-year-old boy whose dark curls and pale eyes resembled his mother's much more than the man whose slick, sandy hair was brushed into a duck tail. His muscled tattoo seemed aflame in the hot sun: a broken heart with *Born to Lose* written under it. Jack always rolled his shirt sleeves up one cuff too high, so the world would know he was born a loser.

I couldn't stand him, but Madeline still had strong feelings for him. "He deserves his money, though," she whined defensively, her voice high-pitched like an angry hornet. "He's a good mechanic, works like a nigger, has to put in long hours since he got his own shop."

"Why don't you spend the night?" Madeline implored, her eyes slightly out of focus.

"I'll go ask Mama if I can stay," I told her.

Mama had on her Saturday martyr's mask, the thin-lipped downward twist of her mouth occasionally taking a break to dangle a cigarette. Her eyes assumed the martyr's stance, rolling Heavenward while she stooped to pick up the dust pan. "No, ma'am."

"Mama, please. She needs me. I've been talking to her about the Lord. Why can't I?"

"Because I said so. Period," Mama snapped. "Looks like you'd want to stay here and help your own mother clean the house. Looks like a pig pen."

I picked up the newspapers Rhett piled on the floor beside their bed when he finished them every night, scrubbed the bathtub, swept my closet floor and lined my shoes up under my dresses like Mama did. I tried not to pout because I thought I could still talk her into letting me spend the night if I pitched in and helped her.

We had just finished our fantail shrimp and French fries when Rhett called to say he was coming in earlier than he'd thought. Mama's tight-lipped face softened and her eyes lit up as she fingered the phone cord and laughed softly. "Um hm," she answered several times, her tone saying "I can't talk now."

I didn't give her an inch, kept moving closer and closer just to rattle her, get even because she wouldn't let me go to Madeline's. Mama tried to be nonchalant, as if there weren't a connection to the phone call. "Rhett oughtta be here by the time *Perry Mason*'s over. I reckon you could stay at Madeline's if you really want to since Lucinda's gone this weekend, but be careful."

"Careful? It's not like I wanna go ride the roller coaster, Mama.

I just wanted to stay with Madeline since she gets so lonesome," I groaned.

"There's roller coasters, and then there's roller coasters," Mama said as much to herself as me, but I shot out the door to tell Madeline at last. I rapped on the door, but there was no sign of anyone inside. I felt a tightness in my stomach, a mixture of relief, disappointment, and concern for my friend. I decided to finish my library book on the courtyard bench, keeping an eye out for Madeline and spying on a boy I'd discovered. He was too old for me, a chain smoker who sat on his porch and picked a guitar some nights. The strumming called me to the window to peer across the darkness toward the orange coal of his perpetual cigarette. That's all I knew about him except that I was potentially in love because he had sideburns like Elvis.

I saw the white turban before the bus stopped, watched Madeline make her way down the steps and saunter toward her apartment. Madeline's gait wasn't jerky; she moved smoothly across the emerald velvet beneath her. Her eyes had a faraway look, but the smile that took over her face told me she'd seen me wave from the bench. She turned and came toward me like some turbaned African princess in the last light of day, her slight frame and the fact that she was short didn't match her demeanor—her carriage erect as if she were ten feet tall.

She tucked me in, insisting I sleep in her bed. "I'll take Timothy's because this bed is much more comfortable. I always use it as a guest room."

As far as I knew I was the only guest she ever had. She had taken the turban off and let her curls hang loose around her pale shoulders. "Why are you always treatin' your hair, Madeline?" I asked. "I think it's beautiful."

Her eyes fluttered appreciatively. "It's this natural curl. I hate it too tight. Let's say our prayers now," she whispered. Later, in the middle of the dark night, I sensed her presence and forced myself awake. She stood over me, staring wildly—her voice shaky, "I can't sleep in that bed. Mind if I crawl in with you?"

"Sure," I offered and moved as far over to the edge of the mattress as I could. When she began to chain smoke, I gave up on sleeping and we talked through the night.

"Promise me you'll walk my baby to school every morning,"

she pleaded. "These niggers are gonna start trouble, I guarantee you. They ought to have sense enough not to rile the white people with all those bombs going off on Dynamite Hill. Looks like folks could learn."

She was obsessed with this fear, certain that Timothy would be the one child kidnapped or murdered or whatever she imagined was going to happen to us. After a while, I tuned out her fright, studying the frizzy hair that glistened in the soft moonlight pouring in through the Priscilla curtains. I wondered why she was so afraid of colored people, especially if Rhett was right when he swore one of her parents was colored. I never knew. I never asked. It was not something people besides Rhett talked about. I also never pointed out to her that colored people were not the ones bombing Dynamite Hill.

Once school started, I saw less and less of Madeline. Lanni and I did our back-to-school shopping at Loveman's Department Store, trying on everything we saw in *Seventeen*. We bought a Banlon sweater set on lay-away. We shared it, both agreeing to wear it every other week. I learned to recognize labels like Bobbie Brooks and Jonathan Logan and tried not to grin when Mama would gasp, "That's sharp! No wonder, it's a Jonathan Logan." She worked hard to remember the "in" name brands and say words like sharp, which was Lanni's adjective for everything that year.

I wanted to hold my chin up like Lanni, refuse the shame of living in the project and insist on being more than people expected of us on the city bus we rode from school. Ladies with tightly lacquered coifs and bright, manicured fingernails jabbered about their work at the shops downtown. Having endured the polite condescension of their customers all day, they enjoyed being superior to people who got off at our stop.

Holding on to the pole at the top of the bus and ignoring the men who gaped at us, we smirked at the colored people in the back. I was grateful to have someone to feel superior to, but I knew better—felt ashamed of passing on the pecking order.

A wiry freckled woman—her thinning, bluish hair teased three inches in a girlish bouffant—said to another as we made our way through the crowd toward the steps, "I couldn't live shoved together like sardines in that hell hole. These housing projects are a disgrace to the city."

Her friend quipped, "They'd be too many flies on yo' honey," which brought gales of laughter from the bus. Laughter ringing in my ears, I pulled the cord to signal our stop. Descending the back stairs (used mostly by colored people), I felt naked. I watched the bus disappear in silence and felt as if every eye in the frame-like windows looked through me.

After that, Lanni and I rode a later bus six blocks farther to the stop her aunt would take if she rode a bus. Pretending we lived in College Hills was worth the walk back every time, left us gleeful about our triumph over the sales clerks from dress shops who were probably on their way home to beer-guzzling husbands and houses no better than our apartments.

I walked off the confusion, the ambivalence of adolescence, going round and round the maze of streets in the housing project, studying the neatly trimmed lawns, clipped hedges, and the sturdy playground equipment. We had the essential ingredients of the 1950's recipe for happiness. Yet there was a gnawing hunger in the eyes of the residents one didn't see in the sagging houses a block or two away. The project dwellers' eyes told of—not once but over and over—the helplessness of having to ask "the gov'ment" if they could plant flowers or hang a picture, or even breathe it seemed.

In contrast, two blocks past the project, men in shirt sleeves mowed their own lawns, bordered by freshly painted picket fences lush with roses. Children played in their driveways, shooting hoops at garages that rattled with the heavy basketballs, and women leafed through magazines while they lounged on metal gliders that didn't squeak.

I went to the Methodist Church with Lanni on Sunday night, where we debated issues like Communism vs. Capitalism during Fireside Chat. "What is the difference in living in a housing project or living in Russia? You say they live in those high rises and can't put their own pictures on the wall. Did you know we can't hang pictures on our wall in the project?" I asked Eric, our youth leader, a student at Birmingham-Southern whose pock-marked face and already receding hairline gave his eyes, behind the horn-rimmed glasses, a premature knowledge of hurt. Eric looked pained by my question, embarrassed for me. His fierce eyes squinted, then winced. His pale forehead wrinkled with thought, "You have a good point there, Bonita, a good point. I can't imagine a spirited girl like you being restrained that way. It must be difficult. What do you do instead?"

I answered softly, "Put 'em in scrapbooks." I thought of my stacks of Elvis and James Dean magazines, the way Lu and I had covered the walls on Southside with their photos.

A chubby boy with an ever-present sneer chimed in, "My brother's a cop. He says niggers tear those places up quicker 'n you can build 'em. They ain't got no pitchers to hang maybe, but they ram their fists through the wall fighting, pee on floors . . ."

"That's enough, Hiram!" Our leader Eric insisted. "This is one topic you're not bringing back to your favorite subject. We're talking about the project in this neighborhood, not one for Negroes!"

Hiram crossed his flabby arms and glared at Eric's flushed face under bushy, red hair.

"Lanni, why do you think people in Russia wanted to live under Communist rule?" The earnest youth advisor continued.

"Me?" Lanni asked, truly astounded he'd think she had an answer. The group laughed nervously, glad to have the comic relief since Hiram tried to keep things stirred up. Lanni fiddled with a zipper on her purse that stayed stuck. We called it her tightwad's purse. Lanni was so beautiful. Everybody brightened just looking at her blush, then laughed. We were totally distracted from the hardships of our Communist peers staring at sapphire eyes intensified by a matching cashmere sweater and the shiniest hair at Tremont Elementary.

"That's enough for tonight," the leader said, "Let's get that hot chocolate."

"Gotta watch them intellectuals. They'll brainwash you," Rhett said when I told about the discussion the next night at supper. He had taken up preaching occasionally again and didn't like it that I continued to go to the Methodist church at night with my friend Lanni instead of going with him and Mama. Lucinda refused to give up Fireside Chat, too, but Rhett made us go with him to church on Sunday mornings. "We ain't got room in this family for no pinkos." He winked when I tried to discuss it.

He must've stayed on the bandwagon two months this time, long enough for Lucinda to have a steady boyfriend at Cheaha Mountaintop Baptist. Herschel O'Donnell and his family had lived on a farm in Lineville all their lives, seemed more content than most folks we'd ever known. Lucinda quit wearing makeup, gave up the cowboy hat and pulled her lush blonde curls into a severe braid that crisscrossed around her scalp like Herschel's mother. Herschel constantly talked about marrying my sister. Though he didn't give her a ring, he seemed eager for marriage, downright obsessed.

We went to a revival somewhere almost every night during the summer, then came home and prayed together as a family on our knees. After we each prayed aloud, there was a long silent prayer period when I considered whether people in Jesus's days prayed on concrete floors or soft, dusty dirt. Then Rhett, as head of the house, would offer up a prayer of thanksgiving for how good he was being now. Lucinda and I sang in a quartet with the preacher's two daughters, harmonizing on the chorus of "I saw a man. I heard Him say . . ." Details like "the nail-scarred hands that bled for me" brought tears to my eyes every time, which would trigger a shout from Sister Conroy. The emotional frenzy was far more intense at puberty than it had been earlier. I was terrified I might begin to shout like her. Lanni's aunt didn't invite me to lunch often once I began to witness again.

Since Madeline had at least listened to me, I had just about worked up the courage to witness to our neighbor on the left who slouched in his undershirt and appeared in the kitchen window at the first sign of a nubile body. I was, under his watchful eye, digging up the hard red clay along our fence to plant a row of zinnias that Eric, the youth director, had insisted I get permission to plant. I was told as long as I kept them at the border of the chain-link fence, zinnias would be acceptable. The point was not to interfere with the mowers. I hummed the tune about touching the hem of His garment as I stuck the rusty fork into the brick-like dirt.

A few scattered raindrops splattered the lawn, not enough to give up planting. They were just teasing rain, Mama would say. I remembered when my cousins had made me go outside in the rain to hear the Devil beat his wife. The smell of fresh rain invaded my senses, and the heavy clouds looked downright pregnant. I liked finding other ways to use that word. I was learning words like ominous and portentous in my vocabulary book, which were just about to come in handy.

I looked up to see the thundercloud off in the distance, its lower edge black, in sharp contrast with the silver edge at the top where the fierce sun struggled to come out again. While I peered at the clouds, I saw a yellow light coming toward me, then pulling slowly up our street. I knew—before I saw Rhett—that my world had soured again, felt it in my gut. He rode up in a taxi as mysteriously as the dark cloud had come out of nowhere to usurp the blue sky with its lacy clouds. When I saw Rhett's eyebrows pointing toward the bridge of his nose, I knew he was drunk. I ran, screaming, inside. I locked my door and sobbed, refusing to answer his knock. I didn't come out until Mama came home, even though I knew he had fallen asleep, could hear him snoring. I made my own decisions about church from that day on.

Something in me shut down, but I saw later in life it was a healthy thing in a way. I cut an important tie with Rhett. I quit allowing his drinking to affect my religious choices, refused to be connected to his unpredictability about something so important to me. I relied more and more on my diary, told less and less to my friends. I didn't tell my family anything anymore, didn't think I could trust them.

Lucinda never mentioned Herschel again, but she began to have those long, tearful telephone conversations again in the afternoons. The mysterious nature of her behavior gnawed at me. I knew something wrong was happening, but was glad she went to church every Sunday night now, even when I didn't because she liked the youth leader, too. "He respects my mind," she explained, "doesn't even seem to know I have a body."

"Or a peaches and cream face," I added.

"I like a man who makes you think," she said, twirling her long thick hair. I wondered why she never had dates who came to pick her up at home, but sneaked off to meet some creep, probably some magazine salesman.

# Chapter Twenty-four:
# Living a History Lesson

DEAR DIARY, SEPTEMBER 2, 1957

*Some old women got in a fight out in the alley this afternoon. Jigger looked real cute when he came to take Lanni to the hay ride.*

When I woke up that September morning in 1957 to the sound of birds and the smell of bacon, it might have been any other day. I didn't know that, years later, I would see a familiar desk on exhibit at the Civil Rights Museum and be flooded with despair and guilt that I had not done more to change that ugly day and the times around me. Like all the others, I was frozen into denial as thick as hypnosis.

Mama made my back-to-school dress, then dipped it in thick, gooey starch, "to give it body," she said, pressing it until it stood out in the closet as if it had a body of its own. I slipped into it, loving the swish of crinoline underneath.

I packed my freshly sharpened pencils in my book satchel and looked in the mirror to see if my enthusiasm for the day was visible. I didn't want my friends to know how much I loved school, had longed for it all summer. The tiny swell of breasts and the zits scattered across my chin had brought with them a fierce concern for what my peers thought. That concern wasn't strong enough to stifle the longing I had for learning, for the encouragement and reinforcement I got from teachers and from friends like June. Teachers had seemed amazed last spring that I could do as well academically as the kids whose parents taught at the college. After all, I was just a grunt from the project—not expected to be much more than educable.

I tried to hide from my mother the extent of my shame about our poverty, the sense of humiliation I didn't understand, but sometimes my adolescent turbulence spilled over. When I turned in the mirror to be sure my slip didn't show, I wailed, "It doesn't hang right, Mama. They'll know it was homemade!"

Mama's mouth fell open, her eyes brimmed, then turned to fire. "You think I like stamping cigarettes for less than a dollar an hour until my hands are raw and still not having a decent income? You've been poutin' ever since we moved here, but our apartment's in walking distance of my job and your school. Do you expect me to get blood from a turnip, girl?"

"Why do you think I saved my ironing money all summer to buy my own sweater set at Loveman's?" I whined, resisting the urge to remind her that she couldn't drive even if she had a car. "Looks like, with Rhett living here again, we'd get ahead, Mama. How can you stand it when he gets drunk and loses his money shootin' craps? I'd kill him if I were you. He asks for it all the time."

"I don't understand it any more than you most of the time," she whispered, her face softening. She hugged me longer than usual, "I wish I could come with you today, baby. These are crazy times!"

"Mama," I said, rolling my eyes and pulling away, "I'm in eighth grade, for Heaven's sake."

"I know, but this is a big day. There may be trouble at school. The papers are full of it, say there may be a race riot, but it's probably hogwash. Just be careful," she said, lighting a cigarette.

I went to Madeline's to pick up Timothy, my nervous little charge, who shivered and sucked his thumb behind protruding teeth. He was so sweet that I hated to turn him loose with other second-graders, much less folks intent on a race riot.

Madeline warned me, just like Mama had: "The niggers have really been acting up, and the Klan's gone crazier than usual. You go straight to school and back. Don't talk to anybody, and mind your own business. You don't know what all might happen. Please take care of my baby."

Then she gave him a big, sloppy kiss and held on to him longer than I had time for. She was probably heading for the bus downtown to see her pharmacist. No wonder Mama had told me to watch out. Madeline really looked like what Rhett called her, a dope fiend: eyes red and scratchy, hair wild like pictures of Medusa in our reader.

Timothy and I made our way down the street that bordered "the colored quarter." I didn't pay much attention to the warnings because I had heard about being cautious before. We had never seen anyone around but older people who merely sat on the porch in rockers. I was intrigued by the street's smells of turnip greens and sweet potatoes cooking in the afternoons and the cool darkness at the windows. The warnings had made me curious more than anything, certainly didn't frighten me since there was always talk. We heard the bombs go off on Dynamite Hill, but they weren't ever close enough to hurt us.

There had been rumors that summer about integration. I had heard nothing to recommend it. Ms. Tombrello, my Sunday school teacher, had told us that integration was wrong. "No matter what *The Upper Room* said, if God had wanted us to go to school together we would all be the same color," she informed us smugly. I had begun to question some things and tune the rest out. For example, why wasn't she Catholic like all the other Italians I knew?

Timothy's eyes looked like the miniature Chihuahua on the back of comic books saying, "Please take me home." He held my hand tighter than usual, kept looking behind as if someone were following us.

"What are you looking for?" I asked my puppy. "Nothing back there but little first-graders. You're a big boy, now. Second-grader!"

"I can't understand why Shuttlesworth would want to cause so much trouble if he's a minister."

I could hear Mama's voice echo somewhere inside me. "There's ministers, and then there's ministers." Timothy looked so small, so scared, I wanted to calm him down. I told him in as soothing a voice as I could muster, "Honey, relax."

"Mama says he wants his daughter to go to our school, that he might be there with them this morning. If he is, there'll be trouble. The Klan's already bombed his house a bunch of times, but he ain't scared of nothin.'"

"Well, baby, take a lesson from him. No use to be scared. We're just minding our business, going to school like any other day. Everything will be fine. They have good schools of their own, and I read in the paper their teachers are paid more than the national average. They don't want to go to Tremont. Trust me." When I took his pale hand, his shaking subsided. As Timothy and I made our way up the long street through the colored quarter, I assured him (and myself), "All this worry from grownups is more talk."

I believed myself; however, I avoided the shop where we normally stopped for jawbreakers, afraid I'd get in trouble for being an integrationist. When we passed, I saw a plump, mahogany hand pull the curtain back and wave to us. I glanced at the woman who usually waited on us, her face—normally cheerful—sagging with sorrow this morning. As we rounded the corner, I could see why.

There were hundreds of angry, red-faced grownups all around the school and flashing police cars everywhere. They chanted, "Two, four, six, eight. We don't want to integrate," carrying placards with slogans reading, "Keep our schools white." The safety patrol hurried us across the sidewalk before I could read the others. Mr. Gleason, our principal, walked quickly with a megaphone, insisting, "All students go inside the building immediately!" He had pitched for the Birmingham Barons years ago, was locally famous and enjoyed strutting in his gray and white two-toned shoes. Ordinarily, he shook hands and smiled like a politician, but today his confident smile twitched above his red bow tie.

Timothy and I arrived just as the minister and his family did, amidst a wave of hate-filled white faces: a blur of sagging jaws and yellow teeth. Those in uniform, with billy clubs raised in the air, seemed more intent on frightening the colored family than the riotous crowd. Another placard read NIGGERS GO HOME!

When I caught a glimpse of the minister's daughter as the pushing and shoving started, tears sprang to my eyes. Her serene ebony face glowed with radiance as if she had built a protective screen around herself right in the middle of hatred and violence. When a fat, toothless man spat on her cheek, she never flinched or touched his slime but kept walking. She was so like me—my age, my size, just a different color. I often recalled that lovely face as I walked through the muck around me and swam the troubled waters of that time. The recollection always brought the shimmering light that I came to believe was my shield.

Why had I been warned to watch out for the colored people? The violence was coming from whites, their mouths erupting with curses, their arms flailing wildly, their bodies surging left and right like churning waves about to engulf us.

The principal shoved us inside the entranceway where a tight-lipped teacher with a lacquered bouffant hairdo ushered me upstairs and Timothy down the hall. Through the long windows beside the staircase, I saw a motorcade of rusty, overloaded cars decorated with Confederate flags and outraged faces circling us. Farther away, standing at the top of the hill away from the crowd with his arms crossed I could have sworn I saw Phil standing with Doc who was smoking his pipe, nonchalant as ever.

Instructed not to discuss the commotion outside, we followed the normal routine of first day back to school. The minister and his daughter were turned away. When I saw the newspaper at home, I looked hard for photos of Timothy and me, but I never saw them. Tremont Elementary remained lily white for another six years.

We had no idea that our event was just the beginning of far more violent acts. It was like the previews at the picture show.

# Chapter Twenty-five:
## Testing Allegiance

OF COURSE, LUCINDA HAD MORE excitement at high school and no-body had time to hear my story. She was breathless, flushed when she came in and slammed her books on the table. Her face struggled between martyrdom and delight, mouth jerking from the strain of deciding whether to go up or down or both. "I got in a fight in the locker room!" she announced.

"No!" I nibbled.

"This morning we had all kinds of trouble at the high school. Must have been a thousand people showed up with chains and bricks, some of them in Klan robes! It was something!" Lucinda's eyes glowed as she told her story.

"We had a little trouble, too . . ." I began.

"They beat Shuttlesworth, sent him to the hospital with a con-cussion. Somebody cut his daughter's lip with a chain. I saw it smack her right across the face, and a bunch of boys in homeroom said the Klan tried to set their cars on fire. It was awful!"

She talked so fast I couldn't even ask a question. "Some big ol' girl on the basketball team was bragging at P. E. that her daddy was one of the Klansmen. I told her I'd be ashamed to admit it, and then a whole gob of 'em came after me. Those bitches called me a nigger-lover and I told 'em, 'Yeah, and proud of it!' I had two of 'em shoved up against the locker, ready for a head banging when the coach broke it up. I can't wait until MYF. Won't everybody be proud of me!"

"I dunno," I muttered, reeling with confusion. I didn't know whether to be proud of her or terrified of the cross the Klan might burn in our yard. Then she disappeared into our bedroom with the phone and locked the door. I tiptoed to the door and cupped my ear.

"I can't remember the boy's name who had the knife," I heard her say, recounting every detail of her day. I had almost given up guessing who she had called when I heard her voice change, "I love you, too," she cooed. "I'll call you back tonight . . . . What? Okay, then later, after midnight." Her muffled giggles and whispering finally nauseated me into giving up guessing.

Mama and Rhett were half way through dinner when Lucinda slid the suspension slip across the table toward Mama who took it up like a serpent, instinctively knowing something was up. "What's this?"

Rhett snatched the slip of paper and pushed his screeching metal chair back from the table, his fury quick as a trigger. "What's goin' on here?" he demanded.

"I got in a fight, which is none of your business. You're not my daddy," Lu spat back.

"I'm the one that's raised you, by God, but I ain't raised no white trash. Fighting in school like common folks is not what I've taught you. My family don't take to that mess."

"I'm not your family, thank God!" Lucinda yelled. "I stood up for what's right, and I'm proud of it. Your folks would be, too, if they weren't ashamed to claim their Indian blood. Don't even know what tribe they came from. Cowards. They ought to be fighting for their rights!"

"You shut your mouth, girl. My grandma left the reservation because she fell in love with a white man and wanted to be with his people. Ain't nobody ashamed. It's complicated. You don't know everything like you think you do!"

The formica table wobbled when Rhett bumped it on his way toward Lucinda, his hand raised with such vengeance I could see its impact would be hard. "Duck, Lucinda," I warned.

She did and lessened the impact of the blow meant for her face. A red whelp of a hand print sprang up on her shoulder, bringing all four of us into a frozen halt like children playing Freeze. "Oh, no," I moaned.

"Who you calling a coward, girl? I fought in two wars for this country. You saying I'm not American?" I had never seen his face that red when he was sober or the blood veins in his arms so huge. Mama started for Rhett, but Lucinda's scathing voice was too quick. "So you didn't raise a fighter? Don't you ever touch me again, you sorry, womanizing scumbag," she defied him. She didn't appear to be ruffled like Rhett, but calm, determined.

"Go to your room, Lucinda," Mama said firmly. "Right now. Do you hear me?" Mama went toward Rhett, blocking him from moving toward the stairs. Then she put her arms around him and sobbed. I cut on the television. My current hero, Bart Maverick, made my escape into make-believe possible for the moment, but I was unprepared for what the next day would bring.

Locked out of my room, I settled on the sofa for the night where I overheard Rhett and Mama. He swore, "I'll leave the day I allow somebody living in my house to talk to me that way."

Mama fired back, "My name is on the lease here, hot shot!" Then she paused long enough, I knew, to light a cigarette, "I know Lucinda can't behave that way, treating us both with disrespect, but I need time to think it over. Now that you got that steady job with Birmingham Transit, you can't just up and leave when you get ready. Ever think of that?"

"I've thought about it, yeah. It's a dangerous job now, baby, with all the boycott talk and folks getting riled up. Sometimes I just want to drive without having to be somewhere. It gets on my nerves trying to keep on schedule. I got ahead yesterday and went in a café to get coffee. When I got back, there were two colored guys in suits on the front seats. I just let 'em ride there. Nobody on the bus. What did it matter?"

"Maybe that's what Lucinda wondered, *What does it matter*? I was kind of proud of her myself."

"Don't you let her know that, Pearl. There's trouble coming. Maybe as bad as the war with all these bombs going off and people refusing to obey the law. We gonna have to punish her for talking to me that way. I mean it." His voice rose again.

So did Mama's, "You deserve some of it, Rhett, but not from her. It ought to be from me. You haven't always been do-right-daddy, you know."

"I heard plenty from you over the years, Mama. I ain't been in trouble for a long time, have I?"

"It's those eyes that get you in trouble. You know just how to cut 'em."

It wasn't long until I heard their door click. I enjoyed being able to read *My Friend Flicka* as long as I wanted to. If I'd had a horse to take care of instead of myself, I might not have been a bookworm.

I heard Mama knock at Lucinda's door a time or two, but there was no answer. I tried the door, too, when I went to the bathroom, but I was sleepy and so tired.

The next morning Rhett picked the lock. We were startled to discover that Lucinda was gone. Mama wanted to call the police, but Rhett said we should wait an hour or two, at least until daylight. About the time the sky began to lighten across the courtyard, we had a call from Grandmother Byrnes, who told Mama Lucinda had run away from home and had come to her place in the middle of the night. She said Lucinda wanted to live with her. Sure enough, Lucinda's side of the closet was bare. Shocked, I felt the chill of early morning on my thin arms and the empty sadness of autumn in my bones.

I wondered how Lu could leave our new bedroom furniture, which was made by Bassett, just like my home economics teacher said you should purchase. Mama had listened to me and the furniture salesman who, naturally, wanted her to have the top of the line in order to charge more. The bed had a small wooden panel missing from my side, so we got it half price at Railroad Salvage. I made up the bed with the dusty rose silk spread we got for Christmas and propped the flowered shams against the headboard's gap. How could she have left me?

Rhett left in a huff, pumped it for all the drama he could. He slammed the door behind him hard enough to rattle the whatnots in the living room, his broad shoulders disappearing into the foggy morning. He liked that hat, made him feel like a policeman I figured.

"I swear he's competing with Lucinda for an Oscar." I giggled nervously. Mama and I faced each other over cold cereal and a life that had to go on. Her puffy eyes squinted from the cigarette more than usual, her lips locked in a downward turn.

"He's embarrassed for Grandmother Byrnes to know he can't control his daughter. Men need to be in control. It's hard on him when he's not drinking, especially. It's like he needs a reward for good behavior."

"Maybe I'll draw him a trophy."

"Make it an Oscar." Mama's laugh was half-hearted. "I don't know what's got into Lucinda," she sighed. "Reckon it's that Methodist church y'all go to gettin' her all stirred up?"

"Look at me though. I ain't fighting," I assured her. "Besides, we talk about not fighting, about non-violence as a means of protest at MYF, if that's what you mean."

"Why doesn't she have dates anymore?" Mama quizzed. "Does she still talk to that girl Tommie on the phone?"

"Some. But there's somebody else she talks to that makes her cry. She won't tell me anything about it."

"When? Tell me when she talks to this somebody," Mama said, brightening as if she might solve the mystery of Lucinda over breakfast. It energized her to be diverted from the sadness she couldn't face and go on to work. I could see her body inflating like a tire, her shoulders leaving the slump behind.

"Sometimes after school. Sometimes in the closet late at night. She whispers a lot, usually while Skycastle's still on the radio."

"What's Skycastle? A fairy tale for teenagers?"

"You know, Mama, over in Lakeview. I've told you about it. It's that glass studio perched in front of the fig tree where we used to play in the back yard when we lived there. Lucinda loves Tommy Charles, the disk jockey. She stays up late until he signs off singing that song "Beware my Foolish Heart." She even called Tommy Charles one night and giggled for half an hour!"

"Hm," Mama said, scraping cereal from the bowls. "Give me some time and I'll get to the bottom of this. For now, let's you and me go on with our business like nothing's happened. Don't tell Lanni a thing, you understand? Lucinda will be home by the weekend. Mark my word."

"Yes'm."

But Lucinda didn't come home that weekend or the next. I missed her something awful, but Mama helped fill the void. She talked to me more than she ever had. She cried all weekend, then told me why she felt so bitter that Lucinda had moved in with Phil's family.

"Oh, baby, I've never told y'all the whole sorry story. It breaks my heart to have worked so hard to make my way without much from Phil or that hateful mother of his. Priscilla's a gem . . . well, sometimes she is, but I can't see why Lucinda likes Grandmother Byrnes enough to think she can live over there. I'm glad she can ride the bus to school, get an education so that she'll never end up as helpless as I've been. Phil owes her some attention since he's her daddy, and Grandmother's her family, so what's the harm?" She asked wearily.

I scratched her back as we lay in bed watching the last hour of Miss America, cheering for a beautiful girl from South Carolina. "I knew," Mama continued, "Someday I'd have to explain things to my girls, but I meant to wait until you were older. I was so young and ignorant when I met Phil. I was fresh off the farm, but he was handsome and charming as Satan himself. I didn't even know he was ten years older than I was, didn't care either because I fell hard."

She paused, went to the dresser and began twisting her hair into pin curls. She checked my response from the round mirror, making sure the beauty contestants who prissed around in swimsuits didn't rob her of my attention. "When Phil asked me to marry him, my folks were thrilled because he'd been good to them. He even helped them out financially when Daddy almost lost the farm after the Depression. They may have been more charmed than I was," she laughed, a dry sad sound.

"We went to a Justice of the Peace, a friend of Phil's, in Tarrant City and then on down to Savannah for a honeymoon. He bought me an ivory silk dress, a shade called moonglow. I remember it so clearly."

"Savannah sounds romantic, right on the water and all," I sighed, watching the contestants parade in gauzy evening gowns on the flickering, gray screen and the sweet face of Miss Mississippi, my favorite.

"We lived in a nice brick home in Huntsville with a spiral staircase, where I dreamed my daughters would be married someday. Phil worked out of town a lot, but I knew that was part of his life as a contractor. Lucinda was already born when I found out about Priscilla and her family." Mama fired up a Pall Mall almost as fiery as her eyes. "The whole wedding thing was bogus, the license, the certificate, everything. We tried to work things out, but most of the rest you know, darling, because you've lived through it. Priscilla was going to divorce him and go back to her teaching job, but then Robby came along. Such a hopeless mess," she sighed. "And now my ungrateful daughter runs over there, disgracing me, wiping away all I've done to raise my girls in spite of Phil's lies and deceit and irresponsibility toward you."

I sobbed when she finally cried. I would have done anything to comfort her, to offer healing. I promised, "Someday, Mama, I'm gonna write that story down. At night, when I can't sleep, I think about being called to be a writer, like a preacher, you know? And I'm gonna tell on lots of people who've been mean to you and Ida."

"Ida?" She puckered her mouth, squinted.

"It's like Jesus said. What those bombers do, they do to Ida, too. I'm too scared of them right now to do anything, but when I grow up, I will."

Mama hugged me so tight I ached. I wasn't sure if she was laughing or crying or both when she said, "Oh, Bo, I love you, baby. You just might set the world straight." We held each other close throughout the night. We were bonded that night as women, no matter how young I was. We were never quite the same again. I never felt completely a child after sharing that burden with her, easing her grief through my reassurance of what a wonderful mother she had been and what a great woman I was gonna be.

# Chapter Twenty-six:
## Secrets Revealed, Promises Made

LUCINDA CAME HOME SOON ENOUGH. Two weeks of Grandmother was all she could take. When Mama pressed her about how she got to Grandmother's, Lucinda finally admitted to both of us that she'd been going out with a college boy. "I couldn't tell, you, Mama. I knew you'd say he was too old for me, but I love him. I swear I do. You will, too. Ask Mrs. Lollar about him. He worked at her office last year, and that boss of hers says he'll be a great lawyer someday."

"Did she introduce you?" Mama inquired, politely. She was intent on digging up information. "It is hard for a mother to find out her daughter knows a boy well enough to be in love when her mother's never laid eyes on him."

Lucinda laughed loud, tense herself. "I met him at church."

I jumped in the search, "Who is it, then? Tell me? Is it that guy Lester, the lecher?"

"No, silly," she smirked.

"Where's he live?" Mama asked, suspicion hooding her eyes.

"Down the street," Lucinda said, then tried to change the subject. "Reckon I'll need a sweater tomorrow?"

"How's a college boy living here?" Mama continued. "His family live here and can afford college?"

"He has an apartment here temporarily. Some kind of special arrangement," Lucinda answered.

I interrupted, beside myself with curiosity, "I know there's only one other college boy at church besides Lester, but that's Eric, our youth leader. He's not even handsome with that red curly hair, all skin and bone. Surely . . ."

Lucinda stopped me, blushing purple, "Looks aren't everything," she proclaimed.

Then I knew. It was Eric! He was my hero first. If it weren't for me, she'd never have gone to MYF. A combination of jealousy and shock churned inside me. I blurted, "He's not your type, Lu!"

"Who asked you? Mind your own business, boney Bonita, always leeching off my life. Go find your own boyfriend if anybody can stand you."

"Don't you light in to your little sister because you're on the hot spot, Lu," Mama warned. "How long you been seeing this boy?"

"Mama, don't you think I've answered enough questions for one night? Let's save some info for the weekend, ok?" Lucinda swished out of the room, the sound of her crinolines welcome in my ears because I'd missed her so much. I even moved my clothes over more than half way in the closet.

Mama let Lucinda sleep late on Saturday morning, but I helped Mama with the laundry and cleaning like I'd been doing. Mama was jumpy, chain-smoking. I should've known there was more than smoke in the air, but I didn't until Mama told me to go outside and play when Lucinda slouched to the breakfast table in a gauzy, low-cut nightie that looked like the evening dress Miss Georgia wore in the recent contest. I said, "Yes'm," but I went in the living room instead and stood in the doorway so I could go out quickly if she caught me listening.

"Where'd you get that thang?" Mama snapped.

Lucinda blushed, then stammered, "Grandmother gave it to me. No, I mean, Frances Terez. Phil bought it for her, but she said it was too fancy."

"Why'd she give it to a child then? I'll give her a piece of my mind."

"Oh, Mama, don't. Please," Lucinda pleaded, a look of guilt taking over her eyes before the confession. "All right. I lied. Eric gave it to me the night he took me over to Grandmother's. I guess he felt sorry for me."

"Um hm," Mama said. "Was it new or a hand-me-down from his wife?" Her cigarette dangled as she shuffled cards and spread out a hand of Sol. The muscles in her chin worked hard to appear calm, but I could tell she was headed somewhere with the question.

"Huh?" Lucinda asked, a fake stupid look clouding her radiant face.

"I been talking to Lanni Lollar's mother this week. Found out a lot about this Eric." She stubbed out the fragment of cigarette, pushing it hard enough to make the ashtray skid across the table.

"Mrs. Lollar said he's a good boy, but he was married until a few months ago. Mama did a good imitation of Mrs. Lollar's soft, sad voice: 'Imagine a kid like that divorced when he's just barely 21.'"

"He's 23! I was dating Herschel when it happened, Mama. His wife was pregnant when he married her, but she had a miscarriage. He didn't love her. They had to get married. It wasn't about me. I swear," Lucinda's voice trailed off. Mama's eyes, hard as steel, were a force to be reckoned with.

"Listen to me, girl. I'll not have you ruining your life before you're seventeen years old. Mrs. Lollar said he's misguided on the racial issue. He quit working for their law firm and took up with that colored lawyer, been hanging around with those trouble makers and going to all those secret meetings. She said the Klan burned a cross somewhere because of this Eric. You have no business seeing that man. I forbid it, and by God, I mean it!"

Lucinda's face registered shock, then anger. "Look who's talking," she gloated.

Mama's face looked as if she'd been slapped hard by the accusation, but she recovered quickly. "Yeah. That's right, Little Miss, you should look who's talking. An expert from the school of hard knocks, so you'd better listen to me."

"Why did I come back to this dump!" Lucinda spat, flying up the stairs in swirls of gauzy cotton like some fallen angel. I looked at Mama, remembering when I'd wondered if she was a honky-tonk angel, but the grief in her emerald eyes was like looking into the sun. I had to turn away. I washed the dishes quietly, the rhythm of card shuffling the only other sound in the morgue-like coolness of the concrete kitchen.

Lucinda promised she wouldn't see Eric again, so she quit going to MYF, but I didn't. He never let on about anything, but he seemed tense around me for a while. Once he figured out I wouldn't blow his cover, he was overly nice to me. I admired him so much I could almost forget how bony his knuckles were or how his limp-wristed hand flapped when he got excited about our lesson and talked with his hands. His pale, freckled skin was almost translucent, giving him an undernourished look, but his blue eyes were so clear, so passionate I could almost see his appeal. I was so well trained in denial that it was no time until I had screened out thoughts about him and Lucinda. I was riveted by his questions for us concerning racial injustice and the teachings of Jesus.

I only thought about all that on Sunday nights, shoved it away into the refrigerator of denial I had almost perfected. Even when we heard bombs, I usually thought it was thunder until I heard the news later. I pretended it wasn't harmful, that everybody could walk away like Rev. Shuttlesworth. I wasn't always successful with this pretending because I worried about the bombings involving children and the elderly. I also wondered if the victims might not retaliate, and we always lived near a colored quarter, near enough to feel the ground shake and hear the bombs go off.

However, the part of the racial trouble that seemed most real was bus riding because that was a part of my life every day, especially now that Rhett was so involved.

# Chapter Twenty-seven:
# *Losing Elvis and More*

I CONTINUED TO RECORD life's normality in my diary, filling it with commentary about whether Elvis should be drafted like any other boy his age. Lanni and I languished because we knew our hero would be drafted, would be reporting for military duty. We interrupted our mourning on January 8, his birthday, however. Lanni knocked softly at the back door, carrying the cake her mother had worked on for hours. The thick, white icing was covered with song titles: "Hounddog," "Heartbreak Hotel," "Blue Suede Shoes," "Don't Be Cruel," etc. In the center was a chocolate icing guitar. Just above it, a butterscotch army hat loomed over a row of caramel gold records, the emblems of our hero's fame.

After we squealed over her mother's creativity, Lanni said, "It breaks my heart to know he'll have that G. I. haircut and look just like all the other boys."

"Well, not exactly, there's something about his looks not limited to hair," I said, surprised at the sly edge in my voice. We giggled self-consciously, moved our car coats to the sofa, and sat at the kitchen table in solemnity.

A father figure to many of the city's teenagers, Duke Rumore cooed into the radio to soothe our adolescent sorrow. Rumore's voice blared from the rock 'n' roll station, which played exclusively Elvis the whole afternoon. The radio star exuded warmth and maturity the way I imagined that mythical father with slippers and pipe would do in the evening as the family gathered around the hearth. I didn't tell my friend that, but said instead, "Elvis will never be able to re-capture the momentum of his career. This is really doomsday in a way . . ."

Of course, I had read this in a magazine and was prepared to hold forth, but each time a new song began one of us insisted, "Shhh, shhh, this is my favorite!" Elvis crooned right through our fickle chatter since we couldn't be quiet for more than a verse or two.

"'Hounddog' was the first record I ever bought," I said, "but I fell even more in love with the flip side, "Heartbreak Hotel." I didn't try to explain the evil prickles that ran up my spine when I imagined Elvis in a hotel calling me baby. I never told Lanni why I loved "One Night with You." I didn't even tell myself, just allowed my mind to drift through scenes of forbidden kisses and tearful farewells.

Lucinda banged the screen door as she charged into the kitchen, helping herself to cake without asking. She rolled her eyes, the May-belline-thick eyelashes fluttering in disdain. "I can't believe y'all threw a party for Elvis! I think I'll go upstairs and shroud myself."

"Good idea," I muttered.

"What does she mean, 'shroud herself'?" Lanni asked, intimidated by the older sister bit.

"It has something to do with a funeral," I whispered, not wanting Lucinda to have the satisfaction of hearing.

After cake, we bopped in the living room. "It's good exercise," Lanni instructed me, her breasts jiggling in the tight sweater. She took the mink collar off and tied the fur string to the chrome frame of our red vinyl kitchen chair. "Don't let me forget this. Aunt Mary would kill me," she squealed.

"I thought you were worried we'd steal it," I stumbled awkwardly through the steps Lanni taught me.

We signed each other's white loafers and dated them when Duke played the last song. To keep the party from ending, I found my autograph book and began a page: This is a day we shall never forget!!! Then we took turns, recording the intensity of our misery over the possibility of losing Elvis. We had no idea that our grief touched on our own loss of youth—the freedom and innocence of childhood.

That night, I turned the volume down, so Mama wouldn't make

us turn it off, as low as it would go on the pink Motorola radio to listen to Tommy Charles broadcasting Elvis tunes from Skycastle until midnight. I told Lu, "I imagine the little glass studio in the sky." I could have seen the DJ from the room where we huddled with Granny and our new daddy when Phil brought the pumpkin pie mix. Instead of laughing seductively, into the pink princess phone like she usually did at bedtime, Lucinda lay quietly across from me, on this night devoted to Elvis, keeping watch.

As Elvis's hurt filled the room, I thought of other nights with jazzy blues filling my ears from The Club Rose and sunny mornings when the sound of Ida's gospel tunes floated through the fresh scent of starch. I also thought of Johnny's curly hair and Smoky Arrington's lips.

Lucinda reached for my hand, squeezed it. I told her, "Elvis was poor, but he made it."

"Yeah," she whispered, "His example gives me a thirst for the American Dream. I vow to use my brain the way Elvis used his songs to break out of the trap."

"Uh, oh, somebody's been reading college boy's textbooks," I giggled.

She took her soft hand back. "Just wait and see. You'll be surprised! I learned a lot from Eric. I'll tell you a secret if you won't tell. He says that D.W.'s company, the steel mill Phil inherited interest in, gives dynamite to those guys who do the bombings."

I gasped for breath. "Maybe that's why he shot himself."

"I doubt it, sweetie," she whispered.

"Remember when Rhett and Phil were fighting?" I insisted. "There was something about dynamite."

"Yeah, like Phil had heard at Rotary that somebody who knew what they were doing could make good money just delivering dynamite. I remember now," she answered like a Mickey Mouse Clubber solving a mystery.

"Did I ever tell you I saw Phil and Doc watching the crowd at Tremont when Shuttlesworth came?"

"Hmm," she answered, scratching my back until we fell asleep.

Dear Diary,    April 4
*I didn't even study for that spelling bee. All those brains are in*

*there. I'd never make it. I don't know what I feel toward Jimbo, but I like him in a strange way.*

April 5

*Ahhh. I won the spelling bee! Lanni's spending the night. I sure was shocked when I won the spelling bee. Lanni and I went to church. Mother had to whip me (do do). I started laughing and here she came to let me have it again. But it's all over now and I just don't care either way. I sure do wish Jimbo had come to church. Ummm. He's a doll!*

April 10

*I can't keep in key with our music class, and Lanni has the nerve to tell me all the time! Tomorrow is the final spelling bee at Hemphill. I'd love to win and go to Washington, D. C., but I don't think I will. Well, may the best man win!*

RHETT swore he saw Lucinda downtown when she should have been at school, but Mama told him he was crazy. "Pearl, I saw her with my own two eyes in that red jacket with that cowboy hat pulled down over her eyes. I'd have chased her down but I couldn't just park the bus."

Mama's eyes flashed, "Rhett, every high school kid in Birmingham has a red jacket like that movie star had. It suits the rebel in 'em. Quit imagining things. We have enough real troubles to worry about."

However, when Mama opened the letter from Lucinda's principal a few weeks later, she looked as if she'd stuck her finger in a socket. Lucinda had skipped school as Rhett had suspected. "Mama, I thought he was just picking on her," I sobbed, quick to absolve myself since I knew there would be real trouble now.

The principal's letter told Mama that Lucinda couldn't pass eleventh grade even though she had all A's in her courses. She had been absent too much.

I watched Mama's lips go through the stages of digesting this news. Shock, at first, then a pucker that stretched into a false grin of denial. "I'm sure they've made a mistake."

"Probably," was all I could muster. Mama's denial was shaky, followed quickly by anger. She threatened to beat Lu within an inch of her life, but the worst Mama had ever disciplined was a pop or two with a "keen hickory switch." I was busy making meat loaf when Lucinda clomped in the back door, sullen as usual.

Her pout dried up quickly, replaced by desperation. Her eyes registered true regret instead of her usual glaze. "I only missed 31 days, Mama, and the limit was 30. I just miscounted," Lucinda told the face of disappointment Mama turned to her. I never saw Mama's eyes so defeated, as if all the muscles around them had collapsed.

Mama's shoulders were deflated even more, as if a mountain had plopped down on them. One cigarette dangled from her mouth while another one burned an inch-long ash on the table where she'd left it. "I've scraped and sacrificed all my life to see that my girls had an education since I didn't have any choice about droppin' out of school, and look at me . . ."

Her voice trailed off and the lips went into the martyr's twist. Giddy, I wanted to laugh, but I knew it wasn't funny this time. I kept my back to them and continued washing the platter in the sink just as hard as I could. Tears replaced the urge to giggle when I heard Mama's shaky voice ask, "Why, baby, why did you do this?"

"To be honest, Mama?"

"Yeah, if you still know how after falsifying your report card," Mama sighed.

"I only did that last six weeks . . ."

"Like that matters, Lu. Same as that one day matters."

"Mama, I did it because I knew I could get by with it. I hate school when it's so boring. Look, I made all A's without even showing up half the time this spring."

"Bonita says you got dressed every morning and walked as far as your bus stop with her and Timothy. So what in God's name did you do all day?"

"I drank Cokes at the drug store downtown with my lunch money, read magazines. Some days I went to the library and just read all day. It was fun."

"Fun? Who else was along?"

"You don't have to have two people to have fun."

"Lucinda, you didn't answer my question. You sound like a . . ." Mama faltered, continuing in a flat voice, "like a lawyer."

"Mama, don't bring Eric into this. This is my problem. He had nothing to do with my choices."

"Yeah, sure," Mama continued in the flattened tone.

"I don't have to endure these accusations," Lucinda sassed, knowing Mama's steam was gone for the moment. "I'm leaving this dump for good. Soon!" Her voice rose to a frightened shriek at the end, which belied her bravado. She stomped upstairs and slammed the door.

Mama waited a few minutes before she quietly lifted the receiver, but I could hear the dial tone across the room. I figured Lucinda was too smart to call Eric just yet. She still had Rhett to face. If Rhett ever lit into Eric, the non-violent, Lucinda's boyfriend would be a goner. I grated cabbage for coleslaw and chopped tomatoes the way Mama loved it.

Lucinda apologized at the dinner table, "I shouldn't have said what I did the way I did. I'm going through a lot," she quivered. "Where's Rhett?" She looked around as if she expected him to jump out of the shadows.

"Working an extra shift for one of the drivers who was too scared to drive in the colored quarter anymore. The guy quit his job without serving notice, so some of the drivers are picking up his slack for ten days."

After she'd picked at the food enough to please me, Mama lit a cigarette, blew the smoke out thoughtfully and said in her conspiratorial voice, "Let's not tell Rhett about this just yet."

# Chapter Twenty-eight:
## Bon Ami and Bus Driving

*GOSH, I missed the first word in the spelling bee. Gee, I felt like a fool. I hope my teacher, Mr. Cason, who drove me there isn't too disgusted. I sure did want to impress him. He's so cute!! The word was ABSENCE, and it made me think of Lucinda. Tonight Lanni and I put our hair in two ponytails and painted on some freckles like Eric's with eyebrow pencils and went through Kroger's acting like idiots. We had more fun!*

Almost asleep, I groaned when I heard Mama resume the ongoing investigation with Lucinda. "I should've listened to Rhett. He swore he'd seen that red jacket and cowboy hat going in that hole-in-the-wall hot dog place at lunchtime. Where've you been going instead of school?"

"Downtown," Lu said like that would explain anything.

"Is that Eric workin' downtown again?" Mama's voice sounded like a lightbulb had turned on in her head.

"Not now," Lucinda triumphed, "but when he worked for that colored lawyer, I volunteered as a research assistant, helped him at the library. Sometimes I'd go pick up lunch for the staff since colored people aren't even welcome in stand-up-and-eat places. They all said I have a high aptitude for law, would make a great paralegal."

"I thought you weren't seeing Eric anymore," Mama pounced.

"Since you forbid me to go out with him and Bonita's such a

tattle-tale, I started seeing him in the daytime some days instead of going to school. College boys don't have to go to class from 8 to 3. They have time —"

Mama butted in "—to make trouble!"

"He's not a trouble maker! Eric got a scholarship to law school in San Francisco. And I'm goin' too, just wait and see," Lucinda threatened, marching in our room as if she were leaving right away.

"Now you're going to California instead of running away to some fancy boarding school?" Mama scoffed, following behind her.

"No way I can take a scholarship to boarding school now since I failed a semester," Lucinda said slyly. "Like I would've won one anyway. Let Tommie go up there and live with those queer girls in a dormitory. Or join the WAVES. I'm ready for a man in my life!"

"Bite your tongue, you little hussy," Mama snapped. Now Lucinda giggled, but I saw her eyes struggle with fear, even before Mama's hand slapped her hard.

Lu's quivering mouth made a great big hole like a puppy makes before it howls, "I hate you! Both of you," Lucinda spat, the handprint turning beet red against her pale skin. I didn't know whether Lu meant me or Rhett, but I was scared to ask.

Then Lu screamed loud enough for the entire courtyard to hear, "I hate school, I hate this place, I hate everything about my whole stupid life!" She sobbed as she collapsed on the bed.

The face Mama turned to me was not comical now, but creased with worry and slack with helplessness. The life left her eyes as she sipped a glass of iced tea, hands shaky. Then she trudged toward the bed after my sister like a monkey on a chain.

I took the Bon Ami to the ring around the bathtub and scrubbed as hard as I could, concentrating on each speck of dirt. I was proud there was one thing I could do something about. After a warm bath, I slept most of the night.

More and more, Rhett swore his job was like a policeman's in a world headed to hell in a hand basket. When he took off his hat, the imprint on his forehead suggested a ghost of his headband that made me want him peddling jewelry again. Face flushed, he popped a beer and propped his feet on the coffee table, newspaper in hand. "I'm gonna try drinking two beers a day like social drinkers, for medicinal purposes," he announced too casually while taking one out of the small paper sack.

Mama, stirring a watery gravy, seemed unsympathetic. "You ought to have to walk six blocks through the colored quarter, then stand on your feet eight hours a day . . ."

"Baby, are you even listening to me?" Rhett folded the paper and threw it across the room. "I'm sick of reading all this crap in the papers after living through the tension all day, every day. Thought I might get myself killed today."

Mama's head jerked to attention. He had her ear now. "What you talking about?" She squinted through the smoke, then sniffed.

"Remember that kid Ida used to bring to work sometimes? I think he was her nephew. He's on my bus every day since I've worked this shift. He's retarded or crazy or something, but he's harmless. They call him Jim Jim. Big and fat, he gets on and waddles to the back of the bus. He wears a chartreuse bathing cap that looks like glow-in-the-dark against his black face. He'll ask everybody along the way, 'You got a bathing cap?' Most of the folks are regulars. They either smile and nod or ignore him, but today three high school boys got on at 24th Street, down by the high school."

By now, Mama had gone back to the gravy, but I'd finished setting the table and moved closer to Rhett, hooked.

"They laughed at him, telling him, no they didn't have no pretty cap like his. Then the big guy, built like a linebacker, grabbed at the cap, pulled on the strap that goes under the neck and made it pop the goofy guy like a rubber band."

Tears sprang to my eyes, remembering how I'd redden when boys popped me that way or thunked my ears.

"I let that pass. Just boys pulling pranks, but then Jim Jim started crying: big blubbery crying. The scrawny guy with peach fuzz on his face hollered, 'Nigger Baby. Nigger Baby.' He chanted it to the tune of 'Pretty Baby,' you know from that movie with June Allyson?"

I nodded, beginning to feel the tightening in my tummy a good story always induced, but this tightened more. The cruelty sent a surge of adrenaline through me like Mama's asthma medicine seemed to do for her. I wanted to cry and fight at the same time.

Rhett, inspired by my absorption, continued, "When the other boys picked it up and sang along, I glared at them, hoping they'd settle down. Some folks looked amused, others pretended it wasn't happening or looked to me for direction. I stared some more. Finally old Jim Jim settled down some as if the song wasn't about him. Then the big boy stalked to the back of the bus and moved the separating sign in front of Jim Jim behind him. Just then I was making that big turn on 12ᵗʰ Avenue, but when I heard him say, 'Get up, nigger. That's my seat,' I felt a tightening like I felt with bullets whizzing overhead in the war. I knew I'd have to fight this. I rared back in my seat and announced, 'A driver is like a ship's captain, boys.' Then I parked the bus, 'Nobody touches that sign but me!'

"The bus was silent as a tomb when I marched to the back. I jerked the sign up and repositioned it in front of Jim Jim. 'I don't want to hear no more!' I barked like a drill sergeant. Those boys didn't even look at each other until they got off the bus, slinking out the door. Only one of them had the nerve to pout. I left a cloud of exhaust in their faces, and the pouty one shot me a bird."

I smiled, "I wish you'd punched him in the nose!"

Rhett grinned, warming to adoration, and popped another cold one. "Jim Jim makes me think of Moon when he was little. Fellas at school always picked on him. Mama swore there was nothing wrong with his mind, that he just couldn't talk plain."

"He's tongue-tied," I said.

"Yeah, but that's not all. He's off, too. He always has been. The boys called him Savage Little Indian because of that coal black hair and red skin, but they cut that out when he grew to be 6 foot 6. Once he discovered moonshine, his face got redder and rounder, but folks quit messin' with him. He started carrying a knife, and he knows how to use it. Word travels. I still worry about him all the time."

"I wish he didn't worry Granny Youngblood to death."

Mama called her royal highness Lucinda down to supper if she could get her nose out of a book long enough to eat.

"Take that hat off at the dinner table," Rhett scolded.

Lucinda scowled. She took that smelly, suede hat off and placed it in the center of the table where families on television had arrangements of lilacs and roses with candles on either side. "Mama, I need to talk to you," she announced, waiting just long enough to arouse curiosity, "about something private."

# *Chapter Twenty-nine:*
# *Eloping from Trouble*

ONCE DINNER WAS OVER, Rhett took his newspaper to the bedroom, where he read every night until he fell asleep. No matter how much he drank, he could read a newspaper.

I washed dishes very quietly as Mama and Lu settled in the living room, talking low. "I am old enough, Mama. I love Eric as much as I hate school and, and . . . this place."

I could feel Mama wince without looking. Lu could be so cruel. How could she love Eric? He wasn't handsome. Mama tried a new approach, "Your education is important. Nobody can take that away from you, baby."

"A woman doesn't need an education if she marries an educated man, Mama. Eric will be a good provider I guarantee you."

"There ain't no guarantees on some things, young lady."

"He leaves for California in a few weeks, and I'm going. Period. Remember those slides Katherine showed us? It's beautiful there, just like in the movies!"

Mama muttered something I couldn't figure out. Then she said, "Your daddy's never met him."

Lu grumbled "So? Which one, anyway: Phil or Rhett? Who cares! Neither one of them, that's for sure!"

After a silence, "Lucinda, I'll not have you eloping from me! Because you'll do it anyway if I don't say yes, you can elope from Rhett if you want to because he'll never hear of it." Mama's voice seemed lighter, almost joyful, "I want to help you with your trousseau. That's something every mother and daughter need to share."

The next weekend, they went to a fire sale and came home with an off-white gown and negligee, a plaid sack dress for traveling, and a white chiffon dress with a lace jacket. I was told to go play with Lanni, but not to tell a soul. I was in on the secret now but excluded from what Mama called rituals like oatmeal facials and egg shampoos. I was losing my sister, and Mama didn't even notice. I toyed constantly with the fantasy of telling Rhett or Phil or both.

The day finally came, and we were up early to help Lucinda dress for her wedding before Mama had to leave for work. Lu might as well have been a queen the way Mama treated her: breakfast in bed, a facial with egg yolks and a hot oil hair treatment with warm olive oil and a weed called lavender. Her head wrapped in a turban of towels, I painted her toenails a sweet pink shade. We had just settled in downstairs where Mama's coffee was perking when we heard a commotion.

Rhett's face was pale when he jerked the door open. Behind him, there were several folks who seemed to be following him, some with cameras around their necks. He slammed the door. Fumbling with a cereal box, I wiped sleep from my eyes. I felt my heart accelerate, as if I'd been shot like a Huntsville rocket from morning haze into full attention. Rhett closed the blinds and took a frantic swig from a pint bottle in his jacket pocket. He looked caught when he saw us peering at him. He didn't usually get home until afternoon.

Then sheepish, grinning at Mama. "Hell, Mama, this is a day for a bubble drink." That's what he called big snorts of whiskey.

Mama seemed to know this was something bigger than the nagging session it would normally elicit. Mouth ajar, her face turned pale, too, her shoulders tight. The bobbing cigarette as fiery as her squinting eyes, she stammered, "What's going on out there?" She headed toward the shade to see for herself.

Rhett grabbed her arm, jerked her back. "Don't touch that shade, baby. I'm in big trouble. I shot a man. Those reporters followed me home. Don't tell 'em nothing," he glared toward me and Lucinda as if it were suddenly our fault. Staggering, he scraped a kitchen chair across the floor, turned it backward as if to shield himself, then faced our three puzzled faces waiting, like a firing line, for more information.

"What . . ." Pearl began.

"I shot a man," Rhett whispered. "I had to. Self-defense. I need to call my boss and tell him those reporters followed me home." He jerked the phone and dialed quickly, talking so low we couldn't hear. Then he slammed the phone down, took another slug of whiskey and took his chair back.

Mama lit a cigarette off the end of her old one. Lucinda rubbed olive oil on her feet and legs. I just sat with my mouth hanging open like a bird waiting for the worm. Rhett's voice was low, almost a whisper. "My boss said not to make a peep. He will send somebody over to make a statement, somebody from public relations who knows the law and all that. I'm not really in trouble because there were witnesses, but it's a mess because of all the boycott business and everything. A white man can't shoot a colored man without raising a stink nowadays."

"Rhett, quit stalling. We want to know what happened!" Mama found it hard to be quiet when she was exasperated.

"Remember that goofy guy named Jim Jim?" We nodded.

Lucinda squealed, "Not those same high school boys?"

"No, baby, these were colored guys. Maybe kin to him. I don't know. I hadn't seen Jim Jim since I've been working night shift, but he got on after midnight with a couple of guys looked to be in their 20's. They'd been to some jazz club down on Fourth Avenue where the dancer had showered Jim Jim with attention."

"That's probably putting it mildly," Mama chimed in, rolling her eyes, mad at the boys already.

"Best I could gather it was Jim Jim's birthday. They kept teasing him about how much money he had in his new wallet. He pulled it out of his pocket, wrapped in that bathing cap, and flashed the bills a few times, and they laughed and jabbed him in the ribs. Just foolishness."

"Why'd you shoot them?" I croaked.

"I'm coming to it, baby. Down on Vanderbilt Road in Norwood when the first two guys stepped off the bus ahead of Jim Jim, this older guy pulled a knife on Jim Jim right at the back door and said, 'Gimme that money, boy!'

"I braked the bus and headed back there to straighten them out. I didn't have to, but it wasn't right what he was doing. Jim Jim ran like a scalded dog! Then that scoundrel came after me with the knife. He was drunk, scared, trapped, but he looked dangerous, too. I didn't think about it. I just automatically did it, just like overseas. I must've been thinking somewhat though, because I shot the hand with the knife in it and kicked the blade under the seat. Then I knocked him out cold and drove straight to the terminal like we're supposed to if there's trouble. I don't know how those reporters got wind of it."

"So, who witnessed it?" Mama asked.

"That old guy who rides to the end of the line with me every night. Just for company I think. Thank God for him tonight."

For a minute, we all sat there frozen in the early morning light. Then Mama said, "Girls, go upstairs and make sure the shades are closed. Then clean up that mess in my room, so Rhett can get some sleep." She turned to him tenderly, "You must be worn out, darling." She removed his cap and massaged his temples.

"Hurry up, Bo, before we get nauseated," Lucinda grinned. We hurried to get the lotion and towels and breakfast tray out of sight, and Lucinda brought the chiffon dress in our room instead of Mama's. We hadn't expected Rhett home until later, so we had set up in their larger room.

"Lock the door." Lucinda giggled as she laid out her white gloves and purse. "Eric will be here in another half hour or so," she squealed.

"Such a glorious day," I sighed. "I can't believe Rhett almost ruined it."

"I can," she muttered.

"Let me brush your hair," I offered.

"Okay," she smiled, "but I think Mama's gonna put it up in a French twist."

We heard Mama call in sick, saying she'd try to come in later, then we heard them come upstairs and shut their door. "Maybe I can go to school a little later, too."

Lucinda shot me a knowing look, but she was already engrossed in her reflection in the mirror. She did look astonishing. The white chiffon fit her like a glove, cinching her waist and accentuating her bust line. Her hot oil treatment had worked: her golden hair hung around her shoulders smooth as silk against the creamy skin. "Wow! You look like a movie star!"

"Betty Grable or Marilyn Monroe?"

"Prettier than Grace Kelly even. I'm gonna miss you," I whispered as I hugged her close.

"Me, too," she said, stroking my lifeless hair. For the first time, I realized that she was scared. Happy but scared. I wanted to yell, "Yap, yap," and scrape my paws on the windowsill and turn my head from side to side as I wagged my tail and tried to say, "Please take me with you.'

When Mama opened the door quietly, her eyes lit up. "The hero is asleep with the help of his whiskey," she twinkled. "And those reporters are gone. I'm ready to groom the bride!" Mama's eyes were wet when she pulled the silky hair and began to twist it. "It's almost time," she said, glancing at her watch. The last thing Mama did was put the little pill box hat on Lucinda's hair, sprayed stiff as a board. She pulled the veil over the sassy eyes that Lucinda turned to her and kissed her lightly on the lips. "You'll never forget this day, Lu. You're gonna have a lot fun. Enjoy it while it lasts."

We went downstairs to wait, and Mama agreed I could go to school late. Lucinda opened her suitcase and re-arranged the clothes several times, admiring them. The sight of them seemed to ease her nervousness, but she kept looking at the clock. Finally, she sighed, "He's really late. What do you think has happened?"

"I don't know, honey, but I'm glad you're leaving town. There are plenty of folks who think he's one of those outside agitators."

"I know it, Mama," Lucinda admitted. "I can't wait for California!" Her worry turned to radiance instantly.

Mama packed a straw basket with white cupcakes she had made. We had topped one with a paper doll bride of mine and one with a groom. Lucinda's tears threatened her mascara, but Mama assured her all brides have to have tears. "Might as well get some practice early," she grinned.

When Eric finally arrived an hour late, we were all on edge. He immediately began to apologize when Lu introduced him to Mama.

"I slung a rod, then I borrowed this car from the man who tried to repair my car and it ran out of gas," he said, pointing to the dilapidated car that rattled at the curb. "So sorry I'm late, but it's working fine now except I didn't want to turn the engine off, you know? I don't know anything about mechanics. I'm a philosopher!"

He said he wasn't sure the car would make it all the way to Trenton, Georgia, but that's where rush-up marriages are easy to get. "We don't even have to do a blood test there."

"You sure your parents approve of this?" Mama asked.

"Yes. My mother's been ill, and my dad just sent his blessing. You know I've already been married once?"

"Yep," Mama said, her eyes scanning his bony shoulders in the white sport coat, drenched in sweat. His teeth were the same glistening color, and his shy smile could touch any woman's heart. Including mine.

"Tell you what, chillun'," Mama said, "Rhett's a good mechanic. I really hate to miss this wedding myself, and I hate worse than that leaving Rhett here after all he's been through today. Why don't we all run away?"

Eric looked shocked but relieved, and Lucinda ruined her mascara crying like a little girl. "Mama, I felt so guilty leaving him out and Bo, my little flower girl/honor maid."

"Go switch the car off, son, and give us 20 minutes," Mama said, her cheeks like roses, eyes shining.

"Me, too?" I squealed, bounding up the stairs behind her. Already, I knew I would wear the silk dress Mama had re-made for my senior tea. It was a teal blue with gold designs, something Helen had discarded with an empire waist that disguised my tummy but made me look pregnant, too. When I came back down in my baby doll pumps and the new dress, Lucinda tore herself out of Eric's arms long enough to sting me, "You look four months p.g. The people at the courthouse will think Eric's marrying the wrong sister."

They both laughed, but I was quick, "Maybe he is!" By then, we heard Mama clomping down the stairs. She was beautiful in a beige linen dress with a veiled hat and red high heels. Rhett, looking dazed and sleepy, had a tie thrown around his neck and his preacher's suit coat over his shoulder. He was grinning from ear to ear.

"So Pearl caught y'all eloping, huh? Of course, I remember Eric," shaking his hand vigorously. "Found yourself a beautiful bride, didn't you, son?"

"Yes, sir," Eric beamed, forgetting he'd never seen Rhett. Lucinda just smirked, rolling her eyes at Mama who grinned like she'd just treed Jesus. I couldn't believe how well the surprise was going. Leave it to Mama.

Rhett sat in the front and told Eric how to drive. He took over the whole scene, never realizing he was only the mechanic. "Tell you what, boy, it's an easier drive over to Meridian than climbing those mountains into Georgia in this rattletrap."

"The mountains are more romantic," Lucinda protested. "I was looking forward to that."

"Sometimes practical is more important than romance, little girl. Let this be your first lesson as a young bride. Yours too, boy!" Rhett slapped Eric's scrawny shoulder. Rhett offered him a swig of whiskey.

"No thank you, sir," Eric said nervously. It was clear he didn't like being caught between Rhett and Lucinda.

"Well, I hope you don't mind if I do," Rhett knocked back a good slug and let out a war whoop that made Eric jump. "This has been one hell of a day. So you're going to California? I was stationed at Terminal Island during the 40's, really loved it. Beautiful country. Broad-minded folks. I used to date a Catholic school teacher who could drink me under the table on Saturday night and haul me to church on Sunday morning. It was an educational experience for me, living in California."

"Yes, sir, I'm sure it was," Eric answered, barely audible over the rumbling old car. "I'm actually from Nashville, but I was given an excellent scholarship to law school at Stanford. I wasn't about to turn it down because of the distance."

"A lawyer in the family, huh? We just might need you, son, any day now." Rhett chuckled to himself, then dozed until we stopped for gas. He insisted on paying for the gas and for our lunch at a barbecue place where he insisted we all have malts. He, of course, had a cold beer. Rhett was silly as I'd ever seen him, giggling like girls at school when the idea occurred to him. "I bet you anything they'll think this is a shotgun wedding with all us along!"

Eric reddened, "I assure you, sir, that is not the case."

"This time," Mama couldn't resist adding. Lucinda kicked her under the table.

Eric's blush turned closer to purple, but Rhett didn't even catch it. He was busy going on about California, the land of opportunity and how every man's dream was that his daughter would marry a fine young man.

I allowed my straw to sputter at the end of my malt just to create a distraction. I dreaded having the man who married them think so poorly of us.

Actually, nobody in the office let on if that's what they thought. They were gracious about everything. As we walked down the steps outside the office, the chimes struck three. There was a slight breeze, and the sound of the bells was mellow, comforting. I wished the three were significant, that I could be leaving with Lucinda and Eric. I met him first, after all.

By the time we stopped for a shrimp dinner at some place Rhett knew, he could barely stand up. Even Mama had a mixed drink before dinner. Ugh. Mama made Rhett sit in the back with us and let Lucinda sit up front with her groom. I heard Lucinda say to Eric, "Sure hope you don't need that mechanic now."

"Don't worry," he said. "The guy at the service station said it would do fine. I just got nervous after the other catastrophe. We'll be in our motel before you know it."

She flashed him a radiant smile and slipped her arm around his neck. Rhett was snoring on Mama's shoulder, and I was watching for rose bushes along the streets to explain the sweetness of the air outside the car on a spring night in the Deep South. The scent of roses and honeysuckle had the only kind of intoxication that interested me.

# Chapter Thirty:
# Graduation

THAT WEEKEND, I made a big production of keeping all the *Photoplay* magazines, organizing the dresser where I'd have twice as many drawers, and arranging the clothes hangers in the closet where my dresses wouldn't be smushed together anymore. Anything to keep the lily that grew in my throat from swelling more or to hold back the tears that watered it.

I turned to my diary:

*I wish I could have someone to love me. If I were only old enough to have someone to protect me. I want someone who's built tall and very masculine, someone I have to stand on my tiptoes to kiss goodnight. It won't be long until I'll be graduating, and that's a big step in my life. I hope I never get in any jams like getting pregnant and all that.*

LANNI was dating my cousin who was a freshman at the university. We had lied to him and my aunt and said she was 15. He looked like a cross between Troy Donahue and Tab Hunter. She had to stand on her tiptoes in heels to kiss him. I was so envious of her and Lucinda.

All our neighbors and my aunts assumed Lu was pregnant. "So how's the little bride feeling?" They'd ask me pointedly.

"Not so hot," I quickly learned to say, just to whet their appetites. I'd count the seconds it took for their minds to work on another way to pry. "The damp weather in California doesn't seem to agree with her," I'd add to make them wonder.

I had other games, too, to take my mind off being alone for the first time in my life, without a sister to snuggle with at night. I put myself to sleep imagining myself at the ocean's edge in white chiffon and lace, dancing in the moonlit arms of a "dreamboat." Soon, my diary became my companion, a far less exhausting friend than my sister.

I recorded endless details of my crush on my teacher, Mr. Cason, a tall man with sandy colored, curly hair and twinkling blue eyes who recognized my potential. He was very affectionate toward me, but always appropriate. His presence eased me across the bridge to high school without a big sister and helped fill the gap where a responsible father should have been.

Dear Diary   May 23

*Gee!!! I got out of the hospital today after a whole week. Strep throat is a very dangerous illness because of the high fever you run. I went to the Senior Tea at 2:00. Would you believe it? I thought my dress was beautiful, and I must admit I looked fairly well. It was truly a gala affair. All the girls were dressed in such splendid taste. Mr. Cason looked like a doll. He had on a suit and white bucks.*

May 28   Graduation Day!!!

*Today was a day I'll never forget. I got up and dressed and got my hair fixed. I looked fairly well I thought. We started down the hall at 9 a.m. on the dot. Everything went along smoothly. I wore a white sheath. I cleaned out my desk and then went into Mr. Cason's room and gave him a big bear hug and said goodbye. He was so sweet. He told me I should go home early, get some rest. When I walked out of the building, my tears just spilled over, and I bawled all the way home.*

Mr. Cason was the first of many such encounters as I made my way toward wholeness. I had crushes on doctors, ministers, bosses, etc.

# Chapter Thirty-one:
# Singing My Mother

1999

IT'S EASY TO TOUCH THIS BODY, its chill familiar by now. My mother looks peaceful, her dignity restored, in a pale blue silk dress my sister made. She and I busy ourselves with Mama's makeup, asking the woman who did it to come line her left lip a little and put some blush on her hands so they won't look yellow. Mama's faux pearls and earrings add the right touch.

Just before it's time for friends to join us at visitation, my daughter takes our hands, "I want to tell you both something." Her brown eyes brim with tears; her full lips tremble. "After you called from the hospital, I had a vision or something. I was out on the balcony at the beach, and Meemaw came to me the way she used to be. She was with her sisters, the ones she's been talking about who've already died. She was kicking up her heels and laughing and smiling like she did when I was a little girl. She said to me, 'My voice is beautiful!' It touched my heart so because I asked her once why she never sang and she told me that her teacher told her she couldn't sing. She said after that she never was much for singing."

My daughter's sobs are faint, sweet. I take her in my arms, loving the softness of her. I tell my sister over my baby's strawberry blonde hair, "It's the kind of thing she used to shame me for, but she's realizing more and more her own psychic power. Like Grandmother's."

I stroke my daughter's hair, wiping away her tears, "Thanks for telling us about that. I'm proud of you," I whisper as we see the first clump of visitors hovering at the door.

I always thought these two hours would be the worst of my life, but I am amazed at how uplifted I feel when all the friends and family begin to gather in the unreal parlor. I introduce friends to family I've told stories about—mixing these two different worlds of mine.

My stepfather has always thought it disrespectful to laugh and talk and have fun when somebody dies. I've argued with him that funerals are for those left behind, for healing the hurt. He isolates himself in a chair toward the back of the room, but everybody goes by to talk to him. Before he knows it, he's enjoying the attention, glowing from the love they pour on him.

And when I take a good ol' boy and my friend he calls his bride over to the coffin and show them my mother, it elates me to see their response when I exclaim, "Isn't she beautiful!"

"Yes," the friend answers, but her husband really agrees, looks right into Mama's face, at the good cheekbones and her smooth forehead's perfect shape, accentuated by the hair style. My eyes linger on the pink nail polish.

"I painted her nails while she was in the hospital, filed them in the emergency room," I tell them. "She was particular about her nails."

"Particular about her looks period, I'll bet," the husband says. Then he's making his way toward my stepdad whose hand he shakes and says, "Oh, man, you got you a pretty one."

My stepdaddy's eyes light up, the proud grin overtaking him. "I did, didn't I?" He says as if it's just occurred to him. "She was a beautiful woman!" He shakes his head. Then a flashy cousin is swooping down on Rhett to give him a hug, and my friend leads me back to the coffin.

"Now, I want you to remember this. Look at that beautiful woman and remember that look in your stepdaddy's eye. They had some gooood times, I guarantee you. Remember that," he advises me, and then they're gone and I'm surrounded by cousins that I love all talking at once and laughing at stories about Mama.

When it's all over, I'm too tired to swim with my sister and my daughter, who had planned to visit by the pool after dinner. "We had three different people bring us dinner tonight," I tell them, opening pones of cornbread and peas and fried okra. I kick off my shoes and pour myself a tall glass of wine. Later, while I'm cleaning up in the kitchen, I indulge in a drink. The name of it—a buttery nipple—has drawn me like a magnet for the last six months. I surprise myself by sleeping like a rock.

Next morning when I get up, I put on Joan Baez's "Will the Circle Be Unbroken?" I play it maybe a hundred times, singing along. I have laid out my navy blue clothes, made sure everything is just like Mama would approve of today. As usual, I'm not ready on time, so I finish my makeup in the car, using the rearview mirror from the back seat while Rhett and my husband swap comments about last night's Braves game. Why doesn't the world stop today, I wonder.

The little church is sweeter than I remembered. The flowers, moved from the funeral home, have been arranged attractively. Mama would have loved all these baskets full of purple irises, daisies, roses of every color, white lilies with pink throats. They emanate a sweet fragrance.

Mostly, I remember the eulogy and holding Daddy up when he sagged as we passed the casket for the last time. Impulsively, as if I could defy the Grim Reaper, I ripped a few drooping lilies off the floral blanket and stomped down the aisle toward the grave.

IT'S BEEN A DAY FOR METAPHOR, one week since Mother's death. When I woke up, I noticed the two roses I took from the casket's blanket. The deep red one, the American Beauty, never opened, but the white one—flushed with pink—flourished. It became a thing of beauty: full, voluptuous.

I'm floating on a tube the kids call a noodle, looking up into a clear blue sky. As I float under the fountain and feel the cool mist on my face, I say to my husband, "I've noticed myself smiling involuntarily again the way I did when our grandson was born."

"A great burden has been lifted," he says. "I think your anger will disappear, too. I think you've been mad at God again."

"Hmm, maybe. I'd do all that caregiving again in a New York minute though."

"I know, and I love you for it," he says. "God does, too. He's bigger than you." Then we're both quiet for a long time, just floating around the pool—something we haven't done all summer. A laid-back Saturday is just what we need. I let my head float in the water, wetting the back of my hair. The cool water refreshes me, restores my soul, the sound of the fountain's gurgling like a brook that goes on forever.

It occurs to me that I'm floating with my feet crossed and my arms stretched out like Christ. The message: I am resurrecting. I have made the sacrifice, done what was intended, and now it's time to move on. *Let go*, I think as I drift.

It's high noon in mid-August in the Deep South. I am astounded by the beauty of a cluster of wild muscadines growing in an oak that hangs over the pool. The sun shines on the perfect round grapes, warming them, filling them with juice that makes them plop off the tree and fall right into the pool. I catch one and place it on my tongue, savoring the feel of it as well as the taste. It explodes in my mouth, the sweet tang of juice tasty. I chew the pulp, spitting the seeds out. Most people don't, but I love to eat the dark purple skin, too. Its rough texture is a nice contrast with the pale green, slippery fruit.

I look up through the green leaves to spot the grapes springing forth wild, untended, unplanned, yet holding the mystery of life. When the fruit is ripe, it is consumed, but it leaves seeds behind. What was it in my gardening class that ripped my heart? Yes . . . that along about August, the plant's main objective is to produce seed. The mother plant willingly sacrifices her life if necessary to produce seeds.

I see the leggy mint on my kitchen window sill, its long tough stem bearing flowers which will turn to seed. This time of year when I float a sprig inside a bourbon or tear a mint leaf for a salad, the sharp, sweet taste and pungent odor have been somewhat diminished.

Last night, the lightning bugs were bigger and more numerous than I've ever seen. As we gazed into the woods at the twinkling points of gold, I said to my husband, "Whose spirit sent these neon-yellow butterflies?"

"Of course," he answered, taking my hand.

When one flew overhead and hovered, its light intense, I looked up and said, "Hi, Mom."

The magical sprouting of wild muscadines alone would not suggest the spirit world stopping to note whether this woman is an island, but a thousand little things like that will make you feel connected to the universe.

My grandson is chasing a friendly butterfly, the first one I've ever seen play with a child. It flutters just out of his reach every time he sneaks up, stealthy and intent, with his little hand cupped. This goes on for ten minutes before his squeals of delight and awe turn into a testosterone-induced attempt at various ways to attack and defeat the butterfly. He takes the little rubber shark out of the pool, its grey skin faded from the summer sun, fills it with water and tries to squirt the butterfly. It has perched on a tree to watch all this. Then it disappears as quickly as it appeared, and he starts looking for lizards.

My granddaughter toddles along the edge of the pool, picking up muscadines. Inside her body are eggs that might contain my great-grandchildren. As she brings the grapes to me, we count. Each time, I tell her, "Thank you."

Her plump little body dances with pleasure. She bends her knees and bobs up and down, clapping her hands, when she answers, "Ta ta," showing her pearlized eyelids.

I try to remember when I was her size, but, of course, I can't. However, I'll never forget my grandmother's muscadine arbor and my childhood delight in popping a grape in my mouth straight off the vine. This is the first summer they have magically appeared in my own backyard. I turn my float around and around. The water is warm, like a great comforting womb.

Years ago, when my father Phil died, there were no friends, no flowers. At home, we were having this pool dug. That gash in the back yard of red clay—not the color of blood so much as the scabs left after bleeding—looked like a giant grave instead of a warm womb where we delve for healing.

I decide I'll make a batch of muscadine wine, let it age, and share it with friends whose hearts are troubled. Each time I sniff the fruity bouquet, I'll remember Mama and be grateful for the way her spirit blessed us with comfort.

# Chapter Thirty-two:
# Singing My Father

## 2010

CELEBRATING THE STRENGTH OF MY MOTHER long after her death, I discovered, at last, the father inside my inner being: my better self, my soul.

I also had to weave the wisdom of a poet friend into my being to grow up. And I had to be reassured by a novelist friend that my story was worth telling and by his wife that I could tell it. Most of all, I had to be spurred for years by my flawed, impatient pool-floating husband to keep revising fiction in order to get at the truth. Along the way, George and I grew into a less entangled relationship where each of us found our own way.

Lucinda and Eric didn't last, but she survived and is thriving on her own, not as the extension of anyone else. If she were to tell you her story, it would be through art. She eventually became a lawyer, too, in San Francisco, then retired and painted. She was known throughout the city for her fabulous openings. Not only were her paintings considered excellent—mostly large florals in bold color—but she also had a following who could afford them.

Finally, Rhett mellowed into a remarkable man who grew beyond the yoke of the Birmingham "city fathers" that stunted the growth of many of his contemporaries. During the decade that he outlived Mama, George and I took Rhett to the Choctaw casino every few months. He loved talking to the Choctaws and to the Mississippi blacks his age about gambling and baseball. He only played the quarter slots, and he and George shared a quarter-century of sobriety. Rhett was too competitive to have a slip.

I tried to get him to tell me about Iwo Jima and Okinawa, but he didn't like to talk about that. He also would never tell me details about Phil and the dynamite and how much he was involved in the bombings. "You don't need to know all that, baby. He's your blood kin, but I raised you."

Instead of standing on my tiptoes to kiss him, I learned to stoop for a goodbye kiss from him once he became bent like a question mark with arthritis. He died at home with me, Lucinda's son and George. While he breathed his last breaths, I was cooking his favorite dish. The house smelled like home and family and love. He faced his final years with the wisdom and spirituality of his Native American heritage, and he faced his final breath with the courage of a U. S. Marine. He knew Lucinda was on her way home, and his sister and her family were coming to lunch the next day. He was content.

Redbuds and daffodils bloom. I plant the bulbs and keep watch. Roses and honeysuckle will sweeten the air long after I'm gone. And voices, I hope, will sing.

THE END

Loretta Douglas Cobb grew up in Birmingham, Alabama during the 1950's, where she was educated in the public schools. She attended Alabama College (now UM) in Montevallo where she was graduated with honors in Engish. In 1972 she earned her M.A. in English from the Bread Loaf School of English at Middlebury College. During graduate school, she taught junior high, receiving notice for her innovative teaching style. Loretta married William Cobb, one of her professors, while she was still an undergraduate. In 1974, her daughter Meredith was born. Loretta joined the staff at UM in order to be a part-time worker, as being a mom was her top priority. She established a study skills and tutoring program, which grew into the Harbert Writing Center, which she founded and directed until 1995. Loretta has published numerous academic articles and given presentations across the country. After her retirement in '95, she enjoyed several years of helping her grandson enjoy his pre-school years. Later, when his sister Sara Beth was born, Loretta had begun a new career as a writer, both for *The Birmingham News* as a freelancer and for a number of fiction publications. Her first story, "Seeing it Through," appeared in *Belles' Letters*, followed by a collection of her own stories *The Ocean Was Salt*. She was included in the anthologies *Climbing Mt Cheaha* and *Working the Dirt*. "Feeling Salty" was short-listed in the Irish International Competition for *Fish*, a literary magazine. Loretta appeared at major literary conferences in the state, and her first book received high praise from reviewers. For the last decade she has been part of the Alabama Readers' Theater, entertaining annually at such venues as Monroeville Literary Symposium and the Scott and Zelda Fitzgerald Museum's Gala. The readers performed for the International Scott and Zelda Fitzgerald in 2014. Care-giving for her parents became a priority for a decade, during which she worked on *How Can I keep from Singing?*